GREYLADY

Clan Wars Book One

Peter Morwood

D1585631

LEGEND

First published in 1993 by
Legend Books
Random House, 20 Vauxhall Bridge Road, London SW1V 2SA

London Melbourne Sydney Auckland
Johannesburg and agencies throughout the world

Copyright © Peter Morwood 1993

The right of Peter Morwood to be identified as the author of this work has
been asserted by him in accordance with the Copyright, Designs and Patents
Act 1988.
This book is sold subject to the condition that it shall not, by way of trade or
otherwise, be lent, resold, hired out, or otherwise circulated without the
publisher's prior consent in any form of binding or cover other than that in
which it is published and without a similar condition including this condition
being imposed on the subsequent purchaser

Typeset by Deltatype Ltd, Ellesmere Port
Printed in England by Clays Ltd, St Ives plc

ISBN 0099 261 618

The Words of the Wise One

'IN THE TIME Before, the Land had its own people. None speak of them now, save for scholars wise in the old words, for the people of Before are gone. They are one with the people of Now, or they are dead.

'The people of Now came up out of the eastern sea, riding the wings of storm into the calm of a still, hot day in summer, and they struck the Land with a storm of war far harder than one of wind and rain. The people of the time Before made war as a game, a hunt, and they bound it around with the requirements of honour so that it remained no more than a savage sport, its prizes the taking of ransoms, hostages, and, sometimes, heads.

'Those who came from the east did not make sport of war. Some said that they came from their last home with only what they wore and carried; but they wore iron, and carried steel, and with those they could take all else they desired. They took the Land, and if they rode the storm-wind in their coming to the Land, they rode tall horses ever after.

'They were *an Mergh-arlethen*. They are the Horse Lords. The Talvalins. And this is their story . . .'

The old man struck once upon the strings of his harp, a sharp, open-handed slap that sent a sharp, melodious discord twanging throughout the high hall. It brought silence as no other sound could do. Lords and ladies, warriors and women, servants, and even the growling hounds beneath the tables, all grew silent as the echoes of those struck steel strings shimmered into silence. In the feast-hall of a great clan-lord, and especially that of Halmar, *ilauem-arluth* Talvalin, none save a singer of stories might behave with such casual impudence. No, not even the King himself, though his guards flanked him forty deep. But for those whose minds held history, all things were permitted – if their songs met with approval.

The old man stilled his harpstrings with a caress of that same striking hand, then stroked his beard and moustache so that they might better spread their silver sweep and fall across his cheeks and chin and chest. There was a softness, a benevolence, about so fine and wise a gentleman, one with a broad brown brow and white whiskers and rosy cheeks, wearing the wrinkles of many smiles about his eyes. Except that there the softness died, for a wide white seam of scar crawled down from his hair and clear across his face to hide itself within his beard. In its wake, one of those eyes was milky-pale and sightless, half-hidden by a black slouch hat. But the other burned with an ice-hot sapphire blue, the freezing fiery remembrance of what was done in recompense for the loss of half his sight.

Then before the high hall grew too cold, the old man smiled; and with that smile the hall warmed again, and people smiled in turn, and forgot that for a moment one and all of them held in their breath for fear – no, surely not fear, it was no more than interest! – of what this ancient one-eyed man might do, of what he had done before. His slender fingers reached, and spread, and touched, and music rippled like the mantle of Heaven, ennobling all who heard it be they lord, or servant, or only dog panting beneath the table or cat dozing by the fire. He looked at Halmar Talvalin, and inclined his head not with the acknowledgement of command, but with that small nod of someone who had at last made his own decision. The soft notes of a simple scale chimed out, and he said:

'This is how it was . . .'

I

Invasion

FARREN MOVED QUIETLY through the green shadows of Gelert's Wood, making no more sound than the sigh of the dying wind as it stirred the treetops. He was a hunter. Of bees, for their honey; of birds, for their eggs; of mushrooms, of rabbits . . . Of anything in fact not quick enough to get out of his way and yet small enough to be hidden in the capacious pockets of his hunting-coat.

That made him a thief. Gelert the High Lord of Prytenon disapproved of hunting without his permission; and since that permission was seldom if ever given, it followed that he disapproved of Farren. But he and his people still bought the eggs, and the honey, and all the other things that Farren and people like him brought to market, and had the good grace not to question how such commodities had fallen into the poacher's possession. They would have disdained to hunt such little, tasty things themselves, preferring bold, dangerous beasts like stag and boar and the great wild oxen. It was a matter of honour.

Of course, if they caught him in the act of poaching even those little morsels without the permission they never granted, that same high lord and his warrior-vassals would have seen him tied wrist and ankle to four strong horses before they were whipped to the four horizons. That, too, was a matter of honour.

So Farren moved quietly through the woods.

At least there was no need to move as quietly as usual. This was one of those times when the poacher could well believe that he was the only thing moving at all, quietly or otherwise. After last night Gelert's Wood and every living creature in it seemed to be holding their breath, in case too much activity might invite the storm to return. It had built all yesterday afternoon, darkening to a slate-skied evening, and after dark it had come howling up out of the deep sea to lash against the coast of Prytenon with thunder and lightning, wailing wind and horizontal rain. The worst storm so far this summer, in a year already grown notorious for them.

It was said here, near the coast, that all dry land had once been open ocean, and the Lords and Ladies of the Deep Sea were jealous of their loss. To the superstitious, and those who made pretence that they had some knowledge of the wizardly arts, it must have seemed as though those Lords and Ladies and all the other demons known to dwell beneath the sea were trying once again to fling their cold, wet realm across the land like a smothering, choking cloak.

They had done so before. Though Farren had never been there himself, he had spoken to travellers from the Cernuan Westerland. They had told him how a man could stand on the roads that led only to empty cliffs and hear the bells of Kerys ringing, ringing, in the cold green water forty fathoms down. The Lords and Ladies of the Deep Sea had reached up glistening, foam-laced arms one night and dragged the city below to be their plaything. Every brick of every building, and every man, woman and child who had been sleeping in them. All the roads to Kerys ended there, on the cliffs above the sea. Forty feet of the city wall curved along the cliff-edge, with the great gateway set square in the middle of it. But the gates swung loose now, rotting in the salty air, unbarred, with no one left to bar them or anywhere to stand beyond them on two hundred feet of empty air, straight down into the waiting water.

Farren had thought it typically Cernuek, nothing more than a good story. For all he knew, there had never been a city called Kerys. And even if there had been, and it had fallen into the sea during a storm – as he had seen great chunks of headland do before, without the weight of buildings to encourage them – there was no way in which the bells would be in any fit state to ring after a drop like that. He was a sensible man, was the poacher. At least in the daytime, and in still air.

Last night, with the gale hooting like mad laughter around the chimney of his cottage and the heavy, hard-driven raindrops pattering and scrabbling like wet, drowned fingertips against the barred shutters of its windows, Farren might have believed anything. Even that the sea had risen from its bed and come roaring in five miles from the shore to invade the land at last. The sound of ringing bells would have driven him under his own bed, shrieking fit to match the storm outside.

4

But that had been last night. Now that the wind and rain had passed, leaving the air rinsed and clean under the warmth of a cloudless blue sky, Farren knew that the only risk a land-dweller could run from the sea was in building his house too close to the edge of it. And as for going out on it in a boat, Farren left that to other, braver people. He liked to dine on fried fish as well as anyone else in his village, but not to the extent of chancing that the fish might dine on him. Not that Farren was a coward, or anything like that; but he sometimes had too much imagination to really enjoy the battering of storms at night.

It was the sort of day when larks sang – and they did – and bees buzzed – and *they* did – and the fortunate few with nothing better to do could wander through the warm woods and lie by the seashore and do nothing at all, except to leisurely hunt for gulls' eggs and the other things that fetched a better price at market than was justified by the minimal effort of their finding. Had it not been for the remote risk that one of Lord Gelert's vassals might have been abroad to see whether the lord's lands had suffered any damage, Farren might have whistled. That, however, would have gone beyond well-being and bravado into foolhardiness, chancing not only his arm but the other arm and both legs as well. So he kept quiet and let the birds do his whistling for him.

Farren's usual custom on these jaunts was to gather nothing on his way out – though he might mark the location of, say, a nest of wild bees or a good stand of mushrooms for future reference – in case of who he might meet exercising horses on the empty beach when he reached the shore. It was only on the way back to the village that he would gather in whatever harvest he had spotted. Fair was fair, and if he was caught he was caught. But once back under his own roof, no Prytenek warrior who might have pursued him would demean himself by entering a peasant's home to search for such things as he would not have troubled himself to gather up in passing. Indeed, if the great man's humour was good, he might buy up such produce without waiting for market, and even pay a little extra for the fun of the chase. Fair was fair, and another matter of honour.

The lords of the land regarded everything as a game, a rough and often fatal sport, whether it was war, or political argument, or the workings of the laws that they themselves had passed. If one remembered that the first and only rule was that there were no rules, then those games were easily played. For a peasant, that was what he could expect from honour.

Farren yawned; the warmth of the damp, heavy air was having its effect on him, especially after a night that had been mostly sleepless. Even though he was almost clear of the forest, there was more than a mile of sand-dunes still to be crossed, dunes held in place by bracken and heather and needle-pointed marram grass. No matter how fierce the storm-wind blew, those dunes weathered all of it, and if their vegetation cover was stripped away by a particularly fierce gale, it was capable of growing back almost while he watched.

Farren was halfway through the dunes when he yawned again. The heat of the reflected sun had been beating up at him since he first set foot on the sand, and slogging through its shifting heaviness had made his task no easier. A nap would be pleasant enough, and it wasn't as though he had to *be* anywhere. He had slept in the dunes before, for one reason and another; a mattress of fern and heather laid into a hollow scooped in the sand could be as comfortable to weary bones as the straw pallet of his own bed, and with fewer creatures living in it. Things to be stolen would still be there when the heat of the day had faded somewhat. That was what he told himself, at any rate. Far off in the distance beyond another three or four steep slopes of sand he could hear the slow rushing of waves as they ran up onto the shore of Dunakr Bay. It was a lazy sound, no encouragement to effort, and without thinking any more about what else he might be doing with the day, Farren the poacher made himself a nest among the bracken and fell fast asleep.

'Land!' yelled someone. 'Land-ho! *Land!*'

Bayrd ar'Talvlyn raised his head from the deck, and peered over the gunwale of the ship. There was no land anywhere that he could see, and he squinted blearily at the dance of sunlight on water. It was beautiful, in its own way, but for him and for his stomach the only beauty was that the water itself was near enough flat calm. It had been anything but these past few days, and last night had been the worst of all. Bayrd was no sailor.

There were times when it felt as though he had been almost

everything else. At twenty-seven years of age he had been married twice – once for dynastic reasons and once for love – divorced once, widowed once, and without children to show for it in either case. His clean-shaven, regular if not especially handsome face was unmarred by that, and his straight nose was unmarred by the usual stamp of a warrior who has seen battle. A man whose helmet-nasal had taken the blow from an enemy's weapon and transferred the shock to the nose it was supposed to guard invariably had a somewhat flattened, cynical look. From the expression that usually lurked in his grey eyes, a glint suggesting lazy amusement at everything the world had to offer, Bayrd ar'Talvlyn managed the cynicism quite nicely without any reshaping of his features.

For all of that experience, he had still managed to avoid travelling aboard any vessel larger than a river ferry before, and this first encounter with the realities of ocean voyaging was enough to have soured him against it for the rest of his life. And there had been times, during the storm, when he thought that life might have been measured in minutes.

He sagged back onto the deck, salt-stained and soaked, but mercifully clean. All the vomit that he – and probably everyone else aboard except the crew – had spewed everywhere had been washed away by the massive waves that had gone roaring through the scuppers like wild animals released from captivity. His guts gave another aching experimental churn, but there was no longer anything there for them to work on. He was grateful for that. Death would be preferable to a repetition of what he had gone through this past twenty hours.

Bayrd sneezed – it hurt, but right now very little didn't – and stared up at the lookout post at the masthead as it described slow arcs across the blue sky. Then a slow, rueful smile began to spread across his face. He might live to be a sailor after all, or at least a landsman able to travel by ship without shaming himself at the first roll of the vessel. No more than a week ago, just watching that movement would have sent him hurrying to the leeside railing. Now it was merely restful.

At least there was still a mast for him to watch, even though its sail was no more than a decorative fringe of canvas hanging from its yard. He could vaguely remember the sail giving way, with a sharp bang and then a long rending sound that was so like and yet unlike the thunder splitting the clouds above. It hadn't been worthy of more notice than that, not at a time when Bayrd thought he might die and hadn't really regretted the prospect. Death in battle he could have faced with equanimity.

At least, he reconsidered, probably. Though he was old enough, the likelihood had yet to present itself, for all that being killed on someone else's behalf was a common ending for *arluth* Albanak's people. Bayrd gazed up at the sky some more, soaking in the heat of the sun as he might have done in a tub of water. Lulled by the creak of cordage and timber, a sound that had annoyed him once but was now a soothing counterpoint to the lap of water against the hull, his eyes grew heavy as he began to slip into a doze that was half a hypnotic trance brought on by the slow, regular swing of the mast. Then his eyes snapped open again as the questions came tumbling out of his subconscious; questions for which he had no answers.

Where was *the Lord Albanak? Where was everyone else? Was this the only ship to survive the storm. . . ?*

The possibility of being alone was almost as frightening as that of being drowned. He sat up with an abrupt jerk that sent stabs of protest through his overworked abdominal muscles. Bayrd gasped, winced, swore viciously as if that would alleviate the pain or at least make him feel better – it did neither – and scrambled squelching to his feet.

Then he swore again, by the Father of Fires and by the Light of Heaven, but this time with a deal more reverence. His grip on the taffrail was tight enough to suggest that he might have fallen down without its support, but that fall would have been from surprise rather than weakness. As he looked from horizon to horizon, his jaw sagging like that of the merest yokel at a fair, Bayrd realised that he had seldom been so *not* alone.

There were ships everywhere.

They surrounded his own vessel as closely as gnats around a lantern on a midsummer evening: big, beamy merchant ships and little fishing-boats, handsomely appointed ocean-going pleasure yachts and even three lean, rakish battlerams. Out towards the east they clustered closely enough that the reflected dapples of sunlight on water had almost to fight for space. Dozens of them.

Scores. Hundreds . . . His brain rejected the thought of thousands, but for all that, his eyes suggested such a number might not be so far from the truth.

Bayrd had not been of sufficient rank to attend the Lord Albanak's last council, but the word had come down: *Take ships. As many as are needed.* He would not have believed that there were so many ships in all the world, much less that they could all have been gathered here after such a storm as last night's. But here they were. Narrowing his eyes against the atrocious glare of the new-risen sun, Bayrd hunted for something familiar: a face, a robe, a banner. Anything to tell him that the others of his name had made the journey as safely as he had.

Those that still had mastheads – or masts at all, and Bayrd began to understand how fortunate his own ship had been in that regard – were flying pennants. It was perhaps too dignified a word for the scraps of cloth hanging in the near-still air, but since they carried the various clan and family Colours, it was good enough. Some were hard to see, what with the glare and all, but the scarlet and green of ar'Lerutz was plain enough. That was a banner indeed, a forty-foot length of silk usually hung from a citadel to celebrate high or holy days. Hanging as it did from a snapped mainmast, most of the fabric trailed across the surface of the sea; but its Colours were undimmed.

Once Bayrd's eyes had sorted them from the glitter of reflected light, clan ar'Sanen's sombre purple and dark blue were just as striking; even though they were less handsomely presented. Someone had been sent to the top of their ship's mast with two buckets of the appropriate paint and then, for want of courage to stay there – or maybe just for want of a brush – had emptied the pigments in two long streaks down either side of the ship's tattered mainsail. Bayrd wondered idly where they had found such things, or taken the time to load them aboard, then dismissed the thought as pointless. None of these were the Colours he wanted to see.

Nor was the Lord Albanak's green tree on blue. Bayrd eyed it, raised one eyebrow and, with no one to see him and report the expression back to unfriendly ears, allowed a sardonic grin to cross his face at the implications of what he saw. No makeshift pennants here, or hasty splatters of paint. Albanak-*arluth*'s dignity would never have allowed such half measures. The

9

Overlord's symbol was flaunted on a sail so complete and undamaged that it must have been kept in reserve and rigged only when the storm was over.

It said more about the workings of the Overlord's mind, and the esteem in which he held himself, than Albanak probably realised. Little of that did him any credit.

Do you really think we'd believe that you and you alone survived the storm unscathed? thought Bayrd. *Or that we place more value on your peacock display than on our own survival of last night? You're too obvious, my lord. And it lessens your grandeur instead of adding to it, no matter what you might think.*

Then he saw what he had been looking for, and felt a surge of relief in his chest and his throat as though he had been lost in a forest and emerged not only to safety but close to his own home. The pennon was tattered, having snapped savagely against itself for Heaven alone knew how many hours, but the Colours it bore were still bright. Blue and white, separated by thin stripes of black that served only to make the brighter tinctures more distinct. They meant little enough to any outside the blood, but to Bayrd they were as comforting as shade on a hot day or fire in the depths of winter. Those Colours had been defended for years, as a rallying-point, a line of safe retreat, even a place to gather for a last stand that would mingle the blood of the family with the blood of its enemies, and do honour to both. Bayrd leaned against the rail of the stubby, ugly ship, waving at people who were still too far away to see him, and if he had been younger or older, he might have cried with relief.

Clan ar'Talvlyn was still alive – and if whoever was doing that yelling was telling the truth, they would have a land to live in again.

They had come from Alba of the south-east long, long ago. It was a vast open country, an ocean of endless grass and endless sky, where trees were an event and the most obvious feature of the world was the horizon at its edge. Apart from the blue heaven above and the green land below, there had been little else to look at – and since one was out of reach, they took the name of the other.

Alba meant *The Land*, and Albans, the Dwellers in the Land, had been their name ever since. If the old stories could be believed – and they couldn't all be lies – the Albans had become capable horse-masters just as soon as the first father developed the first blister from walking to visit a married child who had moved too far from home. It was only necessary to look once at the wide plains to see that *everywhere* was too far from home.

The truth of it was probably more complex than that, but their skill with horses could never be denied. It became a saleable commodity; first the trained horses, then the training of horses, then the trained horsemen themselves. It was not an unusual sequence of events. The Albans became mercenaries, selling their talents as mounted archers and heavy shock cavalry to the highest bidder; but after that, they became unusual. Indeed, they became unique. Because they stayed bought.

It was a troubled time in the many little domains of the Old Country, in Tergavets and Vlekh and Kalitz, Drosul and Yuvan and Vreyar. A time that became known as the Age of the Country at War. Philosophers and historians mocked such a sweeping designation, claiming that there had never been an Age of the Country at Peace. Small rulers rose and fell like flowers in the springtime, jockeying desperately for power and prestige, their followers turbulent and chronically untrustworthy men who could all too easily visualise themselves as rulers in their turn.

Thus it was also the age of the mercenary, the hired sword, whose contracts became increasingly elaborate and complex as months became years and border skirmishes became full-scale battles in an undeclared war. It was a merchant's war, fought with silver as much as with steel. Courage was purchased with coins by men not bred to bravery, and a common tactic before battle became the attempt to buy an enemy's mercenary cadre by the offering of better terms. Some battles were won that way, without a sword being drawn or an arrow being loosed, when a greater or lesser percentage of one side changed their allegiance to the other.

But not when there were Albans on the field. Their contracts were as carefully worded as those of any other mercenaries, but once they were signed – and the Albans signed in blood, a touch that observers thought no more than melodrama the first time they saw it, but never more than once – the clauses were honoured to the letter. They never ran away, they never changed sides, and they never broke their word. The contracts were signed in blood, and the service they promised, whether in victory or in defeat, was as often paid in blood.

What had begun as simple business acumen among foreigners seeking work, to be honest when honesty was rare, became more than that. The honouring of a contract became the honouring of anything. A given word was kept, duty was faithfully maintained – and that was only to the petty kings and merchant princes who scrambled over one another like crabs in a bucket, each pulling all the others down so than none could reach the top and escape from the never-ending cycle of conflict. Having seen the deceit born of coins whose value could be lessened simply by putting less silver into each minting, the Albans resorted to a currency that could not be cheapened. It made them trusted, respected – but never really loved. There was always the air of superiority about an Alban when he dealt outside his immediate name-kin, the sort of superiority that irks ordinary men with ordinary failings, as though their worth was being silently called into question with every look, every word, every breath . . .

Time passed and the wars ended. Those who could not accept peace in life found it in the grave, and the kings and princes who remained found trading more profitable than raiding. They raised palaces instead of war-camps, built towns instead of burnt them, made laws instead of threats, and settled down to profit from this new Age of the Country at Peace. And the historians and philosophers . . .

. . . Wisely kept their mouths shut; kings whose grandfathers had been bloody-handed brigands did not take kindly to scholarly little jokes at their expense, and had painful ways of saying so.

Loved or not, the Albans came to be relied upon by their employers in a way those petty kings did not – or would not – trust their own families. The mercenary horsemen became bodyguards, the last line of protection against ambitious retainers, or were granted small fiefs along debatable borders so that they became lords in their own right and the first line of defence against ambitious neighbours.

They married, but their wives seldom came from among the local people: lords they might have become, but they were still no more than hired servants. Instead, the women and children they had left behind began travelling up from the steppe country to join their menfolk. The families grew and intermarried, so that name-kin became blood-kin; they made alliances with one another as lordly houses might, and became clans; but otherwise the Albans stayed where they were. They remained bodyguards or border guards, neither asking for advancement nor expecting it since such conditions were not in their contracts, and the privileges they had received already were no more than equivalent to the land grants and golden battle decorations given as service rewards to lesser men. They had no Alba, no Land of their own to live in – but what they had was more than enough. They had their honour.

Until *Hospodar* Skarpeya became the king's advisor in Kalitzim.

The Albans were honourable, trustworthy, decent, honest, obedient, lacking in all but the most ordinary and forgivable human vices and, when not slaughtering their various employers' enemies, were reputedly kind to children and small animals. They were, in short, sickeningly wholesome, and tended to be just as sickeningly righteous.

There had been rumblings of discontent about them among the other retainers for a long time now, but those noises had been dismissed as no more than envy. It was not a dimissal guaranteed to win them any support among the noisemakers. Especially when Skarpeya appeared on the scene and the Albans began making noises in their turn.

The reason was simple enough: the Albans disapproved of sorcery. It therefore followed like night after day that they disapproved of Skarpeya, because he was rather more than just the king's political confidant. Skarpeya was a wizard. Whether he was good or bad – in whichever sense of those words – mattered not at all to the Albans. They disapproved on principle, and said so loudly.

And once too often.

That was what had Bayrd ar'Talvlyn – and every other Alban man, woman and child who had survived the storm – floating about in their mismatched fleet. King Daykin of Kalitz had listened reasonably enough to both sides of the argument. Then – quite unreasonably in their opinion and in direct violation of several early-termination clauses – he had torn up all the Alban contracts and given them twenty days to be beyond the borders of his realm, or lose all their possessions and be enslaved.

Those twenty days would not have been enough for them to return to their ancestral plains, even if any had wanted to. After two hundred years of reasonable comfort, of eating meat that they hadn't needed to hunt first, and bread made of flour that someone else had grown and ground, the prospect of returning to the wilderness had been distinctly unappealing. The Albans who moved westward had grown soft; or at least, sensible.

Daykin's impossible restriction had been deliberate, the justification for it no more than an excuse to act against retainers whose honesty unsettled him, no matter that it had been good enough for generations of his ancestors. That callous reasoning – and the repudiation of mutually agreed service contracts – had been enough for Albanak, Overlord of the Alban clans. He did nothing for ten days of the allotted time, then issued his commands.

'Ride north,' he had said, 'and take ships. As many as you need. Enough for all of us.'

Bayrd and the other warriors of Clan ar'Talvlyn saw very little of that raid. Instead they were sent south and east from Kalitz, escorting a vast gaggle of wagons that were as mismatched in their way as the ships. Those wagons were supposedly carrying the families and blood-clan of ar'Talvlyn, ar'Lerutz, ar'Sanen and three others, to draw the eyes of Daykin's other soldiers away from the seaports of the north.

It was a mad gamble, far removed from any of the cool, considered stratagems that had won the Albans their military reputation. Perhaps because of that very madness, it worked. The ar'Talvlyn horsemen let the empty wagons scatter in a hundred different directions towards Tergavets and Vlekh, and swung back under cover of darkness, riding like a storm towards their prearranged rendezvous on the Droselan coast.

That was the only time in the whole dangerous undertaking when Bayrd was almost killed. He had never before swum a horse out towards a ship standing offshore in deep water; and he had never dived under the beast's belly to secure it with straps so that such a valuable resource could be winched aboard. The only familiar part about the whole undertaking had been when the horse, hoisted clear of the choppy waves, had expressed its displeasure of the whole procedure by lashing out with its hind legs.

An iron-shod hoof had whipped past his face, peeled a long strip of skin from his forehead and came that skin's thickness to removing any further need for hats in his wardrobe. Like the rest of his clan, Bayrd ar'Talvlyn had worked with fiery-tempered battle horses all his life. He had learned to sit astride a saddle, and not fall off too frequently, almost before he could walk – and that sensation had become entirely too familiar. War horses were trained to kill, and you were trained not to let them kill *you*. If the training went wrong and your brains were kicked over the landscape, that was just too bad – and your fault. It was as simple as that. Even so, there was something lacking in glory about being kicked to death by your own mount.

Two nights later the storm hit the fleet, and demonstrated that there were still less glorious ways to die . . .

There had been about thirteen thousand Albans in Droselan and Kalitzak service, and all – with their families, their horses and their goods – were supposed to have been aboard the motley fleet that must have included everything that could float along hundreds of miles of coast. As the ships gathered together and began moving towards the still-unseen shoreline, Bayrd wondered how many of them remained – and how many horses, how many bows, how many swords. All those things would be needed, sooner or later. When he issued his last commands, *arluth* Albanak had made one thing quite clear: his people would no longer be given land to live in. Things given could be taken away; they had seen as much. From now on, *they* would do the taking.

Aware that he was no more than an obstruction on deck, Bayrd got himself out of the way as sailors began hurrying to and fro with lengths of rope, lengths of canvas, lengths of wood, and all the other mysterious impedimenta of their trade. They looked busy and willing enough, and some of them looked downright happy – but not one of them looked or sounded Alban. So how, he wondered idly, had they been persuaded to serve as crew on a blatantly illegal voyage?

Then, as Bayrd sidestepped a trio of sailors carrying what looked to be a new sail, he chanced to glance straight towards a large, broad-beamed merchant vessel. Both its masts were shattered, hanging from one side of the hull in a tangle of cordage, and it was being towed to shore by one of the battlerams whose banks of oars made them independent of the need for wind. Despite the damage and the mess, it looked familiar, and Bayrd frowned as he tried to remember where he had seen such a ship before.

The frown vanished as recognition took its place, and he began to laugh for the first time in many days. That was a treasure-ship, something his troop had been assigned to guard in Tanafen harbour three years before, on the memorable day when he came as close to seeing action in the king's service as he had ever done. Which had not been very close at all. The presence of *this* treasure-ship went a very long way to explain both the presence of the Droselan seamen and their cheerful disposition, and it also told him why Clan ar'Talvlyn had been sent to risk their necks escorting what had felt like a fool's errand.

Overlord Albanak was nobody's fool; distracting King Daykin's attention from the north had been for another purpose than just to let the clans and families escape. He must have known where that ship was docked, and might even have been faithfully drawing up the assignments to guard it on the day King Daykin decided to exile his most faithful retainers. Those details didn't matter any more. The old fox had known, and that was enough.

As Bayrd's quiet laughter subsided to a grin, he made a mental note for the future. When the honourable overlord of an honourable people decided it was time to set his honour aside and start to take instead of waiting to be given, he didn't waste time with half measures.

And with an unknown landfall just beyond what horizon he could see from the level of the deck, it was no time for half measures in defence. Better to be armed and armoured and not need it, than be caught trying to ward off an arrow with nothing but a wet shirt and a surprised expression. As he stalked towards the cluttered cabins in the stern, he finger-combed the long, still-wet strands of hair from his shoulders and fiddled at the nape of his neck for several minutes, trying to retie the warrior's braid that had come undone during the storm. After three useless attempts he muttered venomously under his breath and gave up, tying it back instead in a lank horse-tail that he knew would be the very devil to unpick once it had dried.

Bayrd had always felt envious of men and women who could put their hair in braid without needing to see what they were doing. There were no women on this bucket, and no men of his own blood-clan. Though he liked to look neat in his armour in case someone like the Lord Albanak saw him – neat troop-leaders were noticed, and got promotions – he wasn't so desperate that he would ask just anyone to tie his braid.

Men of other lines never touched a warrior's hair except when using the braid for its final purpose, as a handle for his severed head. With the weight of that implication behind it, to do so at any other time and for any other reason was an insult cancelled only by blood. Killing one of the crew at this stage was a fairly pointless exercise.

And while being the man who started a clan-war over the same trivial matter would get him many things, promotion and advancement – except to the top of a tall, sharp stake – were not among them. As he ducked into the cabin where he had stowed such of his gear as survived the storm, the thought tickled Bayrd's somewhat quirky and peculiar sense of humour, producing a bark of laughter that made a pair of passing sailors drop a hundred feet of rigging on their own feet, very hard . . .

Bayrd ar'Talvlyn stood ankle-deep in the ebbing tide and super-vised the unloading of the forty horses his ship had been carrying. Legs dangling, they hung from the cargo-nets slung around their bellies as resignedly quiet as pet cats picked up by children. Bayrd favoured them with a crooked grin, not fooled for a minute. Rubbing the still-raw scrape between his brows and mindful of what had almost happened when these same docile beasts were loaded, he stood well back.

There was a pile of gear on the beach, from this ship and many others, and Bayrd was not the only one to have been burrowing in it before landing. Many of the other warriors had come to the same conclusion regarding armour – theirs – and weapons – other people's. There were already several fully armoured *kailinin* trudging heavily about on the beach, waiting for their horses, and from what he could see of them, Bayrd felt that he had got the better part of the bargain.

He had chosen to wear only half-harness – combat leathers, a light helmet, his lamellar *tsalaer* and its pair of plated sleeves – until he felt less weary, or at least until one of his horses was on shore and able to carry part of the weight for him. The battle harness was not especially heavy in itself, but to men bone-weary from being battered by a storm, it was heavy enough.

There were other reasons why he had left off his mailshirt and armoured leggings: for fear of what seawater might do to their steel. All the rigid metal parts of Alban armour were lacquered against wear, weather and the occasional drenching, but that didn't mean it could be treated casually. A crack in the lacquer, an invisible eating-away beneath it – and all of a sudden you might find that one of the iron scales was no more than a puff of rust, and there was a blade in your guts. All for the want of a little care.

Bayrd backed off as Yarak was swung over the side. Of the five horses he owned, she was by far his favourite – and for all her dainty looks, by far the most dangerous if the devil bit her. Bayrd wouldn't have had it otherwise. The little grey mare was a pure-blood Ferhana, quick as a cat and eager for anything, whether it was hunting or war. She had cost him eight months' pay, and he had lost weight in the saving of it, being reluctant to spend on himself what might go to buy the mare that few days sooner. One day soon, Bayrd intended to get back all the money he had spent, and much more besides, when he put Yarak out to stud with some of the other clan-lords' high-mettled stallions. But not just yet.

Yes, and while you're dreaming, you might start thinking about another marriage, one to a high-clan lord's cseirin-*born daughter.*

One that would bring him into line for lordship of a clan of his own. The ar'Talvlyns were low-clan, and had been since they left the plains of Old Alba; if they hadn't achieved lordly status yet, they never would. Bayrd shook his head and laughed to himself. The hurt was fading, if he could think about taking another wife. It had been such a stupid accident, so avoidable . . . The cargo-crane's ratchets slipped a few teeth with a metallic screech, and Yarak whinnied nervously.

'Gently, damn you!' Bayrd roared at the sailors working its crank. 'Hurt the horse, and I'll hurt you!' He meant it, and not just because of any risk to his investment. Mahaut had helped him buy the horse, and when she had been killed by that drunken cart-driver – *may his spirit long wander between the winds!* thought

Bayrd, though even the curse was growing automatic and its venom attenuated by time – he had thrown himself into his work, gained two levels of rank, and lavished any affection that remained on the little grey.

Sometimes she returned it, nosing after apples or sap-sugar lumps with her velvety muzzle; and sometimes, out of sorts with the world, she responded by using him for target practice with her razory hoofs. Just like a woman. But then there were times when he too could be out of sorts, and he understood the way she felt. He could guess the way she would feel when her feet hit the water, although from her lack of squirming, the sea-voyage had taken some of the ginger out of her. It was just as well. There was a quarter-bred Andarran stallion to be dealt with yet, and three nondescript riding horses, and Bayrd had no desire to see Yarak take off down the beach in an excess of opinionated high spirits.

For one thing, there was far too much beach. She would be over the horizon before she ran out of hard, smooth, flat sand, and until she did, Yarak would see no reason to stop. If the idiot sailors had been any good at their job, they would have beached their ship the way so many others had done, throwing the rudders over at the right time so that now, with the tide receding, the vessels were beginning to heel over. Other *kailinin* were able to disembark their horses by slanted, sanded gangplanks. Why was he the only person dealing with a crane, and one operated by idiots at that?

Sorcery would have been a good idea: a softly spoken spell to float the horses and the baggage and the passengers safely to shore – even though Bayrd had been told that the power of sorcery was greatly exaggerated by those who didn't know its limitations. *Hospodar* Skarpeya knew.

In fact, bringing Skarpeya would have been a good idea, except that everyone else was blaming him for their exile, and not the true guilty party, King Daykin of Kalitz.

Bayrd kept his thoughts very much to himself on that matter, but he had met the man in the city of Kalitzim, when most of the others had not. It had been a strange encounter: Bayrd had known who he was, since the wizard had been pointed out at a distance on several occasions. But he hadn't been able to disapprove of him in the reflex, unthinking way that seemed to be required. There was nothing to dislike; or rather, he amended, nothing had been apparent from their brief meeting.

In fact, since Skarpeya had admired the horses being exercised in the ring, making enough knowledgeable comments that he plainly knew what he was talking about – and had praised Yarak most of all – Bayrd had come close to actually liking the man. He was a sorcerer, *an-pestrior*, something detestable. Liking him, or even thinking about not *dis*liking him, was all wrong.

Wasn't it?

'You think too much, ar'Talvlyn.'

Mahaut's father had said so more than once, and had not meant it kindly. 'You think too much, and about the wrong things.' Now there was real disapproval, if you wanted to see it done properly. He was not the only one to use that very phrase, either before or since, but Esak ar'Doren seemed more able than most to put his own twist of venom into the words. Bayrd had a sharp, quick mind, and plenty of willingness to use it both for his own good and that of others – when he was allowed to do so, and that was seldom enough. In a junior officer of low-clan birth, it was a trait that seemed to make people nervous, or suspicious, or even downright angry. Sometimes all three at once. Even though Esak was of a clan no more important than the ar'Talvlyns, he considered that his ambitions were higher than theirs and required all the help he could provide: cash, political contacts – and his daughter, married advantageously to bring in more of both.

In fact, disapproval was wrong. It was nothing so strong. Not hatred, and certainly not loathing; just irritation and dislike, the level of emotion a man might feel when he wants to swat a fly in the room and it won't oblige by coming close enough.

And Bayrd was out of reach. In all the years and throughout all the changes since they had left the steppes and become what passed for civilised – in that they now killed people who were not their enemies because they were paid to do so – one thing had stayed the same about the Albans. The rights of their women remained as they had been when the scattered name-families lived in the wide grass country, when survival in a land that could turn harsh and savage depended on equal responsibility for that survival. Depending on the family, those might be only the usual domestic privileges – which in the ordering of the home and the raising of young children outranked those of any man short of the clan-lord – or they might have all the rights of a linefather short of commanding in war. Arranged marriage was not unusual, but it required the agreement of the son – or daughter – in question, and, like sons, the daughters always had the rights of choice or of refusal in the matter of marriage, even to being permitted to wed an enemy if the possibility of such a situation arose. Several lasting alliances had developed out of such marriages – and several vicious small wars, but it was always considered that those might have happened anyway.

There had been some attempts at change, certainly, when some of the menfolk saw how meek and demure the ladies of Kalitz and Drosul seemed to be by comparison with their own women. But others saw what lay beneath the façade: pretty decorations for a rich man's house, and a source of children for his posterity, but nothing else. Small wonder the Droselan cities had so many courtesans: they were the source of companionship and intelligent conversation that Droselan men no longer sought at home – because they didn't expect to find it, rather than because it wasn't there.

When Mahaut decided she would accept Bayrd ar'Talvlyn's offer of marriage, there was nothing her father could do about it. His claims that she was marrying beneath her station fell on deaf ears. For one thing it was patently untrue, the two clans being of equal rank, and for another, it was apparent not only to them both but to other members of their two families that Esak ar'Doren's concern was not so much for Mahaut as for his own advancement. To attach his daughter, and his daughter's name, and thus his name and that of his clan, to someone more important than a low-clan *kailin*, no more than a Captain-of-One-Hundred in the Guard Company of a little foreign king.

Things had not gone the way he intended, and when they were free at last of Esak's whining – by the Lord Albanak's decree, for the sake of peace in their house and in his – Bayrd and Mahaut were happy for the two years before the accident. And afterwards . . .

Afterwards her father blamed Bayrd. He listened to the accusations no more than he had listened to the complaints, or at least gave no sign of listening, although inside, in his darker moments, Bayrd ar'Talvlyn wondered if they might not have been true.

21

Yarak's hoofs splashed into the shallow water, and she started to struggle for the first time so that he hurried forwards to release her from the cargo-net. The grey mare snorted and stamped, splashing him, but didn't try to bite a chunk out of the hand with which he patted her nose. That was encouraging at least. Bayrd led her out of the sea and saddled her quickly – the saddle and bridle had been laid out ready on top of the rest of his gear – then hobbled her with a loop of leading-rein around one foreleg. Assured that she wouldn't be going anywhere without him, he returned to the ship and yelled for them to send the next horse down.

It was going to be a long afternoon.

Farren the poacher awoke from a sound sleep with the sun in his eyes, flakes of dried bracken crunching between his teeth, and an uncomfortable awareness that the sand beneath the bracken had managed to insinuate itself grittily into the damper crevices of his person. He yawned, scratched, stretched, and stared up into the cloudless sky.

High above him, white flecks slid and spiralled lazily across the blue: gulls returning to the sea after spending the stormy night well inland. Farren hastily examined his clothing. No, there were no white spots to match the ones overhead. And anyway, that was supposed to be lucky.

'Lucky for the washerwoman,' the poacher growled. The gulls yelled derisively at each other, but he ignored them. All was calm, all was peaceful, and there were no sounds save the distant crashing of the waves and the cries of potentially profitable wildlife. He relaxed again, suspecting that the storm last night was to blame. Farren had never been fond of windy weather, with or without rain to keep it company. It had made him sleep badly, when he had managed to sleep at all, and now he was starting awake at every little sound. Ignoring the abrasive scraping of sand in his crotch, he punched the makeshift mattress of bracken back into a more comfortable shape, and settled back to snooze a little longer.

Then he sat bolt upright again, frozen like the wild animals he so often hunted, with the instinctive knowledge that neither the sun in the heavens nor the gulls in the air nor the waves on the shore had been the cause of his awakening. Farren's eyes widened in

22

shock. It had been a sound, something more felt than heard, something from so deep in his sleep that he had no memory of it, and no recognition either.

Then he heard it once more, and this time he was wide awake: but there was still no recognition of the alien noise, a long, grinding crunch rumbling up from the beach, slicing through all the other noises of the summer afternoon like a razor through fine silk. Something massive had run up the beach and slammed into the bank of shingle and pebbles separating the land from the open sea beyond. As all his scornful dismissals of the old tales came rushing back like waves through a breached sea-wall, a spasm of superstitious terror cramped his guts. The Lords and Ladies of the Deep Sea did not need a storm to help them leave their realm – and then, with an embarrassed grin, he realised that whatever he was hearing, it was not the sound of gigantic footsteps. The grating boom came again, and then again, each time closer together, until those individual impacts merged into a single constant mutter of noise.

Farren rose cautiously from his nest in the bracken. Though his sharp ears could hear something that might have been the beat of hoofs, it was a thin thread woven into the blanket of sound rolling in from the sea. This was not just some Prytenek lord exercising his horses along the flat, open strand of Dunakr; and to the poacher's mercenary mind, that meant it might be something worth knowing, either for personal use or because the High Lord Gelert might pay well to learn about . . . whatever it was. Either way, he moved more furtively than usual. It was just as well.

He had seen ships before, but only as scraps of bright cloth far out at sea when the sun struck colour from their sails. Those had been no more perilous than butterflies, or chips of bark floated in a children's race across a pond. These were no butterflies.

Some were driven by the wind in their sails – or their remnants of sails – others were towed either by their better-canvassed brethren or by the low, long vessels that moved in a swirl of oar-foam and paid no heed to the winds of the world. By this way and by that they rode in towards the shore, iron beaks and wooden hulls cresting each breaking wave until they slammed deep into the land like a predator's claws into its prey. The long curve of the shoreline was crammed with ships, and there were more – many, many more – drifting silently from the heat-mist out in the bay.

There had been raids before. Sea-robbers from across the eastern ocean occasionally appeared like wolves in a sheep-fold, seized whatever could be found within half a day's march of the coast, and then made off with their booty before the High Lord and his men could descend on them. After many years of harassment, the people of Prytenon had given up hoping for a swift response from Gelert's people – whose predecessors for generations back had been no more effectual, seeing all this as a game that they would or would not play depending on their mood – and adopted their own simple solution. They moved everything they couldn't stand to lose a full day's march inland.

As Farren huddled behind a tussock of sea-grass and watched the ships begin to disgorge their cargo of people, it was plain even to the uneducated poacher that a day's march was no longer an obstacle. This was no raid.

It was an invasion.

2

Claiming

B AYRD AR'TALVLYN SAT on a heap of baggage and chewed slowly on a piece of smoked and salted beef. It had all the tenderness of a slab of wood, though fortunately somewhat more flavour. He rinsed the accumulated saltiness from his mouth with a small, careful swallow of watered wine, and peered into the pottery flask in an attempt to see how much was left. From the gurgling sound it had made as he drank, not much. That was a problem.

Bayrd's military talents lay less with grand strategy than with tactics, and more important still, with logistics and supply. An army might march on its stomach, as various wise generals had said in the past – and would doubtless say again, it being too memorable an aphorism to waste – but that same army would trip on its tongue if the tongue was too dry. Bayrd had coined the saying himself, only to find that it was considered yet another demonstration that he was a man too clever for his own good. There was little point in offering views and opinions if they were ignored or dismissed all the time, but he kept trying. Sooner or later someone would take notice, not just of what he said and did, but of what he might be worth – and what promotions might come with it. Until then . . . He sighed, and tried to tear another few shreds from the unyielding strip of beef.

Almost all the cargo had been unloaded; it made a fascinating collection of booty, and a demonstration of just how much a people trained for generations in the art of pillaging could make off with in a hurry. But while there was a great deal of food – battle rations of the salty, smoky sort he was trying to gnaw through, for the most part – and a vast quantity of wines and spirits, there was less water than he liked to see. It had been a hot day's work, especially for the *kailinin* wearing armour such as himself, and Bayrd knew that if everyone else had been drinking as much water as he had, the supplies were even lower than they had been when the first ship's prow drove into the sand.

There was water somewhere, the greenery inland said as much; but what else might be inland, what spears and arrows might be concealed in the thick shadows of the distant forest, had prevented the Lord Albanak from sending out a watering-party until everything was off the ships and his people had made at least a start on building themselves a fortified camp. It was practical advice, if Albanak-*arluth* – and the sailors who crewed them – accepted that the only sturdy building material anywhere on this beach was the timber of the ships. But Bayrd could see that the very act of building such a camp might lead to trouble: simply by the builders consuming the last few barrels of water.

He got to his feet, shaded his eyes and looked up and down the wide, flat beach. They were all here. All that remained of the Alban people. There had been losses: people washed overboard or crushed to death by shifting cargo, ships that had left harbour and not been seen again. Thirteen thousand men, women and children had left Kalitz and Drosul. There were maybe eleven thousand here. It had been brutal, but not a disaster; not yet.

A dousing with salt seawater last night; a long day's work in the hot sun with only salt-preserved meats and pickled vegetables with which to break their fast; and soon only wine to quench their thirst. To Bayrd's mind, unrestricted by the needs of lordly high command, *that* was where disaster lay. The rich vintages of Briej, Hauverne, and Seurandec were all very well as plunder, but sliding into a drunken slumber on a potentially hostile shore – even behind whatever wood and sand fortifications could be built on a beach and withstand the turning tide – would likely be a sleep from which these people would not awaken.

Bayrd took a few deep breaths in an attempt to calm himself down, because he knew from experience that if he went to the Lord Albanak in this mood, he would end up shouting. One did not shout at the Overlord; it was . . . inadvisable. More than just discourteous, dishonourable, and a guarantee of being ignored more certain even than the usual sin of being too obviously clever, it might draw much more of Albanak's often-irritable attention than any man of a lesser clan could hope to survive. There were more diplomatic ways in which to convey urgency – if he could just think of one.

Yarak nudged him in the back. The mare had been ambling about, pausing now and then to munch wisps of hay from her fodder-net, or slurp some of that precious water from Bayrd's upturned helmet. Now she wanted the hobble off her leg, because she wanted to run.

'All right,' said Bayrd, fishing in his belt-pouch for a couple of dried apples he had put there earlier. 'Here. Eat this, pushy one, and then you'll get to stretch your legs. Believe me.'

Since the Lord Albanak was notoriously strict in his regard for protocol, he buckled his full weaponbelt around his waist – longsword, shortsword, dagger and all – and arranged a blue *elyu-dlas* Colour-Robe over his armour. When he looked down at it to admire the effect, Bayrd swore under his breath and tried without much success to smooth out the worst creases. He dried the last few drops of water from the inside of the helmet with its padded liner, then clapped liner and helmet on his head, secured the cords of its warmask under his chin, and swung up into Yarak's saddle before the mare had even finished crunching her second apple.

Once there, he scanned the beach until he saw what he had expected: the banner of a green tree on blue, and a glittering assemblage of armed and armoured men standing beneath it. That was Overlord Albanak all right: yes indeed, even after a storm at sea and on the frantic first day of an invasion, he was always one for observing all the social niceties. As if he was more important than even he thought he was. Bayrd allowed himself the sardonic smile that would be most unwise when close enough for the Overlord to see it, then put heels to Yarak's flanks and took off at an easy canter down the beach.

Farren huddled lower and watched. Knowing what was going on, and what he was expected to do about it, were completely different things. He was only a thief and a poacher, his sole claim to fame the amount of money he owed to people, and none of that equipped him to do anything but stare.

There were many horsemen milling about on the beach; not as many as he had seen when Lord Gelert summoned his vassals to

27

make war on the lords of Elthan or Cerenau, but enough that he preferred to watch from the safety of cover. They wore armour and carried weapons with an extravagance that shocked him to the bottom of his thrifty soul. One man came riding along the flat sand – Farren automatically tried to put a price on the handsome grey horse – and he was wearing or carrying enough iron and steel about his person to have made spearheads for a hundred Prytenek warriors. But not one of those warriors would have demeaned themselves or their courage by wearing so much protective armour. It was as if this man and the others like him were afraid to die.

His spear was unlike those of Lord Gelert's men: it was long, light and slender, and ended in a wicked tapering point. Had Farren known as much about the use and function of weapons as he did about their potential value, he would have kept his head further down instead of raising it for a better look. Long spear, long sword, long-hafted axe and a cased bow small enough to be a child's toy; they were all weapons with a long reach, horseman's weapons, to be used from the saddle.

Farren had his first lesson in just how those weapons could be used a few seconds later. The grey horse slackened its pace and the spearhead flashed once in the sunlight as it twirled around to slip into a scabbard behind the rider's right knee. Then the horse exploded forward into a full gallop – straight for where the poacher lay concealed.

Before Farren realised that the little toy bow was even out of its case, an arrow kicked sand in his face and went snaking off through the grass. Another followed the first, coming close enough that its fletching scraped a hot line across his face.

Farren the poacher scrambled to his feet just as a third arrow ripped through the sleeve of his hunting-coat as if the heavy leather garment wasn't there. He felt a sting that was no sand-flea, clapped a hand to his arm, and saw the most unpleasant sight possible: his own blood. On any ordinary day Farren would have tumbled like a shot rabbit from the shock alone, but this was no ordinary day, these unerring arrows were no ordinary threat, and fear of the foreign horseman who was shooting at him put the spurs into his flanks as even Lord Gelert in full cry at his heels had never done. He tripped in the matted bracken at the crest of the next line of dunes and rolled downhill in a shower of sand, but was on his feet and running again before he even hit the bottom, listening in terror for a sound of pursuing hoofbeats that never came.

Yarak's hoofs went crashing through the band of shingle that edged the long beach, and the grey put herself at the first dune as though taking a jump on an assault course. She shot over it with feet to spare and would have charged up the next one with equal ease had Bayrd not reined her in. The Ferhana mare reared back, squealing and pawing the air like the most ferocious stallion ever foaled; she wanted to go, was determined to go, and only the pressure of the bit on her soft mouth was holding her back.

Bayrd ar'Talvlyn rose in his stirrups and sent a third arrow whirring after the running figure. That one probably missed too – though the man fell out of sight, Bayrd knew a stumble when he saw one – and he cursed venomously at his own poor marksmanship. He was doing a lot of swearing today, what with one thing and another, and this was adding insult to injury. Three clean misses at two hundred yards on a still day would have been enough to earn loss-of-privilege penalties had he seen any of his own Hundred shoot so badly.

But he wasn't going to let his horse go charging off over unknown ground, especially unknown ground like this. Sand dunes meant rabbits; rabbits meant burrows; and burrows at a gallop meant a mount with a broken leg. He wasn't risking five thousand crowns' worth of Ferhana horseflesh with a pedigree almost as long as his own for some scruffy peasant who with luck wouldn't stop running for the rest of the day. Bayrd smiled thinly at that thought, because it wasn't strictly true. He wouldn't have risked even the meanest of his riding-horses without a much better reason than this. A *kailin* had six legs, so the saying went, and was responsible for keeping all of them healthy.

At least it had proven something that he could use as reasoned argument for a watering-patrol when he finally spoke to the Lord Albanak. There was nothing out among the dunes except for a single man in the wrong place at the wrong time. Nothing threatening. Otherwise he would have known about it by now. There was already a fourth arrow on the string of his bow, but it wouldn't be needed now and –

Bayrd took one look, yelped, and dropped it. The arrow went end-for-end to the ground and drove a little way in under its own weight, then toppled slowly sideways and lay there.

It was sizzling.

Wreathed from nock to point in a slowly fluttering scarf of blue flame, it was making a sound absolutely like that of frying bacon. Every now and then the barbed head spat fat white sparks that went dancing across the sand, as though it was still red-hot under the hammer of the smith who had forged it eight months before. And yet the wooden shaft wasn't charred, the blue and white feathers of the fletching weren't shrivelled by the flames. It just lay there. Sizzling . . .

This time Bayrd ar'Talvlyn didn't swear. There were some things for which mere obscenity was inadequate, and this was one of those things. He blinked at the finger and reinforced thumb of his leather shooting-glove. Nothing; no scorch-marks, not even a smell of burning – and he had certainly felt no heat. But when he looked down again at the arrow lying on the dune, he could see how the sand on which it lay had puddled into crude glass, a thick green honey that flowed sluggishly for a few inches until it cooled and cracked like dirty ice.

He shivered so that the hair on his forearms stood on end, and at the same time felt sweat-beads forming on the hollow of his back beneath his armour. The fright came more from knowing what had happened, and the shock from discovering that he was capable of such a thing. He had been told – warned, almost – that the Art Magic was not as difficult as it appeared. In its manifestations of raw power, it derived as much from the personal force of the wielder as from words written in an ancient book or circles drawn in chalk or stranger things. Some people, all unknowing, possessed more talent than others, and needed only the right burst of passion to release their potential. Skarpeya had told him that.

Skarpeya had been right.

Bayrd dismounted and bent down to stare, moving gingerly because even though the arrow seemed cool, the half-melted sand in which it lay was still hot enough to throw off a shimmering haze of heat. Drawing his *taipan* shortsword, he poked with the blade until it could be lifted free. Even then he was wary, first dabbing with outstretched fingertips like a cat at a spider before risking his skin by picking it up. And against all reason, it was cool indeed. More than that: it was cold, as cold as a bar of ice. In a sudden spasm he gripped the arrow in both hands, broke it in half and flung the pieces far away, then straightened up, trying to convince himself that it was the coldness which had made him shiver all along.

When he swung up into the saddle and turned Yarak's head towards the beach, he did not look back.

Like most of the other *kailinin* moving to and fro along the shoreline, Overlord Albanak was wearing armour; however, unlike the drab, workaday mail of lesser warriors, he was encased in *an-moyya-tsalaer* of the old style. It was a spectacular full battle harness, its gilded scales laced together with dark blue leather thongs into rigid flat boards of metal, that very inflexibility a demonstration that the man who wore it had no need to run about a battlefield, but merely commanded others to do so. His helmet was plumed with a spray of white egret feathers that had evidently suffered less harm during the voyage than many of his retainers, and its peak and wide neck-guard, thought Bayrd sourly, looked to make a fine sunshade.

However, since the clan-lord was a stoutly built man in what was normally called his vigorous middle years, the effect of that four-panelled cuirass and the broad helmet on top was to make him look like a richly dressed cube. Sitting boxlike on the box his harness had been packed in, itself draped and padded with a handsome bolt of green silk, Albanak-*arluth* had all the easy assurance of a man whose rank and station in life was high enough that all he needed to do was watch others work. Even if he did look like something a child had built from blocks.

As he cantered closer, Bayrd was impressed despite himself and his own worried thoughts. None too fond of the Overlord, for various reasons of his own that had little to do with the man's abilities, it was as well for the sake of morale that someone should have been able to trick themselves out handsomely and not spoil the effect by sweaty labours in the hot sun. Even though he hoped some colour had come back into his face, he was uncomfortably aware that beneath his crest-coat he probably looked – and smelled – less than good.

'Bayrd-*an*.' Albanal swung one arm across his chest and then out in a lazy salute, 'I greet you.'

He always tried to address his retainers by name, as if to make them feel known and somehow important. The gesture would have carried more weight with Bayrd had he not seen the clan-lord turn quickly to one of his retinue and ask who was approaching. Still, even if it rang a little false, the effort had been made.

'I greet you, Albanak-*arluth*.' His own salute was crisp and precise, parade-ground perfect. 'You came to no harm in the storm. It pleases me to see you well.'

So much for small-talk. The forms of speech between a high-clan lord and a low-clan retainer were cumbersome and stilted, very much in the manner of a Kalitzak vassal addressing a superior nobleman. It had developed among successive Overlords of the Alban clans, and the warriors who seven generations past were their equals, but so slowly that it had become accepted. As men rose and fell in rank, it became difficult to find points of common interest to talk about until finally no one made the effort any more. Only one or two clans, the ar'Talvlyn among them, found anything wrong in it – and that, the other clan-lords said, was no more than simple envy that they were low rather than high.

Whatever the reason, Bayrd didn't care for it. Nor had his father, or *his* father before him. But today was not the time to make experiments in social change. Today was for reporting the presence of a possible spy, or at the very least a pair of unwanted eyes. Eyes, moreover, in a head that Bayrd had signally failed to bring back with him, despite – what had happened.

' . . . and shot at him three times.' Bayrd made no mention of the fourth arrow. He had still not quite come to terms with the incident himself, and until then it was nobody's business but his own. If Mahaut had been alive there would have been someone else to talk to, but as it was . . .

He did his best to conceal his annoyance at letting the man in the sand-dunes get away, since none of the others seemed especially worried. 'But I missed. When I last caught sight of him he was still running. At such a speed that whoever rules in this land will know about our presence soon enough.' The reaction was still less than he had expected. 'Lord, I said . . .'

'I heard what you said.' Albanak not only looked unconcerned, he sounded so as well.

It was enough to raise a small niggle of suspicion in the back of Bayrd's mind. There had been a great many ships in the harbours of Drosul and Kalitz just at a time when they were needed. The treasure-barge had been there too, just when Albanak needed enough gold to pay the crews of his fleet. And this shore was more than just the first landfall the storm-driven fleet had reached. Everything had been planned in advance, and the only variable in the equation was King Daykin's decision to throw his mercenaries out.

'We – all of us, and perhaps our families as well – we are expected here,' he said, a flat statement rather than a question, offering the Lord Albanak an opportunity to deny it. Or ignore it, as more usually happened when someone lower than *kailin-eir* put forward a controversial view in the hearing of high-clan lords. For his own part Bayrd felt certain; just as he felt equally certain that as a low-clan *kailin* he would never be told the truth of it all. In that at least he was mistaken. Keo ar'Lerutz leaned forward and muttered behind his armoured hand into the Overlord's ear, and was answered after a few seconds' consideration with a nod of agreement – the unexpected sight of which sent Bayrd's eyebrows up.

'Get down off your high horse,' said Albanak-*arluth*, the inflection of his voice neutral enough that he might have meant only, or a great deal more, than the simple content of the words. Bayrd did so at once, and went on his knees to offer the Overlord proper obeisance rather than a military salute. 'No.' Albanak gestured for him to straighten up. 'Nothing so obvious. I take the intent for the action. Now listen and be still. Gyras, tell him.'

'There is no more room for us in Kalitz any more,' said Lord Gyras ar'Dakkur. 'Nor in Drosul, or even Yuvan. There are too many alliances between those little lords for us to find one willing to defy the rest. Not through any lack of living-space, but because we, and what we represent, no longer fit. Our presence has become a reminder to the so-cultured people of those lands that once, and not long ago, they were less cultured than they would have the world believe. That once they needed us. Now – now they'd prefer to forget we ever existed.

'I – ' he made a sweeping gesture with both hands to include the Overlord and the other half-dozen armoured high-clan lords standing around him, ' – *we* have seen this state of mind take shape, slowly at first and then faster. That is why our departure from Daykin's realm was more disciplined than it might otherwise have been. We were already well down the road of preparing for such an eventuality.'

'And with more warning,' put in Keo ar'Lerutz, 'we might have left the King of Kalitz a memento of his dishonour that he would not soon forget.'

That was unnecessary, even if the words were only a relief of feelings. Bayrd hoped they meant nothing more. Even so, he looked shocked, and didn't try to hide it. Responding to one dishonourable action with another was not the way he had been brought up. Honesty and the keeping of a sworn word was the Alban way, not this twisting of meanings to suit the way the wind blew.

'You are just *an-kailin tleir'ek*,' said Lord Serej ar'Diskan. 'What can you know of high matters?'

Bayrd gave the man a sharp look, not liking the patronising sound of his words. 'My lord,' he said carefully, 'I may be just a low-clan Captain-of-one-Hundred, but I am *kailin* for all that. I know what honour is. And truth. And the keeping of oaths.'

He half-expected to be challenged for what could easily be considered a slur – but if an Alban warrior could not speak his mind in such matters to an Alban clan-lord in the hope of a fair hearing, then there was no longer any point to common courtesy. Ar'Diskan stared at him for several seconds while Bayrd braced himself for what might follow; then relaxed as the clan-lord merely grunted, half-turned to Lord Albanak and rolled his eyes expressively skyward as if suggesting *what did you expect from this one?*

'You may wish to appoint yourself our conscience, Bayrd-*eir*,' said Albanak, and Bayrd hoped that his use of the enhanced honorific wasn't accidental. 'Just don't be so obtrusive about it. I mentioned your high horse before, but it seems you have an over-literal mind. I meant more than just dismount.'

'I have my father's training.'

'A good man. But your faults aren't his. He never thought too much. You do.'

Bayrd stifled a groan as the same old criticism came trotting out again. 'You aren't the first to say that, Lord.'

'I know,' said Albanak. 'And I won't be the last.' Then he gave Bayrd an odd, sympathetic glance, one suggesting that when he had first greeted the younger man by name, he had known it without needing to ask. And knew much more than just the name, too.

'Thinking too much,' the Overlord said quietly, 'is only a fault when it's obvious, Bayrd-*an*.' No honorific this time. It seemed his promotion had been brief, or an accident after all. 'It makes those who seldom think at all feel uneasy. So . . . be more circumspect. And tell me what it is you were thinking.' Albanak looked from side to side at the faces of his other lords, and nodded at whatever it was he saw there.

Bayrd could see their faces too, and the expressions of these powerful men were such that he could easily have wished himself elsewhere. Some were irritated by the presumption of going over their heads to ask the opinion of a low-clan *kailin*, and others seemed more amused that their overlord thought he might say anything of value. It was not that the horse should sing well or badly, but that it should sing at all. Only Gyras ar'Dakkur seemed interested in more than his curiosity value, and that might have been because he was the only clan-lord present able to control what his own features revealed to the world at large. It was a useful art, and Bayrd mentally determined to learn it – if he survived the next five minutes or so.

Though such extreme reactions were uncommon, it was also not entirely unheard-of for an angry high-clan lord to wrench longsword from scabbard and cut down the source of his anger, whether enemy or peasant or just inopportune subordinate. Bayrd had seen it done, just once; but the length of time it had taken to wash spatters of blood out of his clothing had driven the lesson home.

Don't annoy a clan-lord, and if you do, be prepared to duck – or lose your head.

'I repeat what I said before, Lord. This landing was no stroke of good fortune. We were heading for this beach, or at least a shore along this same coastline, in this same . . . domain, lordship, whatever.'

'Province,' said Albanak. 'The province of Prytenon, ruled by one Guelerd, or Gelert as they pronounce it here. Correct so far, ar'Talvlyn. Continue.'

'This Gue—, Gelert, is not just expecting us to somehow arrive on the threshold of his province. He invited us.'

'Where in the Nine Hot Hells did you hear that?' snapped Serej ar'Diskan, his black moustache bristling with fury. Even though such suspicion might have been justified – and it was not, Albanak's approval had made that plain enough – such harshness was impolite even to an outlander. To another Alban, and regardless of any difference in rank, it was boorish to the point of insult – and with ar'Diskan's earlier impudence still very much in mind Bayrd had to make a conscious effort to keep his hand away from the hilt of one sword or the other. His ears went hot when he realised that Albanak-*arluth* and Gyras ar'Dakkur had seen the whole play of emotion across his face, and had almost certainly noticed the involuntary twitch of his right hand before he brought it under control. Yes indeed: Lord ar'Dakkur's skill of controlling his expression was something he should learn, as soon as he was able . . .

'I did not *hear* it, my lords,' he said slowly, addressing the gathering in general rather than Serej so that he could persuade himself that he was not making a direct response to the crudely worded question. 'I merely put together what I saw, and drew my own conclusions. Gelert is at war, or planning a war, and wants warriors he can trust. Not those who might change their allegiance – which must be common here, or it wouldn't have concerned him so much.'

'Well done!' Albanak laughed aloud and struck his gauntleted hands together twice, in what for him was a transport of delight. 'Well done indeed.' Again he glanced at the faces of his lords. 'Gentlemen, if this is what thinking too much will do, then I warrant we can allow a deal more of it. Bayrd-*eir*, you are too clever to lead only a hundred men. Lead a Thousand; you are now *kailin-eir myl'ek*, by my command.'

Bayrd blinked, and managed to prevent a large, stupid grin of delight from spreading all over his face. Not just that someone had finally heard what he might have to say, but that of all people it had been the Overlord himself. If this was how one earned promotion off the field of battle, then he felt certain he could tolerate the strain. Lordship and the elevation of clan ar'Talvlyn became suddenly more than just an idle dream. This time when he knelt and lowered his forehead to the ground between his hands in formal First Obeisance and genuine deep gratitude, the Overlord accepted it with good grace.

'Up,' said Albanak after a few seconds. 'You're right, of course. The lords of this land have always treated war as a sporting event, whether to extend their domains or their herds or to gain influence over one another. They buy and sell the players – the lesser warriors not bound by house-allegiance – in the same way that the Yuvain and the Kalitzak trade in riders for their racing-stables. Gelert has decided to change that. He wants to bring the entire country together under one ruler. Himself. And he wants us to help him do it.'

'You don't trust him, Lord.'

'Why do you say so?'

Bayrd gestured at the rampart slowly rising along the landward side of the beach. It may have been no more than a steep bank of sand from the ditch dug to its landward side, but it was well packed down, mixed with shingle and capped with a wooden palisade of timbers ripped from such ships as could spare them, and more than anything else it was well sited: above anything but the highest tidemark, and following the first line of dunes so that they added to its strength.

'That tells me,' he said. 'He expects only the mercenary army he hired. The presence of their families might suggest a permanence of occupation enough to give him second thoughts. He might try to force us out. And . . .' Bayrd shrugged, a movement exaggerated by his armoured shoulders. 'And you don't trust him anyway.'

'Are you trying for a further promotion?' Before he could answer, Albanak waved the reply to silence. 'Never mind. Though I find myself wondering why *thinking too much* has become such a disparaging phrase. It seems more useful than that . . .'

The Overlord dropped that train of thought and stood up, signalling to one of the retainers who stood just out of earshot of the private high-clan conversation. 'Summon all the clan-lords not already here,' he said as the warrior went to one knee and awaited orders. 'Have them follow my banner to –' he looked thoughtfully inland, then picked a spot and pointed, '– to there. I have something to say. Something important.'

He might have received unexpected betterment of his position, but Bayrd ar'Talvlyn learned at once that unless the Overlord had invited him directly, which he had not, he was not entitled to remain in the company of clan-lords of whatever rank. Lord ar'Diskan pointed that out quite bluntly once the protection of the Overlord's banner moved away, dismissing him with excessive relish and hard words spoken in a low voice no one else could hear.

He planted himself in front of Bayrd and stood there, smiling unpleasantly and toying with his moustache until the younger *kailin* gave him a proper salute and led his horse away, then hurried off to join the rest of the nobility and gentry at the new site of Albanak-*arluth*'s banner. His departure was fortunate, in that it saved him from noticing the thoughtful stare that Bayrd directed at his retreating back.

Clan ar'Diskan was still far above clan ar'Talvlyn – but less so now than it had been an hour ago. And patience was a well-known trait of all the ar'Talvlyns, patience that could be cuddled close and kept warm for years at a time if need be. Bayrd had waited before. He could wait again; and if need be his children – once he had fathered them – could wait after him. One day the right time would come. What that time might be, and what it would be right for, remained to be seen. That was the virtue of patience.

Other warriors began to gather, those not busy with other tasks or of sufficient status to lay their duties aside for a while, and with them came the old people, the wives, the consorts, the children – all who could spare a few moments to hear what their Overlord had to say. Rumour of something afoot had raced through the embryo camp, moving among the clans even faster than Albanak's message. Bayrd sat easily in Yarak's saddle, feet kicked free of the stirrup-irons and one knee crooked around the pommel, watching them. Now and then he saw familiar faces, heard an exchange of friendly words or a speculation about what was happening.

Though he knew, or at least guessed, Bayrd said nothing of it. That would have been betrayal of a confidence, and dishonourable. Instead he waited with the rest, and thought again about what had happened to the arrow. Skarpeya would have laughed had he been there to see it. The wizard had given every evidence of having a sense of humour – another thing about him which had surprised Bayrd. He had never associated laughter and sorcery before. Skarpeya might also have been able to tell him what had happened, why it had happened, and how to control it, but Skarpeya was in Kalitzim and he was here, on a beach in Prytenon, wondering.

Clad in their Colour-Robes of green and white, a small group of *kailinin* rode past; and though one or two inclined their heads in greeting, most disregarded his presence. It was a typical response from his ex-in-laws. He nodded distantly, sufficiently lost in his own thoughts not to take offence. Once Bayrd was widowed, clan ar'Doren had seemed content enough to scatter their relationship to clan ar'Talvlyn along with their sister Mahaut's ashes. Even old Esak's death had done nothing to close the rift, and if that was how they felt about it, well and good.

He was, and had always been, on better terms with his first wife's line. Lorey ar'Harik was still a friend. She had said herself that while their marriage had been a mistake, which it had, the intention behind it – closer ties between two low-clan families for mutal advantage and advancement – had worked. At least the ties were still there, the advantage had worked, and if today was an indication, the advancement was beginning at last. Clan ar'Harik should be pleased.

Bayrd smiled nastily. Even if the next step up might have to be on Serej ar'Diskan's face, the prospect had a certain appeal. He listened briefly to what the Lord Albanak was saying, then ignored the rest. He had heard it before. Indeed, from the few words he had just caught, he had said some of it himself. But when Albanak raised both hands above his head and Bayrd saw what he carried there, he sat up very straight and started to pay attention.

It was a sword.

This sword was not the one Albanak-*arluth* usually wore at his hip. That still hung there, an ornate hilt in an ornate scabbard, and it was a *taiken* longsword, modern – allowing for the hundred years since it was forged – straight and double-edged, with an elegant long taper to the point. The sword in his hands was far older. It was plain steel: unadorned, unpolished, still straight – but with only a single edge and a sharply angled point whetted bright and glinting against the dull grey metal. Its hilt was severely plain, a safe place to grip the blade and nothing more, and there was no guard. This weapon had been made for cutting, not for fighting. There was no need of a guard.

The length of metal gave an impression of stark utility: a cleaver, something created for no other purpose than cutting flesh. Nowadays a sword doubled as both weapon and adornment for the home and the belt of the warrior who owned it. Not that Albanak owned this sword. He held it in trust for past and future generations. Together with his very name, which was no name of his own but the title of his rank, it had been the symbol of the Overlord of Alba for longer than even the Keepers of Years could remember.

Its name was Greylady.

He brought the sword down in a lazy sweep across the ground between his feet. The cut was purely symbolic, without any real force, but Greylady's edge parted the matted grass and bracken and the packed sand beneath as though they had not been there. In the sudden stillness as everyone present realised what he intended to do, the sound of three more cuts was loud enough even for Bayrd to hear, half a bowshot away. Albanak stooped, took a handful of grass, twisted once and pulled. The square of dirt beneath it lifted neatly away like the head of a defeated enemy, and like a severed head, he drove Greylady's point into the centre of the square and held it up so that all could see.

'Here is the Land, and all that grows upon the Land, taken by the sword and held by the sword! Let any who claim otherwise defend it by the sword!'

It was an old, old ceremony, and Bayrd wondered what Lord Gelert of Prytenon would say had he been here to see it, because with those four token cuts he was no longer Lord of anything, save by the sufferance of Albanak. It now only remained to do in reality what had been done in ritual.

Albanak-*arluth* wiped the ancient blade with a cloth of white linen and handed it back to one of his retainers, undid his helmet and handed that back as well. Then he stood with arms folded, and looked in silence at his assembled lords and warriors. There had been no dissenting voice at what he had done, no outcry that it was a dishonourable act to enter a country by false declaration of intent.

Not even Bayrd ar'Talvlyn said anything, though he suspected that some of the high-clan lords around Albanak were expecting to hear both him and others with his turn of mind. But this was a different matter than that concerning the King of Kalitz. No oaths of fealty or service had been given or exchanged, no contracts had been signed, and he doubted that there had been any meeting face to face between Albanak and Gelert, or even between their higher lords. The Prytenek had intended to cheat his own compatriots, and had been cheated in his turn. It had long been known that all was fair in love and war – or the business equivalents of both.

'We were a banished people,' said Albanak at last, his voice not loud but pitched to carry well. 'We left our own lands long ago, enticed by the promise of silver and a new dwelling-place. We took the silver and the place to live, and did honest duty in exchange. Then the silver was withheld, and the land was taken back, and we were cast upon the storm. But our skills remain: with horse, with sword, with bow. With those skills we will hold this new land, and we will not be banished again!'

He looked slowly from side to side, at low-clan and at high, at men and women and children, and seemed satisfied with whatever it was he saw there. 'There can be no going back. There will *be* no going back. Burn the ships.'

3

Challenge

THE SHIPS BURNED. Long banners of dirty smoke trailed low over the water, stinging the eyes if the wind shifted, and filling the air with a reek of melting pitch and scorching timber that was nothing like the homely smell of firewood. Every now and again a sail would ignite with a surprising bright flash of yellow flame, but for the most part the ships, stripped of everything that could conceivably be useful, charred slowly to the waterline, then wallowed, hissed steam, and sank.

Bayrd ar'Talvlyn sat crosslegged at the edge of the beach and watched them burn, coughing occasionally when a drift of smoke caught at his throat. He had taken his armour off again, since there was nothing that had to be done at once, and the sun was warm and pleasant when the clouds of smoke didn't obscure it.

Mevn ar'Dru knelt behind him, fussing quietly under her breath as she tried to work the knots out of his hair. By contrast with the fire and destruction along the beach, their little scene looked improbably domestic, though every now and then Bayrd winced and hissed between his teeth as a particular tangle refused to give way to her fingers without some force being applied. He didn't mind overmuch about those occasional small stabs of discomfort; like Mevn's constant muttering of annoyance – which no matter how it sounded, had nothing to do with the state of his warrior's braid – they were something else to think about. Something besides burning arrows and burning ships, the loss of any chance to retire in good order if events turned against them, and the crooked reasoning which had prompted Albanak-*arluth* to issue such an order.

His own poor ship was well alight, a dance of flames and a crawl of embers, all shrouded in that stinking smoke. It was not as if Bayrd had any say in the matter – though if he had, the vessel would have been left alone. But despite his promotion, clan ar'Talvlyn didn't even rank high enough to have a clan-lord, only a Head of House, and being accustomed to obedience they did as they were told. They were not alone. Most of the ships that flared along the shoreline had common sails, undyed canvas without clan Colours. For the most part the low-clan Albans had followed their Overlord's command without question – just because it was customary to obey.

Others, higher placed, had done so because, like Albanak, they had thought the lack of any means of retreat would stiffen resolve, and make their people well-motivated to succeed in whatever enterprise now confronted them. And almost all the rest had fallen in line, for no other reason than because their superiors had subscribed to one or other of those theories.

Bayrd was scornful, if too sensible to say so. Ever since he was old enough to understand such things, the Alban clans had never needed the outside influence of any person or any situation once they had determined to succeed. Sometimes that success eluded them, as it did other, lesser peoples; but not for any want of trying.

Hoofs thudded in the sand and Mevn's brother Marc ar'Dru came cantering by, riding his handsome black Andarran. Marc was armoured and the horse was armoured, all in full battle harness, all dramatic glinting black. His spear was in his fist and a fine blue crest-coat fluttered bravely in the speed of his passage. Bayrd grimaced – he should have expected nothing less from that one – then changed it to a grin and waved. It was the sort of quick dismissive wave that acknowledged presence without inviting conversation. Marc took the hint and didn't slow down as he shouted back. Bayrd saw his mouth open inside the warmask, but all he heard for the most part was noise rather than words. The only scrap of a sentence that did make sense sounded like '. . . regret it . . .' but he might have been mistaken either at the sound of the words or at their meaning.

If it had to do with the ships – there were more of them blazing now – then it didn't come as a surprise that Marc ar'Dru agreed with him, or that he was stupid enough to yell his views aloud where the whole world might have heard them. And if it was about Bayrd keeping company with his sister again, then it wasn't so much a threat as a warning – if not an especially serious one. He

43

knew them well enough for that. Marc and Mevn behaved like most clan-brothers and -sisters Bayrd had ever met, including his own, expressing any public fondness for each other as a misleadingly spiteful sniping, for fear that anything else should be construed as weakness unbefitting a *kailin* family.

Despite what Marc might have thought, Mevn's presence meant little; she was just the first woman Bayrd had met today whom he knew well enough to decently ask for help with his hair, which after having his helmet on top of it had degenerated into an unruly rook's-nest unfit for a gentleman leading a thousand soldiers – assuming there were still a thousand soldiers available to be led. It was an honourable request, and given their past relationship one which could not honourably be refused. That was all. One of his own line-family would have been less complicated, but they had been busy stripping everything remotely useful from their own ships before putting the torch to them, and in any event his relationship with them was not of the best right now.

Mevn ar'Dru had just been there.

She had been there on several occasions in the past, since he separated from Lorey and since Mahaut died. There was a little more than friendship in the relationship, but not much, even though it was a friendship that had brought them together in one bed or another three times now. But still just friendship. He had needed company and comforting, Mevn had said. And she had wanted to be the one to do the comforting. Nothing else: no offer or expected offer of marriage, or even the socially acceptable arrangement of official consortage. Just company, and comfort, and not being alone when the nights were black and cold and empty.

Marc of clan ar'Dru was another good friend; a drinking-companion, and someone with whom to share opinions about the superior high-clan gentlemen who thought that birth and breeding were everything: above bravery, nobility, wisdom, or even honour. That was usually worth a laugh – even though when it came to brains, their friendship, no matter how long it had lasted, did not mean that Bayrd had to deceive himself into thinking that Marc was any brighter than he had to be. He was a better soldier than a warrior, warriors having occasionally to reach their own decisions about matters. Marc ar'Dru was happiest when he had a

44

superior officer to make those decisions for him, and then tell him what, when, where and why to do a thing. As for the rest of it, he was many things: trustworthy, courageous, honourable, amiable and amusing. But not really intelligent. Never that. Just a friend, whose faults were ignored for friendship's sake, just as Bayrd hoped his own were ignored in turn.

Mevn ran her hands affectionately through his long hair preparatory to putting it up in the proper style for low-clan warriors, the full head of hair plaited into a single braid at the nape of the neck. Bayrd's head jerked back and yelped as her combing fingers found yet another tangle that was still not quite untied. And still it didn't matter. The small concerns were more easily dwelt on than the larger ones, and this latest development was largest of all.

With the exception of perhaps a dozen, all the ships that had come to shore so far had been stripped to the keels and set alight. There was already conflict between those who had burned their ships willingly whether through duty or through agreement, those who had been forced – there were already too many of them – and those who had refused to burn their ships under any circumstance. That it had been mostly high-clan families who had refused, with low-clan vassal families permitted that right only by alliance to and support from their high-clan lords, added just one more unpleasant spice to the stew that the Albans were cooking for themselves.

His own duty done, his own ship no more than dead embers and a half-sunken hull being battered slowly to pieces by the surf, Bayrd watched it all from this safe distance. The foreign crews who had not signed on for this loss of their livelihood were silenced with handfuls of Kalitzak gold from the belly of the treasure-barge, and by the presence of weapons in the belts of the lord's-men who distributed that gold. They trailed sullenly to such of the undamaged ships as remained their property – very few now – and began the laborious task of working them back from this suddenly-unfriendly shore in the face of contrary winds and currents.

Three times Bayrd had seen those weapons poised for use, and only once against the Droselan sailors. The other two occasions had been Albans drawing on Albans. He sighed wearily, already resigned to seeing it at some stage or other, if never so soon as this.

Arguing was what his people did best, and they had been practising the art for a thousand years. Usually at the most inappropriate times. Just like now. It didn't matter that this was exactly what they did not need, to squabble with each other before they had even taken the measure of what hazards might await them in this new land. But in its own way it was typical, as much a prideful part of being Alban as the language, the skill with horses, the honour. Arguments, sometimes about nothing more important than precedence at table, had always played a part in the lives of the *kailinin*, sometimes a larger part than seemed reasonable. But usually they had been able to set their differences aside in the face of a common enemy.

That common enemy had not yet appeared. Perhaps he – or they – never would appear, and Albanak with his talk of dangers and his building of fortifications was being more cautious than need be. No matter about that: concern for his people was an Overlord's duty, just as obedience was theirs. But perhaps, thought Bayrd ruefully, Lord Gelert and his men would arrive on the beach just in time to see the clans and families fall to wrangling among themselves as had happened too many times before.

Too many times indeed: that was why internal alliances, by marriage, by adoption, by blood-oath, were so important. It meant that no one family faced a potential opponent alone. They had allies both in their own family and out of it, and the more there were from other clans, the better. It increased the number of reasonable voices – or the number of swords. That way differences of opinion had a chance to calm down before any of those swords needed to leave the scabbard.

There had been feuds in the distant past, over petty things: horse-raiding, or cattle stealing, or the kidnapping of potential marriage partners of either sex – and sometimes with the connivance of the supposed victim. While it remained no more than a feud that could be amicably settled, everyone entered into the sport of it. But there had been times when those feuds had turned bloody, and at least two occasions recorded in the Books of Years of various clans when the feuds had dragged in more and more supporters from either side until the whole thing had become a vicious small war.

Now the whole chance of their success against the Pryteneks

depended on the fact that they had progressed beyond making war for fun, while the Pryteneks apparently had not. Bayrd hoped that was true. They were outnumbered no matter what happened.

Mevn tapped him on the shoulder. 'I can almost hear you thinking,' she said. 'What about? My idiot brother?'

'Hardly.' And not just the ships, either. There was enough to think about even apart from that. Bayrd leaned forward to where his gear was stacked and pulled an arrow from its quiver, turning it over and over in his fingers. It was an armour-piercer, the polished metal of the head long and narrow like a willow-leaf, and it twinkled as the cobweb marks of honing caught the sunlight. But that was all. No sparks, no flame, no heat. He jabbed it into the sand like a man reaching a carefully-considered decision. 'No, not about Marc. Ow! And never mind the braid. I'll just tie it back.'

'You were never one for fashion before.'

'What . . .?'

'The lastest fashion. For *kailinin*. A loose queue instead of fully braided. Not tied, mind you. Held back by a clip with your personal crest on it. Like this.'

Mevn took a handful of hair and twisted it gently into a single lock by way of demonstration. The result was more or less what she had just unravelled, but a good deal neater. Bayrd shuffled around just enough to give her his full attention, which in this instance involved raised eyebrows and a certain quirk to the mouth that suggested she had to be joking.

'Fashion? *Me*?'

'Um.' She looked at him for a few seconds with her head on one side, then shook her head and let go of his hair again. 'No. I suppose not. Still just the single braid, isn't it?'

'Yes. It was a promotion in rank, not an elevation in status.'

'Albanak must have thought that making you *kailin-eir* was going to cost him money,' snorted Mevn. 'Stupid. It would probably have saved him some, if I know you. All right. Sit still. And don't argue, you know I'm right.'

Bayrd shut his teeth with a click of mild disapproval that he hoped was audible. If the unnecessary severity with which she began braiding was anything to go by, she heard it well enough. It felt as if his ears were being pulled until they met at the back of his head, and if he risked a smile his face would probably split. So much for domesticity.

'You think the Overlord's order about the ships was just as stupid, yes?'

'Yes – ow!' And so much for conversation. 'Was that clumsiness or criticism?'

'Neither. Just another tangle. What were you doing, to get your hair in this state?'

'Drowning. Or it seemed that way at the time.'

'But you'd still keep the ships intact? Even after the storm last night?'

'Yes.' Bayrd turned so that Mevn could see his smile before he said anything more. 'I can still remember a "last night" when I wasn't sure I would ever feel safe with you behind me again. Armed or not.'

'You say the sweetest things,' said Mevn after a moment's consideration. Then she pulled at the length of braided hair resting on the palm of her head, not the savage wrench to chastise his impudence that he had been expecting, but a steady force that drew Bayrd back and back until his balance went and he sprawled. His legs were in a tangle, caught underneath him and still halfway crossed so that there seemed to be nothing below the waist but locked joints. And his head was in her lap. It fitted so comfortably that it might have belonged there. There had been other days when they had both thought the same thing.

Bayrd had to squint as he stared up, because the sun was behind her head and a glowing halo of brilliance caught in her own loose fair hair and turned it golden. Whatever expression was on her face was hidden by the shadow beyond the glare, but he could feel the light pressure of one fingernail against the soft skin under his chin, drawn taut by the angle at which he lay. 'I can be other places than behind you, and you still wouldn't be safe,' said Mevn ar'Dru gently, stroking the nail across his throat from one jaw-hinge to the other. 'If I wanted it that way.'

'You would make an . . . interesting wife.'

'You would make an interesting husband. But not for each other. And I don't think that was an offer to marry, do you? Just an observation. Anyway, I like you better as a friend.'

Sorting out his legs enough that he had only the one pair of knees again, Bayrd sat up, swivelled, went crosslegged again as neatly as a cat folding itself into a meatloaf on a cushion, and gave her the ghost of a bow. 'A pity,' he said.

'About being your friend? Why don't you lie back down again, ar'Talvlyn – but give me your knife first.'

'That wasn't what I meant.'

'Of course not.' Mevn brushed an imaginary grain of sand from the elaborate patterns of her travelling-skirt, straightened its folds, re-straightened them and only then looked him in the eye. Her own eyes were hazel, the browny-green of new acorns, and right now their green shade had the advantage. 'Then you really did mean . . . ?'

'Only if you agree to it.' He wasn't sure what answer he wanted, and certainly there was nothing to be gained by the match, but a man could have a worse wife.

'I don't. I won't. Friendship, yes – but anything else and before too long we really would have knives at our throats. Like those fools down on the beach. If they can think of fighting each other, then they haven't enough to do.'

'You sound like an officer's wife already.'

'I said no. And anyway, now you're just making the appropriate noises. I'll take them as said, because no, no and no. You're a deal too ambitious for ar'Dru to keep up with, except maybe by alliance.'

'Ambitious? Me . . . ?'

'Yes. You. Protestations about fashion I'll believe, Bayrd ar'Talvlyn. You're too practical. But advancement – as I said before, no, no and again, *no*. You have ideas for clan ar'Talvlyn. Or are they just for Bayrd?'

He thought about that in a way he hadn't done before. The clans and lesser families had always been the chiefmost focus of loyalty, taking precedence even over the Lord Albanak, although this present Overlord was clearly trying to change matters in his favour. But that loyalty was supposed to be a two-way trans-action, and Bayrd still remembered the cooling that followed his marriage to Mahaut ar'Doren. That ponderous catch-all word 'disapproval' had been trundled out again, and after Mahaut's father, to have the same response from his own folk was almost more than even ar'Talvlyn patience could bear. But he was stubborn, another and less appealing characteristic and one which the line-family had inherited four generations past from *ar'Ayelbann'r Kozh*, the Albans of the Old Time, on his great-grandfather's side. That, combined with a certainty that he was in the right, made for trouble. Because the rest of ar'Talvlyn knew just as certainly that *they* were right, and the honour of both parties required that each side of the argument be maintained without question. When such stubborn minds clashed, nothing so dramatic as sparks flew; but the Hot Hells could grow cold waiting for one or the other party to back down.

'All right, I'll agree on the matter of advancement. But ambition has an ugly sound to it, one I –'

' -Wouldn't want any of the high-clan lords to hear. I could believe that.'

'If you keep putting words into my mouth, one fine day you're going to hear me say entirely the wrong thing.'

'You, utter a word out of place?' Mevn chuckled at the very idea. 'Hardly. Or should I say, not unless you meant to. Even when we first . . . met, you were looking at everything five ways before you spoke, just in case you let something slip that was nobody's business but your own. And two years has made no difference that I can hear. You know what they say about you?'

'I'm sure you'll tell me. That I think too much?' For once he was able to say the hated phrase without a bitter twist of self-mockery. Mevn evidently heard the difference, because she gave him a considering slantendicular stare from the corner of one eye, and smiled lazily.

'That's one, and common knowledge. True, too. Think too much, and don't talk enough about it. Downright closemouthed.' She reached out to ruffle his newly braided hair, then trailed her fingers across his face until they traced the outlines of his thin lips. 'Though not all the time, I'm happy to say. But no. *I* was thinking of something else entirely.'

'Evidently.' Bayrd caught her hand before she could pull it away, turned it over, and nipped lightly at her inner wrist, just where the veins ran smoke-blue shadows under the delicate pale skin. Mevn shivered, and made no great effort to get free until Bayrd released her himself.

'They say,' she looked at the faint crescent marks his teeth had left, 'that Bayrd ar'Talvlyn has ideas far above his present station.'

'Who are *They*?'

Mevn shook her head, a gesture she combined charmingly with a shrug. 'They. The usual gossips. But this time I think they might be right.'

'Gossips. So?'

'And they say that he has plans to bring his station up and level with his ideas, one way or another.'

'Indeed?'

'Yes, indeed. Oh, very yes . . .'

Mevn ar'Dru sounded drowsy; perhaps because of the heat, for though the sun was sliding well down the sky towards evening, still the sand gave back all the warmth it had soaked up in the course of the day. And perhaps not.

Bayrd watched her curiously. The hazel eyes were heavy with sleep, or more than sleep, because her head didn't roll loosely on her neck the way it usually did when she dozed off. Bayrd knew about that well enough; he had seen Mevn fall asleep before, after enough wine, enough food, or enough loving. That part was hard to remember, because he had been falling asleep himself, wrapped in the comfortable tangle of limbs that looks so complicated because nobody's arm is trapped underneath.

'And you will,' she muttered. 'I know you. You will. A man to watch . . . honourable . . . made lord . . . by his own hand . . .'

Her head nodded forward, and she woke up with a jolt just as Bayrd was reaching out to catch her. If she had ever been asleep at all, and there was no trace of it in her eyes. They were as bright as ever. Bayrd found himself glancing at the arrow still driven into the sand, looking for sparks, flickers of fire, anything out of the ordinary. There was nothing of the sort.

Just the most practical woman he knew, sitting with her eyes closed in the warm sunshine and mumbling what might have been prophecy, if he believed in such superstitious rubbish. That was out of the ordinary enough for one afternoon. Prophecy or not, Bayrd was grateful that no one else had been close enough to overhear. It was enough to lose him his newly acquired promotion, if it reached the ears of any of the high-clan lords; and maybe enough to lose him his head, if one of those lords was suspicious enough.

The worst part was that it was all so much nonsense. Clan ar'Talvlyn might not be a lordly *kailin-eir* family, but their honour – his honour – could match that of anyone better born. Or surpass it; fine gentlemen had nothing to prove, either to themselves or to anyone else, while he . . .

He shook his head. The thoughts were going round and round, and never reaching a conclusion. The fairly earned respect and friendship of his equals was enough and anything else would come from the duty and obligation to a lord that any Alban *kailin* would be proud to owe.

Bayrd sat in companionable silence with Mevn for a few minutes more, then stood up with some excuse about the unburned ships that sounded banal even to his own ears. As he gathered up his gear, Bayrd ar'Talvlyn was uneasily aware of the way she was gazing at him. He tried to convince himself that Mevn's smile of cool amusement was no different to all the other times. She might have been surprised at what had to look like an over-hasty departure, or that he suddenly had nothing more to say on the subject of his intentions for the future, not even curiosity about who had been making such dangerous speculations about him.

Or she might not have been surprised at all.

Bayrd stared up at the star-thick sky as he lay dozing, not asleep enough to ignore what was going on around him and yet not fully awake enough to care about it either. He entertained himself in a dreamy way with what he would or would not have done had he been the Overlord Albanak. His sleeping-place was with the others of clan ar'Talvlyn, but he might as well have been alone. They ignored him, and by silent mutual agreement he ignored them. It was the safest way to guarantee peace.

Even though his cased bow and sheathed longsword were close to hand, Bayrd did not expect trouble. The sentries on the wooden walls were a necessary precaution in what might be hostile territory, but if Lord Gelert and his people were as they had been described, then they would not attack after nightfall. It wouldn't be because of superstitious fears or any religious constraints, but simply because warriors who fought to perform glorious deeds in the sight if their liege lord would find little point in performing any deed, glorious or otherwise, when it was too dark for the lord to see them do so.

The Albans had been like that once, a long time ago when they could afford the satisfaction of profitless posturing for personal reputation and little else in the way of reward. They had become a good deal more pragmatic since then. If a night assault would give them a tactical advantage over their opponents, then they would attack by night; or in a rainstorm, or in a blizzard, or under cover of a fog so thick that they could not see their own spears extended in front of them. They had done all those things while in mercenary service, and some of the younger and more aggressive *kailinin* might have considered doing so again, if any of the clan-lords had known the country well enough to tell them who and where to attack. As it was, they stayed where they had landed, the conquerors and proud possessors of a mile of sand and shingle.

The night passed peacefully; at least, there was peace outside the ditch and palisade of the fort, and any spies who might have been sent by the mysterious Lord Gelert moved quietly enough not to disturb the guards who paced the packed-sand ramparts. Inside was a different matter. As Bayrd had expected, thirsty people had broached the wine-butts long before Overlord Albanak had finally agreed to send out a watering-troop, and though their venture had been successful, by the time they came back with full water-butts the wine had already done its work.

Threats and accusations flew as members of one clan took those of others to task for doing, or failing to do, one thing or another. The charges grew wild; indeed, they grew historical as well as hysterical, questing back in time for new and better allegations. When the ships were burned; before they were burned; after they had reached this Heaven-forsaken coastline; before they landed; before they left Kalitzim – any reason for a quarrel was good enough.

Bayrd finally heard a voice in the darkness declare that if the Alban people were back in the wide grasslands and anyone had suggested leaving them, then he, the anonymous speaker, would have stuffed such a suggestion back into the proposer's mouth with the butt-end of his lance. That was too much even for the legendary patience of clan ar'Talvlyn.

Bayrd pushed back his blanket and propped himself on one

elbow, waiting for the sounds of approval to die down. They more likely meant that the speaker was someone of rank rather than that many people really agreed with what he said, but that didn't matter any more.

'So long as your lance is the only thing you want to ram down his throat,' he jeered into the silence, 'he can count himself lucky!'

There was a satisfactory number of chuckles, some stifled and others deliberately loud, suggesting that Bayrd had merely given voice to what many others had been thinking, but there was also a ripple of gasps – and an explosive oath that could only have come from the original speaker. He could hear an outbreak of scuffling, the sound of someone made clumsy with rage fighting their way free of a tangle of blankets, and a pair of makeshift torches were lit at the nearest fire. The presences of those torches, and someone to carry them, meant that whoever he had insulted was of sufficient rank to have at least one retainer in attendance on him and maybe two – but it was the harsh scrape of a *taiken* coming out of its sheath that warned him he might have gone a little too far this time.

As the hot red eyes of the torches began to make their way towards him, Bayrd briefly considered pretending to sleep. But that wouldn't work; either he would be caught unarmed by whoever was approaching, or someone else would get the blame. And by the sound of the muttered curses heading his way, excuses were not going to be accepted. With the other drowsy figures around him diving frantically out of the way, he rolled sideways up onto one knee and grabbed for his own longsword. Shaking its scabbard free, as an extra precaution he drew his *taipan* short-sword and braced the two blades across each other.

It was just as well.

There was a quick beat of footsteps and a bulky shape surged out of the shadows, swinging a long starlit shimmer of steel at his head. As he jerked his crossed swords upwards, that shimmer caught in the angle where they met and screeched sparks from their edges. Ordinary sparks this time, yellow instead of blue, though Bayrd still flinched as their heat stung his face. The force of the blow jolted him, but he was braced enough against it that he kept his balance until the torch-bearers came running up. There were two indeed, both in crumpled crest-coats, and Bayrd felt a momentary qualm as he recognised the Colours of red and white and the black bear device embroidered on them. They were of clan ar'Diskan, and the man who had tried to take his head was Lord Serej.

Bayrd was shocked, not by the assault itself so much as by its manner. There was no honour in it. No respect. And that it had been provoked was an excuse, not a reason. To attack like this, without warning out of the dark, with formal challenge neither given nor received, was not the action he would have expected from a high-clan lord. And yet . . .

If any man was to have attacked him like this, then of all the armed *kailinin* on this beach, Bayrd would have guessed at Serej ar'Diskan. It went beyond coincidence into the inevitable working of fate. After their encounter the previous day, he felt certain that even if one of them had been here and the other back in Kalitzim, he would have been forced to fight Serej sooner or later. It seemed the time was going to be sooner after all.

The clan-lord gestured a torch closer, close enough indeed that Bayrd had to sway back from its flame, and leaned in to stare at the man who had insulted him. Then he straightened up, stroking at his heavy moustache, and there was a dour smile hiding behind the spread of black whiskers. An idle thought passed through Bayrd's mind, that the man and his crest were well matched.

'Bayrd ar'Talvlyn . . .' His voice matched too, for it was a rumbling growl from deep in the clan-lord's cask of a chest. 'Yes . . . I should have guessed. Who are you, to insult a *man* with such words? Married twice, and how many children have you to show for it? Were the women not to your taste? Are any?'

Bayrd ignored the gibes, remaining in the ready posture of middle guard centre, longsword high and shortsword low, both poised to counter another attack. 'I have memories, my lord,' he said calmly. 'Good memories. Better, I think, than yours.'

'Do you think so, indeed?'

Bayrd shook his head. 'Since you ask, then no, my lord. I look at your face, and I know so. And what if I – or any man or woman in this camp – should have been inclined to make love in a way that you find wrong? At least that involves another person. It's a better thing than loving only yourself.'

'You are no gentleman, ar'Talvlyn –'

'– Gentleman enough for the Lord Albanak to give me *kailin-eir* status and command of a thousand. Gentleman enough, and honourable enough, not to attack out of the darkness like a common brigand. As you have done, my lord. Before witnesses.'

'No gentleman, whatever your rank might be. So you think you have the Overlord's ear, do you? Well, tomorrow I'll take him yours.'

'Is that a formal challenge, my lord?'

'Formal enough for the likes of you. Enjoy the rest of your promotion, *kailin* whelp. And the rest of your life.'

'I have. And I will. More than you have ever done, my lord. Until the morning, my lord.'

He gave Serej ar'Diskan a formal salute with both swords and held it even though the clan-lord snorted and rudely turned his back without acknowledgement, but he didn't relax his guard, much less put the weapons away, until ar'Diskan had lumbered back to his own encampment. As he studied the edges of his blades, looked nervously for any trace of flame apart from that reflected in their polished surfaces, Bayrd could hear the whispered discussion beginning among the others of clan ar'Talvlyn, and wondered whether he was meant to hear the words or not. Too many of them seemed complimentary. It was a strange thing, that he would have to be openly disrespectful to a high-clan lord, and put his life at risk in the process, in order to regain the respect of his own family. But then – he punched at the rolled overrobe that was doing duty as a pillow in an attempt to make it a little less than actively uncomfortable – they were Alban, just as he was. Just not as sober . . .

Gossip flew at its customary speed, and as if what had passed between Lord Serej and himself had been a catalyst for bottled-up angers, before silence and the sleep of exhaustion fell at last over the camp, another half-dozen duels of honour had been arranged between *kailinin* who had taken exception to something someone had said. In at least two cases, they were as a direct result of his own stand. Bayrd ar'Talvlyn stared up at the sky and knew that he, at least, would not sleep. Only the coming of dawn proved him wrong.

Certainly he had slept better. Though the camp had been built well above the high-tide mark, there had been a creeping dampness in the sand which compacted it overnight – and under pressure such as shoulders, heads or hip-bones – into something as unyielding as a brick. Bayrd lay for several minutes in the same huddled position in which he had awakened, with such an ache in all his joints that if he moved, he felt certain that one of them would snap. At least his own groans of discomfort were no louder than those of anyone else, because the entire Alban people seemed to have been tied into one huge knot.

And he would have killed for a bathtub brimming with hot water. Hot *fresh* water, Bayrd corrected himself. The perfunctory scrub in the icy sea last night might have made him smell somewhat better, but it had left him coated this morning with an abrasive film of dried salt.

The muddiness of sleep cleared slowly from his mind, but as it did a shiver ran through him as though a drop of that chilly seawater had just run the length of his spine and Bayrd remembered that, unless he had been dreaming *very* vividly indeed, someone was going to try to kill him for a reason much less real than any tub of water.

'Did I really say that to a high-clan lord?' he muttered aloud, sitting up painfully and cradling his head in both hands. The question hadn't been addressed to anyone in particular, and he didn't expect an answer; but several of the relatives who hadn't exchanged more than twenty words with him in this past year were more than willing to give him all the answers he could possibly need. Lord Serej wasn't over-popular among the lower clans and the common families, and as he listened Bayrd wondered just how much the clan-lord knew about it. Let only half of what he was hearing be directed at *him*, and he wouldn't go anywhere without his personal guards – and a mail reinforcement under his tunic.

Though this was his first ever duel, he wasn't frightened. It surprised him at first, until he realised that deep inside, he knew he was in no danger from Serej ar'Diskan. The man would be trying to kill him, there was no doubt about that. Just as he had tried last night, without challenge or formal defiance, in a common assassin's attack out of the dark. But, like last night, he wouldn't be able to. Bayrd ar'Talvlyn was too good with a *taiken* for that. But

57

he hoped he was even better, because his chief problem was going to be how to put the murderous clan-lord out of action without permanent damage. Doing too much would be as bad as doing too little, since wrong interpretations would be put on it at once.

He would be the low-clan upstart, recently promoted beyond his ability by a generous Overlord, trying to push himself still further by engineering a duel with that same Overlord's most trusted advisor. It wouldn't matter in the slightest whether ar'Diskan was 'most trusted' or not trusted at all: the fixed epithet was as common in politics as in any story told in House or hall, and if he happened to kill the clan-lord, whether by accident or by design, then Serej would be remembered only as having been in the right all along.

And then there was what Mevn ar'Dru had said, only yesterday: that he was gossiped abroad as being ambitious. With such a reputation hanging over his head, even though he knew it to be false, Bayrd absolutely had to leave ar'Diskan alive and mostly unhurt – if the clan-lord's notorious temper would allow him to do it.

Fighting to first blood was an honourable concept, but it needed the agreement of both sides, and Bayrd doubted he would get anything of the sort from Lord Serej. More, if worst came to worst and he had to kill the older man to save his own life – and he was in no doubt whose life was more important to *him* – then clan ar'Talvlyn could easily end up with a blood-feud on its hands, which from the sound of them was not a matter considered by the cheery voices surrounding him.

Heaving himself to his feet, teeth closed on the grunt of pain as his cramped limbs straightened out again, Bayrd stalked down to the cleansing sea to bathe.

Dressing afterwards, he gazed at the sails that were all that remained of the ships which had escaped the great burning. The tiny specks of colour out on the horizon were crewed by Kalitzak sailors on their way home, and grateful to have vessels in which to do so. The others, thirty or so anchored far enough out in the bay to be beyond reach of the Lord Albanak, belonged to the clans who had rejected his command to destroy their only hope of leaving this shore again.

They, it had been let known, would now prefer to be called the Ship-Clans, and they would maintain their vessels for use in trade when the hot-heads on shore decided that trade instead of war was what they wanted with the rest of this new country. Those ships were apparently now their homes as well, since the message had been delivered tied around the shaft of a hard-shot arrow from a ship that was immediately rowed back out to deep water.

Their request was ignored, since already people were starting to call them not by their clan names, but by the simpler title of *an-tlakhnin*, 'The Undeclared'. It was not a pleasant term of reference, since it derived from an old, old insult that implied spineless equivocation in the face of any and all voluntary decisions from getting out of bed in the morning onward. It was all of a piece with the bickering that had started last night, and if anyone had troubled Bayrd ar'Talvlyn for his opinion – they did not – he would have suggested that the appearance of a hostile Prytenek force under Lord Gelert would do everyone a power of good. Either that, or a hearty dose of some physician's opening mixture. Either would serve to give them something else to do.

Bayrd spared a quick glance for that other part of the camp where the red and white banners of clan ar'Diskan fluttered in the morning breeze and his many retainers and body servants surrounded Lord Serej, assisting him to dress and arm. That made Bayrd smile grimly to himself, because while such behaviour was typical of Serej, it was more usual to see even high-clan *kailinin-eir* putting on their own harness. No matter how careful and dedicated a man's servants might be, the only person who needed to be really, totally sure that a battle armour had been fitted properly was the man inside it. It was entirely possible that Serej-*eir* might believe that superior rank granted superiority in all things, even the handling of weapons; but Bayrd remembered that sword-cut from last night, and while there had been weight, it had lacked any true focus of power. A woodsman with an axe could have struck better.

He tucked his shirt into his breeches and stamped into his boots, secured all the laces and buckles, then began sorting out all the various parts of his own armour from its storage box before climbing into it, securing each piece to the next with all the care of one who knows how much he might need its protection later. The combat leathers went on first, padding against the abrasion of the light mail-shirt that followed; then leather leggings plated with discs of black steel; sleeves and a coif, both of mail over more leather, even though for the present he could leave his helmet off and allow the coif to hang loose behind his head; the *tsalaer* cuirass itself, black scales laced in blue and white; and finally the plates of metal for shoulders and arms.

Bayrd performed a deep knee-bend, lunged with one leg and then the other, squatted, stood again, bent over and to either side, raised one arm and then both together, and after all that adjusted a strap here, a leather thong there, and did it all again. Only when he was satisfied that he was flexible enough not simply to move while encased in sixty pounds of metal, but to do so effectively, did he lock the buckles shut and tuck the trailing ends of laces out of harm's way. Once the weapon-belt with its three scabbards was buckled around his waist, he was as ready to fight as he could ever be. Whether he would be ready to appear as one of the principals in a formal duel took rather more thought.

Bayrd gave some consideration to whether or not he should wear a Colour-Robe or even one of the ar'Talvlyn crest-coats, because although he had heard about formal duels, read about them, and been instructed in their etiquette by his father, he had never actually witnessed one. There were certain honours and respects paid from one duellist to the other, and one such token of regard was the wearing of family crests or Colours. However . . .

Given how boorish and ill-mannered Serej ar'Diskan had been last night, he suspected that no such honour would be paid to him, and the thought of matching slight for slight was a tempting one. But then again, as a man suspected of ambition – however false that might be – prudence as well as common courtesy dictated that he observe all the niceties. With that in mind, Bayrd decided on the same *elyu-dlas* that he had worn the previous day when speaking to Albanak-*arluth*. If it had been good enough for the Overlord, then it would be good enough for Lord Serej.

At least, it had been then.

He shook it out, and looked at the once-handsome garment in despair. Yesterday had been bad enough, but when he had wadded it up to make his pillow last night, he had not expected that he would be needing it for a formal appearance first thing in the morning. All he could do was to sprinkle it with water and make sure that most of the worst wrinkles seemed to be running in more or less the same direction, then pull it on over his armour before it dried. To make up for the creases, he put his crest-coat over the top of all, squared up all the visible hems in a hopeful sort of way, and – trying not to think what messages of intent such an array was giving out – decided the ensemble would have to do.

When he looked about him, the faces of his relatives had become suddenly less eager than their voices had been suggesting; because they knew what he wanted. The principal in a duel was accompanied by at least one Companion, the allied or neutral witness who carried his banner and whose presence – officially at least – ensured fairness and honourable behaviour from his own as well as from the other side. Bayrd sighed. He had been expecting too much, too soon. They were more than happy that he should restore his own reputation, and increase that of clan ar'Talvlyn, by putting his life at hazard, but none of them wanted to become directly connected with his actions by acting as his banner-bearer.

Well, no matter; the blue and white clan Colours were on his long robe, and the *halathan* crest of a spread-winged eagle was embroidered in silver at shoulders and collar of the coat. If he went to meet Serej without supporters, flags or banners, there was every chance that instead of disrespect it might suggest a laudable modesty.

Then Marc ar'Dru arrived, in a hurry and slight disarray, wearing half-armour with his own crest-coat over it, and Bayrd realised that he might have a formal Companion after all. He didn't care overmuch for the younger man's carefree grin: it was very much the grin of someone who knew that whatever happened during the course of the day's events, by virtue of being from an independent family he wasn't really going to be involved. Bayrd objected to his expression of bright-eyed eagerness as well, even though Marc was probably more keen just to see the duel than to see anyone actually killed.

No matter that the Albans had been mercenaries in Kalitzak or Droselan service, their service had been peaceful for too long – or not long enough. Fighting, at least in single combat, still had an aura of romance about it: something from the old tales. As if there was anything romantic at all about two men who when all was said and done should have known better, trying to hack each other apart with lengths of sharpened steel.

He wondered sometimes where thoughts like that one came from, because they were most definitely unAlban and inappropriate to any *kailin* who was still, however lowly, by blood and descent a member of the warrior class. At least, Serej ar'Diskan would probably say so – and possibly others as well. Bayrd didn't care. Maybe he *did* think too much, as everyone seemed to claim he did. He didn't care about that, either. He was liked well enough in spite of it, or maybe *because* of it, and he saw no reason to change in an attempt to gain more widespread approval.

Then Marc ar'Dru bowed, lower than was strictly proper, so that a *kailin* concerned with good form might have taken exception, and though he gave no outward sign of how he felt, inwardly Bayrd shook his head. He was only four years older than Marc, but there were occasions when it seemed much more. This was one of them. Instead of the neat braid at the back of his head which custom dictated he should have worn, the younger man's fair hair was caught back in a long plume floating loose in the early-morning breeze around his tanned, handsome young face. So *that* was what Mevn had meant about the new fashion. With that, and the black armour and the crest-coat over it, her brother appeared romantic and dramatic enough for any number of stories.

And Bayrd considered privately that the plume would have looked better clamped to the top of his helmet.

'Are you ready?'

Bayrd stared at the younger man, amazed that anyone could sound so much like they felt. *Light of Heaven, how can anyone be so bright so early in the morning? Especially* this *morning . . .?*

'Ready enough.'

'Then shall we . . .?'

Marc's cheerful voice trailed off at the expression on Bayrd's face. 'Aren't you forgetting something?' he said gently. 'Your manners, perhaps?'

Marc blushed bright red, and his hand flew to his mouth in embarrassment. This was a more formal occasion than most, and required among other things a more formal greeting than the one he had just given Bayrd. 'Er . . .' This time when he bowed low from the waist it was a proper Third Obeisance, which perhaps paid compliment to Bayrd's age and military seniority but was still more than a *kailin* of equal status was entitled to. At least it served to cancel out his earlier clumsiness. 'Forgive me – I, uh, I . . .'

He cleared his throat and tried again. 'Bayrd-*an*, *kailin-ilauan* ar'Talvlyn, I, Mareckh *kailin-ilauan* ar'Dru, whom you in past days have been pleased to name as friend, would hold it both honour and privilege to stand by your side and be your Companion and your banner-bearer in this present matter between yourself and Serej-*eir* ar'Diskan, *ilauem-arluth* and Lord of clan ar' Diskan.'

An honour for whom? thought Bayrd, but he kept the thought to himself. 'It is good for any man at contest to have a Companion to stand by his side in such a matter,' he said, 'and better when that Companion is a friend and not just a retainer of his House.' He bowed slightly. 'Honoured by this, I accept you. Be honoured by this: take up my banner, and be my Companion at arms.'

Then he strode off without waiting for Marc, who for lack of anything more personal to Bayrd, grabbed for the nearest ar'Talvlyn clan banner and hurried to catch up.

The custom of duelling had a long history in Alba – wherever The Land of Alba happened to be at the time. It meant that internecine disputes among the clans could be settled, if it was agreed in advance that the outcome would be accepted as settlement, by two individuals fighting rather than two clans – or two halves of the nation, if it came to that. In the earliest days, that fighting might not end in death or even in the spilling of blood, since it might have been established in advance that demonstrably superior skill was also a demonstration of superior rights in whatever disagreement had prompted the argument in the first place.

It was all very civilised and courteous, and of course like all basically simple civilised activities, it began to attract interference. Rules and regulations began to govern its conduct, and customs and traditions extending supposedly back into the dim haze of long ago might actually have originated five years before as a good idea from one clan-lord with too much wine on board. Before many years had passed, the austerity of judicial combat had become surrounded with the glamorous – and dangerous – mystique of honour.

Once, for a man to have fought in a duel was enough; then it was necessary for him to have won; then, to have killed his opponent. That killing led to blood-feud as often as not, and eventually the formal duel became just one more source of the kin-strife it had been intended to replace.

Bayrd did not intend to observe all of the conventions, only those that worked to his advantage. As the challenged, it was his privilege to meet the challenger at whatever time he felt inclined, so long as it was between dawn and sunset of the appointed day. Nor was there any requirement to duel only with swords: it could be swords indeed, singly or as a pair with the shortsword, as Bayrd had demonstrated to Serej only last night. But it could also be axes, or maces, or even lance and bow on horseback, and there were cherished records in some clans of such combats having taken place, to the credit of whichever ancestor had been involved.

When they reached the part of the fortified camp marked by their red and white flags as clan ar'Diskan territory, Serej was eating breakfast and ostentatiously ignoring their approach. Bayrd was not especially surprised; he knew the strategies well enough by now. This was a standard tactic, though it was usually employed by the challenged as a means of delaying and unsettling the challenger. In *that* case, nothing could be done but wait; in this, with rights and traditions in his favour, Bayrd could insist. But he felt sure that Serej was banking on a low-clan warrior not daring to interrupt the Clan-Lord ar'Diskan on his own ground and before his own people.

Serej, Bayrd concluded, had made yet another mistake.

The delay was intended deliberately, of course. But whether it was a duellist's ploy or just another insult, he was not prepared to stand around while the clan-lord broke his fast, digested the meal and possibly had a little nap afterwards before finally deciding that it was time his injured honour should be avenged.

For his part, Bayrd had eaten nothing, merely rinsing his mouth out with a swirl of tepid water. He had to wound, and only wound, making it grave enough to put Serej out of the fight but not so severe that the man might die of it. At the same time he had to make it quite plain to any observers that the wounding was no accident, but gentlemanly restraint in the face of excessive provocation. To do all that, he would need to be as light on his feet as possible. Not fed, and most especially, not drunk. It was an annoyance.

Life could have been so much simpler if he had really intended mayhem, for then he could have sat quietly, sipping at his beaker of water and counting the number of times Serej ar'Diskan filled and emptied his great wine-cup. Just watching and waiting – while the clan-lord slowed his reflexes and thickened his brain with more of the copious draughts of wine that did him principal duty as breakfast. That would have been an admirable choice even now, except that it was difficult for either side to fight safely when one or the other had been drinking. Never mind the damage it would do to Serej, an accidental stumble onto the point of his blade could do Bayrd's reputation as much harm as any deliberate long swing at the clan-lord's neck.

He sighed, and waved Marc forward.

'My lord ar'Diskan,' said Marc ar'Dru formally, 'you have given challenge, and heard it accepted before impartial witnesses.' They were ar'Talvlyns and his relatives, so that was not entirely true; but given their attitude towards Bayrd, it was true enough. 'He whom you challenged has come freely to this place. Is it your wish that this fight should continue?'

Ar'Diskan looked up from his platter of smoked meat and fresh-baked griddle bread, chewed thoughtfully, spat out a fragment of something and took a long drink of wine before troubling to reply. 'Ah, the upstart and his fashionable friend. Or should that be, more than friend?'

Marc's mouth fell open and even Bayrd, working hard at keeping himself on a tight leash, allowed himself a small blink of surprise. Was this clan-lord so confident of his rank and status that he could insult and possibly end by challenging every younger *kailin* in the entire Alban camp?

Then he looked at Serej's face and realised with a clarity he had not felt before how very mean and nasty the man's eyes were. He had the look of someone who hated well, liked few or seldom, and loved not at all. Small wonder that jab of his last night had gone home so deeply. What sort of life did this man's household have? His wife, his children, or his servants. He was an unpleasant creature, probably better dead – but that would be a duty reserved for someone else.

'So you want to fight now?' ar'Diskan said, and to show his lack of interest in the reply, selected another toasted sausage with the point of his eating-knife and ripped off a chunk with big, square teeth.

'I would not keep you from your breakfast, my lord,' said Bayrd, 'except that I would like to get back to my own.'

'Where you are going –' Serej began to say, but Bayrd silenced him with a quick sweeping gesture of one open hand that was more dignified than anything the other man had done so far.

'My lord, I know the threats already. Can we dispense with them just this once?'

'I would not have thought you quite so eager to go out into the dark, ar'Talvlyn.'

'I am eager to be done with this nonsense.'

'So then . . .' Serej pulled the remains of the sausage from his knife and flung it to a dog. That casual waste – and the animal itself – told Bayrd something about where Lord ar'Diskan saw himself in relation to everyone else. The half-sausage, no matter how small, was a part of their limited supplies, not just for clan ar'Diskan but for everyone – and it had just been wasted. More, the dog was a pet, a small, yappy, curly thing; a hunting-hound would have been more forgivable, since they at least worked for their food. But this . . .

Perhaps something of the way he thought showed in his face, but ar'Diskan leered unpleasantly at him. 'You prefer cats, I suppose,' he said. It was true enough, but the implications of the tone of voice in which he said it meant that there was no need to elaborate any further.

Bayrd did not waste his breath. Instead he backed off just far enough to be out of range of any unpleasant surprises before he bowed to the clan-lord, then set off with Marc to attend to the final preparations for the duel. Such things as pulling up his mail and leather coif, making it snug around his face and over his chin before lacing it shut; putting on his helmet and securing that; fitting the warmask in place over cheeks and chin. And finally, walking with Marc at his side to the expanse of flat sand that the receding tide had newly exposed.

As challenged, he had choice of ground as well as of everything else, and he would have been reluctant to fight over any terrain that ar'Diskan selected. The man was enough without honour towards those he regarded as inferior that Bayrd could easily have suspected him of digging and concealing spike-lined pits.

Marc drove the ar'Talvlyn banner into the sand, stepped back, took Bayrd's crest-coat and Colour-Robe and then, with a small bow of courtesy to the blade, accepted the sheathed *taiken* as well. There was nothing special about Bayrd's longsword, neither history nor name; that was the prerogative of higher clans, or older swords. But it was a weapon for fighting against *kailinin* of any rank, and thus worthy of their respect at all times.

The three weapons each had their separate functions: the *taiken* for attack in battle, the *taipan* shortsword for defence of honour, person and home – and the *tsepan* dirk for dying. It was for a fallen friend, or even enemy, still alive but shattered beyond the aid of any surgeon. But mostly, marked as it was on the pommel-cap with its owner's crest, it was for the man who carried it, so that there would always be a way to hand to ease his pain, and yet no blame for his dying could attach to the merciful hand which gave him this final gift.

Despite what other people believed, it was not for suicide. The Albans had no time for suicide; their lives were fraught with threats enough, and for a man to kill himself instead of striving on while breath remained in his body was tinged, just slightly, with the hint of cowardice. Like the Undeclared, safely out aboard their ships, it was seen as the choice of someone unwilling to make a choice.

The Overlord Albanak was conspicuous by his absence; this duel was a personal matter between the combatants, thus officially none of his concern – and since one of the principals had been recently promoted by him and the other had been recently in the company of his advisors, he was not risking being seen to give active or tacit support to either side.

This was a private fight.

4

Combat

FOR SUCH A private fight, it had a large enough audience. Bayrd watched the crowd gathering, and wondered was it his own unsuspected popularity which had brought them, or that Lord Serej ar'Diskan was so cordially disliked by all except his personal retainers. They stayed well back; a swordblade or axe-haft had been known to snap under the stresses of blow or block, and the flying shards could do more harm among the unprotected spectators than to either armoured duellist.

Despite the formality of the rituals leading up to it, the duelling-ground was starkly plain. Except for the banners planted in the sand, nothing had been done to mark out a perimeter. The reason was simple enough: there *was* no perimeter. This combat could finish in the sea, or in the sand-dunes, or as far up or down the beach as either man could go before his stamina gave out. Bayrd even gave momentary consideration to that as a means of ending the fight in his favour without even needing to lay a blade on ar'Diskan's skin.

Then he dismissed it. There were too many risks. Unforeseen risks, like the chance he would discover too late either that Lord Serej could outlast *him*; or, worse, was far enough out of condition to die from the strain. Or he might turn Serej into a far more implacable enemy by making the high-clan lord look foolish. Or he could lose whatever reputation he might have by making himself and thus all of clan ar'Talvlyn look foolish instead, by spending the entire duel running away . . .

It wouldn't matter that he wasn't running, or that though he might be on the defensive he was also in full control of the conduct of the fight. Bayrd put no great faith in the ability of rumour to transmit truth. Given the choice between an accurate and an offensive way to describe the sort of constant retreat such tactics would involve, malicious tongues would choose the insult every time.

He shrugged, and turned his attention back to the style of ar'Diskan's armour. And specifically its weak spots. Like the Overlord Albanak, and perhaps in flattering imitation, Serej wore an old-style *tsalaer*, red with white lacing, bulky and inflexible. That same inflexibility made it more of a problem than armour hammered from a single sheet of iron. If a blow fell wrong, both were smooth enough to glissade it off without harm. But where the single sheet would dent inward with brutal force under a severe impact or even crack completely, the *tsalaer*'s lamellar boards would just shatter back into separate scales, and they would still be held together by the tough leather and braided silk of their lacing.

Going through to break bone was not an option. He would have to go around. Hamstringing, perhaps, if he could sidestep neatly and let Serej go blundering past him. Or a thrust through one of the bigger man's meaty thighs, remembering always to stay outside the bone and well away from the big arteries running down from the groin. Or . . .

There were several possibilities, though when he discussed them with Marc ar'Dru, as a principal was allowed to do with his Companion, Bayrd was surprised and then sardonically amused to see the young man go slightly green. It was no reflection on Marc's courage; in the heat of a fight he was probably fierce enough, but this cold appraisal of how best to cripple someone and be obviously skilful about it was not to his liking at all. Bayrd ar'Talvlyn wondered how his Companion would react to the first sight of blood.

Then, belatedly, began to wonder how *he* would react as well. He had seen men die before, but for all his expertise with the wooden *taidyin* practice swords, or in exercises with live blades, he had yet to cut an opponent in earnest. Bayrd looked across the beach at Serej ar'Diskan, holding forth loudly to his own Companion and a circle of retainers and hangers-on, and concluded that there could be few better ways to start.

There were other *elyu-dlasen* in the crowd now, red and green, yellow and white – those were Lords Keo ar'Lerutz and Gyras ar'Dakkur in person – and a gaggle of *kailinin* in ar'Sanen purple and blue. Whether as a compliment or from simple curiosity, all the Colours were there, worn either by a clan-lord, a Head of House or by their highest retainers. In the presence of so much power, Bayrd almost bowed in a formal obeisance, but restrained himself for no better reason than that he didn't want to include Lord Serej in the courtesy even by accident.

Then steel rang as it was drawn. The clan-lord's sword grated slightly as it cleared the scabbard. A named-blade, it was called Lethayr, and it had seen three hundred years go by. And three thousand lives, if the stories were true. A long, slightly curving ribbon of bright metal, beautiful in its simplicity, it was dishonoured by the ugly spike and pick of the battleaxe that Serej hefted in his left hand.

That second weapon dishonoured more than his sword; it stained Clan-Lord ar'Diskan as well. The agreed weapon in this duel was the *taiken*. No matter that no one had said so aloud, custom required – and this was a genuinely old tradition, not something created for effect – that it was for other, lesser weapons to be mentioned by name. The use of *taikenin* needed only to be assumed.

Bayrd held out his hand in silence to Marc ar'Dru, and felt the weight of his own sword-hilt laid into it. Another tradition had it that in duelling, the principals did not approach each other with their blades still sheathed: supposedly a token of respectful intention. The truth was less respectful.

One of the classic forms in *taiken*-play was a double cut: *achran-kai*, the inverted cross. Employed properly – which usually meant at the very beginning of a duel – that stroke would end most combats almost at once. In *achran-kai* the swordblade came out of its scabbard without any advance warning of stance or posture, and into a full-force focused cut at chest or throat or eyes; then it swept around almost full circle for an equally powerful downward strike through the upper part of the forehead. It was said that if the first cut was delivered properly, the second was never needed.

As he made the little twisting motion to release its locking-collar and let his sword slip free, Bayrd recalled with almost too much ease that there were also cuts, or combinations of cuts and thrusts and pommel-strikes, for the proper disposal of men armed with axes. Their only drawback in the present circumstances was that each and all of them were meant to kill . . .

That was not an option available today.

Let the man who can least spare the effort do all the moving, his swordmaster had said. So he poised the long hilt in both hands and waited for Serej ar'Diskan to come to him. There had been many small, easily remembered dicta like that, so many that he had begun to suspect Chalad of decorating his private rooms with them. More than a few ignored the combat completely and had to do with watching the opponent even before the fight began, studying strengths and weaknesses in the man as well as in his armour.

Serej's principal strength was obvious: he had physical size and power, with possible endurance to match. His weaknesses were less conspicuous; a preference for strength over skill, as Bayrd had felt in that single blocked cut last night, and thus a possible lack of any but the most basic ability with his fine blade. The presence of the axe bore that out; though a long-handled horseman's weapon and relatively light, it was still no feather. Bayrd knew it; there was one slung from his own saddle on most days. But Lord ar'Diskan carried this one as easily as a riding-quirt.

And used it as readily.

Just as soon as he was within reach, he batted Bayrd's sword to one side with the axe and slashed Lethayr's long blade into the opening. It was a crude beginning – so crude and unexpected that it might have worked.

Who needs achran-kai *any more?* Bayrd thought wildly. If ar'Diskan had possessed sufficient patience for another step forward, he suspected the man would have had him. Even then he had felt the wind of the *taiken*'s passage on his face, and that was far too close. Regardless of what Chalad-*eir* had said, Bayrd ar'Talvlyn broke ground backwards as fast as he was able – and Serej ar'Diskan came after him, as lumbering and unstoppable as the black bears on his crest.

He kicked, sending a great spray of sand at Bayrd's face, and then at once the two swordblades clanked together as he repeated his first move, batting with the sword instead. This time, sand or not, Bayrd was ready – and instead of resisting with braced wrists to block, dropped his own *taiken* under the clan-lord's blade and swung upwards to meet the axe as it came down. He felt the jarring contact up to his shoulders, and heard it too: not a metallic sound,

71

but a dull, solid clunk as steel chopped wood and the keen blade bit a wedge out of the axe-haft just between the long tongues of iron that were meant to strengthen it.

Better . . .

The brief moment of assurance was knocked out of him along with his breath. Not by any weapon, but by the battering-ram impact of ar'Diskan's ironclad shoulder as the clan-lord discarded any more of what he regarded as fancy swordplay in favour of his own armoured bulk. Bayrd lurched backwards far enough that he heard splashing and felt cold seawater seep into his boots, but he rolled with the impact like a barrel sideswiped by a passing ship and thanks to that was not quite where he should have been when the axe came down again. Rather than hitting him square on the crown of the head, it struck the flared neck-guard of his helmet instead, knocking it crooked and briefly blinding him on one side when the warmask inside it shifted.

Bayrd rammed the helmet back up on his head with the heel of one hand shoved under the peak, and with the other, the right, stabbed at the exposed back of Lord ar'Diskan's knee where it was protected only by the leather of his leggings. He cursed as he felt the swordpoint snag and then release immediately after, aware that if he had used his left hand, which had been holding the hilt down near the pommel, those few inches of extra reach would have been enough.

Now it was all to do again.

But there was one thing that could be done right now, and he did it – a quick, savage cut aimed not at Serej, but at the damaged axe. More splinters of wood flew, and suddenly that wicked pick-backed blade was sagging sideways, held in place by no more than a single rivet.

Serej ar'Diskan roared something that might have been an oath or nothing more than a wordless, furious noise, and flung the shattered weapon at Bayrd's helmeted head. Ducking to avoid it, the younger man heard outraged yells behind him, cut through by a shriek of pain as the missile found a target somewhere in the crowd of spectators.

One of the hazards, he thought dispassionately, and took the longsword Lethayr's blade on his own in a series of clanging exchanges that left his ears ringing in sympathy and his forearm muscles quivering with strain. He could see ar'Diskan's teeth bared under the black moustache, and hear his hoarse, ragged breathing. At least the exertion wasn't all one-sided; but he was heartily glad he hadn't tried to outlast this man in a contest of manoeuvres along the shoreline. He would have won eventually, but it would have been a close-run thing, and who was to say what might have happened before that.

Sweat ran down his face, stinging as it reached his eyes. *Hot work. Damned hot* . . . There was still no fear, no sense that he might actually be killed, only a growing anger against Serej ar'Diskan's foul temper and honourless behaviour. If this was an Alban clan-lord, then he, Bayrd ar'Talvlyn, would make a better one himself. The anger built inside him, a thick heavy sourness that he could both feel and taste. Had anyone ever tried to describe righteous wrath to him in terms of a form of indigestion, Bayrd would have laughed in their faces.

He wasn't laughing now.

There was fear behind the rising fog of fury that threatened to overwhelm him, and all his skill, and all the schooled control which kept that skill in check. It was a fear that if he let the anger take over, he would have Serej's head off his shoulders at the first chance he got, and to the Hot Hells with the consequences. And there was a fear that had its birth in memory, a memory of the last time he lost his temper in this country.

The two blades clashed again, grating together as he blocked another cut, and for all the red rage colouring his vision, Bayrd could see how the sparks torn from their edges had begun to burn bright blue in the sunlight . . .

No. . . !

He fought now against his own passions as much as against ar'Diskan, struggling to regain the composed inner stillness that allowed him to focus the force of a cut to best effect. Instead he could find only the heat of rage and the roiling of another force eager for release. It rose through him like a tide, and it felt . . .

Light of Heaven help him, it felt *wonderful. . . !*

There was nothing evil in it, no more than an avalanche was evil, or a tidal wave, or a fire, but the single small cool place that remained in Bayrd's brain knew that if it only flowed along his arms and into the swordblade, then Serej was dead.

Dead too would be any respect he might have now, and any

honour he might have gained for the winning of a fair fight. If his own people – his own *clan* – even permitted him to remain among them, there would be the stares, and the muttering, and the words exchanged behind his back, and the backs turned towards him as he passed. Bayrd had seen it before, in the way they had treated Skarpeya. And in the way for a short time that they had treated him, merely for speaking civilly to the sorcerer.

But it didn't matter, because he couldn't stop it any more than he could stop – no, he didn't *want* to stop, it felt so – O God, he was going to – going to . . .

'Alarm! *Alaarm. . . !*'

Nobody knew who shouted, or why, but everything stopped. That cry, backed as it was by the frantic clangour of a gong brought all the way from the barracks in Kalitzim, was almost the only thing short of an earthquake more immediate to Alban senses than a good swordfight. Over four centuries the urgent sound of the warning gong had meant precisely that; nothing else. It was never used as a casual summons for drills, parades or exercises, so that when the clans and families heard it ring, they knew the message was real.

Bayrd ar'Talvlyn gasped and staggered backwards, his heart slamming against his ribs like that of a sleepwalker woken suddenly on the lip of a precipice. His guts churned, his eyes burned – but it felt as if he could see clearly for the first time in hours. For all the sweat born of heat and fright and exertion filming his body inside the carapace of black steel, he was shivering hard enough that his teeth chattered, and the chilly water halfway to his knees had nothing to do with it.

'Later for you, *turlekh*,' snarled Serej, and flicked up his left hand in a vulgar sign before stumbling off towards his camp, and his horse, and his retainers. That was all he could do. During an alarm, even a high-clan lord in the midst of a duel was required to set aside his private quarrel, no matter how helpless his opponent – and Bayrd, sagging inside his armour, was horribly aware of how vulnerable he was. He could no more have defended himself against Serej ar'Diskan with Lethayr in his hands than against a child armed with a wooden sword. He had seen the frustration twisting the older man's face, for they both knew it.

74

Safe now, and not caring for the moment about what it might do to the metal, he lowered his own nameless *taiken* until its point dipped into the sea. There was a small, sharp hiss like that of an angry cat, and a wisp of steam came drifting up. Bayrd caught his breath, and released it in a little sound that was more groan than sigh. He drove the blade deep into the submerged sand, then folded slowly over its pommel until he was on his knees in the beat of the shallow surf.

There would be questions asked, there was no doubt about it; but at least he had acquitted himself well enough that none of those questions would concern his courage. Or his ability with a sword, for that matter. There had been enough chances for him to kill Serej, chances he had deliberately – obviously – ignored, that his restraint would have been commended by the watching clan-lords.

But what they would have said if the magic roaring up inside him had managed to burst loose, he didn't want to even think.

Bayrd raised his head at the sound of footsteps splashing down from dry land. He looked up at Marc ar'Dru and managed to summon up a sort of smile for his Companion. There wasn't much to smile about, but enough: he hadn't won, but he hadn't lost, and most of all, he hadn't humiliated himself in public. That was enough for one morning's work, with the sun still not two hours from dawn.

'What's happening?' he asked, leaning on his *taiken* to heave himself back to his feet. It wasn't made any easier by the long blade sinking even further into the wet sand, and Marc caught him by the arm as he all but lost his balance.

'Never mind what's happening! What *happened*? To you?'

That was the first. How many times would he hear that same question, or its variations? 'Momentary weakness?' Bayrd ventured, his mouth shaping another smile, but this one was even more feeble than the first. 'Sun in my eyes? Lost my footing?'

Marc looked at him and waited for the real reason, but when he realised he would wait for a long time, shook his head slowly. 'Bayrd-*ain*,' he said amiably, 'you're remarkably full of shit today.'

That would be more easily explained away, thought Bayrd sourly. 'I don't see why – I went to the latrine first thing.'

'Idiot.' Marc punched him in the chest – lightly, to avoid skinning his knuckles on the armour – then pulled a cloth from his belt, the *taiken* from the sand, and began to dry the blade. 'This,' he said, 'will need to be stripped down and rinsed in fresh water before you put it away.' As they trudged out of the sea and up the beach, he shot a critical glance at the threads of water still trickling from the joints of Bayrd's armour, and the streaks of sand left in their wake. 'You too, probably.'

Bayrd knew the sound of a subject being avoided as well as anyone. 'Oiled as well. You forgot that part. At least, the sword will. I could just use a drink, and something to eat.' He produced another smile, one that felt – and he hoped looked – a more honest smile than the others. 'Listen, Marc-*ain*, I'll tell you what happened. Sometime. When I'm more sure of it myself. Now – what about the damned alarm?'

'Oh, that.'

'Yes. That.'

'We have company. Lord Guelerd, I think.'

'We have – ? Why didn't you tell me?' Bayrd's stride lengthened as he accelerated away from this deserted stretch of shore and off towards the camp, and his horse, and his bow, and the Alban people who would need his help as they needed help from all of their warrior sons. Then he jerked to a near standstill as Marc reached out and caught him by the back of the belt.

'Would it have helped?' ar'Dru asked, annoyed.

'I . . .' Bayrd considered how he had felt in the instant that the orgasmic surge of power had stopped just short of its peak, and then begun to drain away. If the world had been ending, knowing that wouldn't have helped either. 'No,' he admitted finally. 'I suppose not.'

'And it isn't an attack,' Marc pointed out. 'I'd have told you that, no matter how you felt.'

'You wouldn't have needed to. I would have known.'

'Oh, would you? How, I wonder. . . ?' Marc gave him a strange look, one that suggested far too many possibilities to Bayrd's guilty mind. After four years, first of mere acquaintance when Marc reached an age to join the Ten which happened to be Bayrd's first command, then friendship, then best-friendship and finally the slightly complicated relationship of remaining two best friends while one was sleeping with the other's sister, he had assumed he now knew young ar'Dru well enough to pass sweeping – if private – judgments on his intelligence. Or more properly, on the lack of it, since Marc endeavoured to do nothing outside his own energetic private life without the instruction of a superior officer.

But after last night and today, when a great many of his previous certainties had been burned away in a swirl of azure flame, it occurred to Bayrd that an apparent lack of brains was nothing more than that: apparent. Because of it, Marc ar'Dru enjoyed a much quieter life than he did. That, in light of his own past half hour, was definitely not a sign of stupidity.

Bayrd felt slightly ashamed of himself, and more than slightly foolish. But he still said nothing. That would come later, if at all, because right at the moment, he had no idea what to say.

Lord Guelerd, or Gelert, or however his name was pronounced, was not quite what Bayrd had been expecting. In fact he conceded that he hadn't *known* what he was expecting, except that it would be different to the Albans who stood or sat or bestrode their saddles all around him. Even there he was wrong.

Gelert had red hair, fox-bright, and he wore it oddly, in a number of thin plaits hanging loose around his head rather than the single braid of low-clan *kailinin* or the three of high. Unlike the Alban hairstyles, it seemed to have no meaning, even though the narrow crown of coppery red gold resting on it had significance enough for any number of warrior's knots. For the rest, his moustache was large and equally red, and it had been greased or oiled into fang-like points that drooped down on either side of his mouth almost to his chest. The man's armour was what caught Bayrd's eye, familiar enough in shape to be almost an imitation of an Alban *tsalaer*; but instead of the customary small scales laced together, it was made of broad strips of coloured leather, or maybe fabric covering metal, with each piece linked to the next by a narrow band of mail. He felt sure that he had seen something like it before, somewhere, but when the answer was not forthcoming, he put the matter aside to ponder at his leisure.

The effect was handsome, but not so impressive as Overlord Albanak in full harness and crest-coat sitting astride his great Andarran charger and backed by a hundred other supporters and

77

retainers equally well equipped and mounted. Gelert and some score of his followers were also on horseback, but the rest, perhaps another hundred, were on foot and carried only spears and axes. Bayrd took note of it. Axemen were dangerous enough up close – he knew that well enough from recent personal experience! – but they were easy meat if treated with the proper caution and lavish showers of arrows from a distance.

Curious to hear what was being said, Bayrd edged forward. Yarak advanced slowly at the pressure of his knee, shouldering people gently to one side rather than running them down. The crowd was sufficiently dense that it was easier to move through it mounted than on foot, and Yarak, like most other Alban warhorses, had been schooled in the gentle arts of moving through packed masses of people without doing them any harm – as well as the far from gentle arts of the battlefield which the fierce little Ferhana mare preferred.

For the past eighty years, Kalitz and Drosul and the other small kingdoms across the sea had been at peace, more or less, and though the Albans had been retained as a mercenary cadre for the sake of prestige and the training of lords' younger sons – and as an expendable striking force if one should be required – they found themselves more often acting as policemen. Worse, they were kept as exotics, wild animals of strange appearance and interesting habits that might be spiced with danger, rather than through any real use their erstwhile liege lords had for them any more.

A glance over his shoulder told Bayrd that Marc and two or three of the others had followed his lead, falling in behind him before the passage broken by Yarak through the crowd had closed again. He suspected that there was another reason why they didn't trouble to force their own passage; the ordinary folk would more readily clear a path for a notorious and savage duellist – even one whose duel had ended so inconclusively – than they would for anyone of lesser importance.

Bayrd was careful to judge his approach correctly: close enough for a good view, and to hear what was going on between Albanak and Lord Gelert, yet not so close that his intrusion would be noticed by any of the other high-clan lords and especially Serej ar'Diskan. Otherwise there was every chance that he, and everybody with him, would be dismissed back to their proper place again among the common herd.

He had no need to listen long. One sentence was enough to understand the looks of surprise that he had seen on people's faces as he rode closer. Lord Gelert was speaking *Alban*. It was an oddly accented, stilted and archaic form, but clear enough, even though he had an interpreter beside him to tide both himself and those to whom he spoke over any difficulties. It answered many of the questions which had been niggling at the back of Bayrd's mind. The armour for one; and the custom, strange to see in this foreign country, of wrapping green branches around the shafts of spears as a token of peaceful parley. That was Alban, true enough; it was also apparently Prytenek. But in the present circumstances it was ironically similar to the ritual by which Lord Albanak had laid his claim to Prytenon, raising a piece of the land itself above his head on swordpoint before the eyes of all the people.

Ancestors. . . ? Marc mouthed at him. Bayrd shrugged. It was possible, in fact it was likely. The oldest legends spoke of entire peoples wandering to and fro across the world 'since the time before time', that condescending term with which Alban chroniclers and clan Archivists dismissed any period of any history not written into their books. There had long been inclination towards keeping records of family doings in each clan's Book of Years. It was the formal clan Archive and its official history, as separate from what songs and stories had to say, but the practice itself had gone on for so long that its origin was not in fact recorded – except in legends and old tales, thus presenting the Year-Keepers themselves with an awkward conundrum. But given that some of the most ancient *ylvern-vlethanek'n* went back a thousand years, it was a wonder that no account had been set down of which clan or family, or more probably which tribe or groups of tribes, had first crossed the sea to make Claim on this place. And who had they Claimed it from. . . ?

With an odd little start, as though the memory had reached up to tap him on the back, Bayrd recalled where he had seen that strange-looking armour before. It had been a drawing in one or other of the older ar'Talvlyn Books of Years, *ylver-vlethanek an-Dirak*, Lord Aldrik's book, from so long ago that even the man's name had dropped from fashionable use.

The drawing had not even been one of the coloured, gilded illuminations to the text, of which there were enough in each book to keep the attention of a nine-year-old boy even when the crabbed handwriting was too difficult to read. It had been no more than a sketch in the margin of one page, some hall Archivist's moment of boredom recorded in fading brown ink for all posterity to see. And here it was, that same armour and perhaps those same people who had worn it then, out of the Archive pages and very much alive. Very much annoyed as well. The guarding of displays of foul humour, whether from politeness or for some more convoluted reason, was plainly an Alban rather than a Prytenek custom. Neither Lord Gelert nor the men around him made any secret of the way they felt.

Bayrd listened hard. He had been fortunate in always having had something of a talent for languages; not fluency by any means, but more an ability for understanding and being understood with only the minimum vocabulary. And this was easier than most. Expression, inflection and tone were a guide as much as anything else, but after overhearing only a few exchanges, it seemed as though two pages of his own mental Archive had stuck together in the turning, for his grasp of what was being said jumped from vague to clear almost at once. He grinned briefly, the private worries he could do nothing about set to one side for the time being. It looked as though those long, quiet, rather dusty afternoons with his nose buried in what the rest of the Household had dismissed as 'just old books' were bearing fruit at last. Many people with a head full of esoteric knowledge never had a chance to use it – but he was using this.

'. . . and I tell you again, Landmaster,' Gelert was saying, 'that the arrangements which were made, and the payments which were agreed, concerned only the hire of soldiers. Not . . . not *this!*'

He waved his arm in a sweep that took in everything: men, women, children, horses, baggage, the hastily constructed field-fortress on the beach . . . and most of all, the still-smouldering ships. 'Why did you burn your ships, Landmaster? How do you and all this rabble plan to leave, once your service is discharged?' His voice sharpened. 'Or do you mean to stay, invited or not?'

He shouldn't have said 'rabble', thought Bayrd. *But perhaps the meaning of the word has changed.* That was pointless optimism;

even if the meaning had changed, the delivery of the word itself remained very much the same.

'We were hired fairly, *arl'th-eir* Guelerd,' said Lord Albanak. 'And we have come to fight. But not for your crown.' Gelert looked startled, then scandalised, but before he could draw breath to say something that he might not have lived to regret, Albanak pulled a gold coin from the small pocket in the cuff of his Colour-Robe and spun it upwards, glinting, from his thumb. 'For *this* crown,' he said as he caught it again. 'And others like them. But if you look out into the bay you will see the only ships that survived.' He spoke smoothly enough, and gave Gelert rank-honorifics enough to satisfy the man's sense of his own importance – but even though he concealed it well, Bayrd thought it likely that the Overlord took exception to being called 'Landmaster'.

That was what his name meant: the name borne by every Alban Overlord for the past five hundred years. *Ayelbann'akur* was the master of the Land. But in a smaller sense, any peasant farmer who owned his own property was that. The new title of Overlord carried a much more satisfactory sense of being lord of the *people*, and it was fairly clear which one Albanak preferred. If a man gave up his own name, the very essence of everything he was, in favour of a title that had been borne by others before him and would continue after he was dead, then it was a very human thing and not to be condemned if that title should mean something.

'Explain what you mean by survived,' said Gelert; at least, *survived* was what the interpreter said. Gelert's own word, in his odd, old-fashioned Alban, had more a meaning of 'deliberately spared from damage' than 'escaped from damage'. The presence of that aspect of intent was disturbing.

'Easily done,' said Albanak, and pointed further out towards the horizon, where the Kalitzak ships could now barely be seen against the brightness of sea and sky. Gelert stood in his stirrups, shaded his eyes, and gazed out for a long time before dropping back into the saddle.

'More ships, on their way here?' The sound of suspicion was a raw edge on his voice, and the interpreter could do nothing to hide it.

'Not approaching, *arl'th-eir* Guelerd. Departing. There go the men to whom we entrusted our lives. They took our gold, for the purchase of all their ships and the hire of their service to crew them. Then when we reached this shore, they stole back every ship they could, and burned the rest.'

There was muttering among the Prytenek lord's-men as the interpreter passed this information back to them, and Bayrd could hear enough of it to realise that this supposed treachery made perfect sense to them. There were some voices raised in discord, but those were talked down by the rest.

'Very well then. We can ignore the ships.' Gelert sounded less suspicious now, but to Bayrd's ear the difference was not worth noticing. Lord of a people sufficiently lacking in honour that they would accept such an explanation without question, he was devious enough to accept it himself while looking at it from all sides to see what might be wrong with it. Not even something so simple as 'is this true or false?'; he was trying to establish to his own satisfaction why Albanak would have told him such a thing in the first place.

In hope of sympathy, perhaps? Or a hope for support above and beyond the payment already agreed with his mercenaries? Even a simple explanation of the truth? Or a lie to hide the traces of some larger plan? Bayrd shook his head slowly and smiled at the weary familiarity of it all.

Before they were exiled from Kalitzim, every Alban warrior from the highest to the lowest had been forced to deal with Kalitzak and Droselan officials whose minds worked in just this convoluted fashion. It became wearing after a time, even though they had had generations to get used to it.

Albans could be devious too, as witness the Lord Albanak; but not all the time. That was what made it work. Albanak for his part was doing a skilled job – as one might who, for most of his life, had been distilling clarity from the most obscure remarks – of letting Gelert apply the doubts and assumptions of his own supple mind to a carefully simple untruth presented as unembroidered fact. That very simplicity was the bait for endless elaboration by those accustomed to look for such things.

'Do you bring your families everywhere you go?' the Prytenek demanded.

'Of course we do! They are our *families!*' It was not Albanak this time, but Gyras ar'Dakkur, and he spoke in a tone of astonishment that anyone should consider doing otherwise. Bayrd wondered how many of the high-clan lords had been primed to respond in such-and-such a way to such-and-such a cue. Probably most of them. That was most likely the meat of the discussion he had interrupted yesterday, with his commonplace quartermaster's concerns over food and water, fresh fodder for the horses and all the other things far less important than this preparation to deceive – but without which such a discussion would have been mere theory.

One of Gelert's men rode forward this time, and irritably indicated the long, deep ditch dug in the sand above the high-water mark, and the palisade and shingle-reinforced rampart running behind it. 'And this is customary when you reach your new liege lord's domain, eh?' he snapped, speaking not Alban of old or new form, but good Yuvain. This was probably the man through whom the negotiations had gone forward, and not best pleased with what had happened, for if Lord Gelert was anything like the shorter-tempered clan-lords Bayrd had encountered, a huge and possibly painful weight of blame would descend on him as soon as they were out of earshot.

'Sir,' said Albanak, 'we are not a seafaring people. The mysteries of ocean navigation are still a mystery. We placed our trust in the sailors yonder,' with a dismissive wave of one arm, 'to bring us to our proper destination. Given how we were betrayed when we landed here, can you blame us for suspecting that they might have gone so far as to set us down in one of your enemy's domains instead?'

Another well-crafted complex statement: trickery, the risk of a worse deception, and in such circumstances a perfectly justified caution. There was more debate on the Prytenek side, pitched too low for Bayrd to hear some of the words themselves, but the tone was one of general agreement.

'Give them the benefit of the doubt,' seemed to be the consensus. 'Let them prove themselves. They may have proved so far only that they can be cheated, but that was a seafaring matter and we didn't hire them as sailors. Their numbers are impressive, but look at how many of this imposing crowd of people are old, or women, or children.'

They were right in that, and it included the first native-born

Alban; a child brought into the world earlier this morning, with the first noise she heard apart from the delighted cooing of her parents being the distant sound of swordplay ringing in her ears. That might have been a bad omen, but Bayrd thought not. He preferred to believe it because the combat had been man to man – Alban to Alban, unfortunately – and not a full-scale battle. The baby could so easily have been born into the middle of one of those. It had happened before, and it might happen again.

But not this time.

Still unhappy, though seeming satisfied enough by the explanations – and their own interpretations of them – Lord Gelert and his party took their leave. The Albans watched them go, those with an interest in such matters noting how the ranks of footsoldiers opened out to let their mounted leaders through, then closed again and turned smartly about to march off after them. Such evidence of discipline made the axeman even more dangerous, but many voiced the comforting assurance that these were probably Gelert's own household guard, and the rest of whatever host he might have at his disposal would be less well drilled. Otherwise, and the conclusion was put forward as though with irrefutable logic, why would he need to hire trained soldiers from across the sea?

It was a pleasant thought, but to Bayrd's ears, over-optimistic. It was also doubtful. From what he had overheard – and what he had not been *meant* to overhear – this was not the last they had seen of the Pryteneks. He nudged Yarak forward again, this time unconcerned that his presence might be noticed by a high-clan lord, because he wanted words with the highest of them.

The Overlord – Bayrd contemplated what would happen if he addressed him as 'Landmaster' and decided not to try – glanced at him as he rode closer and acknowledged Bayrd's salute from horseback with the same careless wave as yesterday. This time it seemed careless more because his mind was distracted by other matters than simply to display his own importance.

'Bayrd-*eir* ar'Talvlyn,' he said. 'I greet you. Not hoping for another promotion, I trust?'

'No, Lord.'

'Yet you were trying for an advance in status this morning. Or so I heard.'

'No, Lord. The matter was of much less significance than that.'

'Oh indeed? I must hear your side of it some day . . .' The implication that Serej ar'Diskan had already been busy was an annoying one, and more annoying still that he seemed to have been believed.

'Yes, Lord.'

'Well, then, what do you want? As you may have seen, ar'Talvlyn, I'm a busy man.'

'I saw, Lord. That is what brings me here.' Albanak-*arluth* exchanged significant glances with a couple of the other clan-lords, then turned back to Bayrd and raised his eyebrows. 'Lord, I would have your permission to take out a mounted troop –'

'– After more water? We have more than enough, surely?'

'No, Lord. To shadow Gelert and his retinue.'

'Shadow them?'

'And make certain that they're leaving.'

'You really do *not* trust him, do you?'

'No, Lord. I didn't trust the man before I saw him, and now I *have* seen him, I trust him even less.'

'Less than not at all . . .? You are something of a philosopher, ar'Talvlyn.'

'Only cautious, Lord.'

'But a sweeping statement.'

'Lord, we can test the truth of it in two ways: by sending out a scouting party . . . or by waiting to see if this camp comes under attack or not.' Albanak gave him a sharp stare, the expression of a man not caring to be told his business by a subordinate – and a very junior one at that – though when he nodded for Bayrd to continue, there was no indication of anything more than interest. 'If not, well and good. But if we are attacked, and lives are lost, then Albanak-*arluth*, I would not care to carry the blame for it. Look at them.'

After the stresses and the strains of the previous few days – the storm, and the landing, the poor night's sleep, the excitement of the duel – and the still greater excitement provoked by whichever fool had sounded the alarm before he saw the parley-tokens wreathed on Gelert's spears – most of the people in the camp were beginning to relax, sinking into a state almost of torpor. It was simple fatigue borne too long, so that now, when nothing needed to be done, nothing was *being* done. A deadly weariness lay over them like an overrobe of lead, dragging their footsteps, loading every movement with more effort than a human frame could bear.

'At least,' said Bayrd finally, willing to compromise for the sake of safety, 'at least if you do nothing else, keep them within the ring of ramparts until we know enough of how the land lies hereabouts to establish a picket-line.'

Lord Albanak looked him up and down, not sure how to respond to advice that, while good, had been slanted in its delivery dangerously close to insolence. After a glower at Bayrd, Serej ar'Diskan muttered something into the Overlord's ear; but before Albanak could respond to whatever he had been told, Keo ar'Lerutz and Gyras ar'Dakkur came forward to put in their respective quarter-crown's worth. Their opinions might have swayed him, or he might have come to his own independent conclusion – or he might have simply had enough of Lord ar'Diskan's venom, which if today was any indication tended to be indiscriminate. Either way, Albanak waved a dismissal.

'This is your suggestion, Bayrd-*eir*,' he said briskly. 'It seems appropriate to me that you should be the one to see it carried out. Gather your Thousand – or as many of them as you can muster.'

Bayrd heard the sound of realism creeping in, but saluted and set about it. There were seventy-odd men of his original Hundred free for duty, but of the Thousand he was now supposedly commanding, he could find no more than two hundred and forty-five. All the rest had already been appointed tasks, by their clan-lords or Heads of House, and those orders took precedence. With a sigh of resignation Bayrd ar'Talvlyn, Captain-of-One-Thousand by the Overlord's command, drew up the three hundred and sixteen of that Thousand in approximate ranks of twenty, and rode towards the hills.

Halfway up the first slope, they met the Pryteneks coming down, and this time there were no green branches on their spears.

The horde of footmen were led by far more mounted lord's-men than had been with Lord Gelert. Indeed there were more men altogether, men who must have been approaching even while the parley was in progress; but there was no sign of Gelert himself. The reason was straightforward enough. If this surprise assault defeated the Albans and drove them back into the sea, he would have no reason to explain to anybody but the dead, and if it failed . . .

If it failed, he could disclaim all responsibility, pass the blame onto one of his liegemen or retainers – preferably dead already, or soon to be that way; Bayrd found his mind was beginning to slip all too easily into the crooked Prytenek mode of thought – and declare that the attack was nothing to do with him. Other thoughts hovered for a moment, then flitted away like so many gnats. Thinking too much was one thing; but knowing when to stop was just as important.

He had signalled the charge without thinking, pulled his bow from its case without thinking, and now he loosed an arrow and spilled his first man dead or dying from the saddle without thinking of that, either. It had all been a series of ingrained responses so long practised that they had become as natural as breathing. There was no time for regret, revulsion, or any of the other feelings that supposedly followed a first kill. There was only shock at how easy it had been, and fear; not for his victim, but for himself. Arrow on string, ringed thumb hooked to string, draw back the string and release. And *thud!* – there you have it: a corpse. It would be just as easy for someone else to do the same to him.

Bayrd shot two more arrows as the distance closed, emptying another saddle but leaving the third still occupied; not with a rider now, just a bloody, screaming thing that fled past him, lost to everything but the shaft that had shattered its jaw. He slammed the bow back into its case, pulled the lance from its saddle-sheath behind his right knee – and lost it five seconds later in the guts of a Prytenek spearman.

Then he was through the first rank of enemy riders and into the open space beyond them, wheeling Yarak about as he drew his bow once again and began shooting arrows at anything not Alban that he could see. The other ranks were charging now: he could hear the snap of bowstrings, the whir of arrows and the startled shrieks of those the arrows hit. That was the sound of warfare: surprise, disbelief, but very seldom pain. The pain came later, if only a few seconds later.

No need to go back to warn the camp. Unless they were all deaf, they knew by now. If a man did not die at once from the spear or arrow in his body, or go straight into shock, the sounds he made could carry for a long, shrill distance.

The Prytenek attack was blunted already, its first element of surprise quite lost. Best to disrupt it completely, and destroy it if he could; break the formation, scatter the horsemen, and after that pull back to an open skirmish line and reduce the footmen with arrows. It was impossible to tell, amid the swirl of men and horses, how many were involved on either side. Fewer than three hundred of his own men, now. There were empty Alban saddles, mute witness to the risk of getting too close to those long-handled axes.

But in exchange, there were very few Prytenek horsemen still astride their mounts, and fewer still of those without the harsh geometry of spear or arrow transfixing some part of their bodies. Most of the remaining enemy were axemen on foot. None wore armour; just leather skirts adorned with pieces of metal that were so few, and so widely spaced, that the squares and discs and diamonds had to be ornamental rather than defensive. Their unencumbered speed was their own best defence, a proof of the old truth that speed could be armour enough, but armour without speed was just an easy target. These targets were not easy at all: they came over the tussocks of grass that clad the low sand-dunes in huge, horrible bounds, with the great, wide-bladed axes whirling around their heads – at least until an arrow, or a spear, or least often a sword or mace or horseman's hatchet, slapped them backwards to the ground.

Bayrd hauled Yarak around, the grey Ferhana mare dancing with excitement on her hind legs and looking out for someone else to kick. For his part, he was looking for his signaller, intending that the man should signal 'fall back' then 'regroup' before the depleted Thousand went in again. If a single collision – Bayrd had enough self-respect not to dignify the hasty action by calling it a charge – had caused this much confusion, then another could do nothing but good. But there was no sign of the yellow-and-black-striped overrobe that a signaller was supposed to wear at all times, and there weren't even any Colour-Robes he recognised. For a long, slow minute there were no Albans in the area at all, only himself –

– And another of those damned Pryteneks, with his damned axe. . . !

Bayrd dropped his bow, grabbed for his sword, tried to duck, tried to pull Yarak into a sidestep – tried to do too many things at once, and finished none of them.

The axe came round and hit him in the side, just below the ribs. It went through the iron scales of the *tsalaer* and the iron rings of the mailshirt beneath, through the combat leathers and the meat inside them, all in a single easy sweep as though none of all those layers of protection had been there.

Bayrd ar'Talvlyn pitched backwards, feeling his feet come out of the stirrups as easily as if he had kicked them free. He saw the sky swing up above him, the white clouds and the brilliance of the sun. Sight meant nothing: he could *feel* something else, something far brighter, and he could feel the shape of it, a crescent like the new moon at dusk, burning at white heat.

The one hand he slapped against the enormous wound in a futile attempt to hold it shut told him the meaning of that burning crescent. It was what the axe had done to him. From front to back, from navel to spine, he had been split open like a fish for gutting. There was no pain. Not even the flare of heat was hurting.

Yet . . .

He had seen enough in the past quarter-hour to know – dispassionately, without any surprise or fear – that he might not live long enough to feel it. The ground came up to strike him across the shoulders, and he rolled over in a tumble of flailing limbs too loose to break his fall. Even the fall didn't hurt.

Bayrd saw the sun spin round above his head. It was moving; he had stopped. Then it fell on him, and burned him, and went black.

And the world went with it . . .

5

Sorcerer

Panting hard, Marc ar'Dru reined his horse back to a walk and patted its armoured neck, raising a little cloud of water-droplets from beneath the leather scales. Both he and the black Andarran stallion were bathed in sweat after their work of the past half-hour. He had personally killed two men for certain, and wounded another five, though he had yet to feel any pride in the achievement. But he was very proud of the way his Ten had outmanoeuvred a full score of Prytenek riders and mauled them badly enough to force the entire group – or its survivors – into headlong retreat. That Ten and the remnants of another went roaring off in hot pursuit to make sure that their adversaries kept running. Marc had been at their head, standing in his stirrups at full gallop and twirling his spear as he sang, absolutely *sang*, with the sheer overwhelming thrill of it all, still young enough to know for certain that he would never die until the day beyond the day beyond tomorrow . . .

He went warm around the ears just at the memory, but what happened next made him proud to think of it. When the Captain-of-One-Hundred's signaller sounded recall – and despite the excitement of the headlong chase and the conviction that they needed at least another hundred yards of pursuit to be quite sure the enemy had broken – all his men had instantly drawn on their reins and slackened their pace and turned hard about to regroup and charge again. And again; and *again*, one final time, driving home the impact with a storm of arrows until all the Pryteneks still capable of movement were fighting not the Albans but just to get away.

That was what discipline in battle was all about; not the skill to ride in straight lines and pretty patterns in review, but the self-control that was both the simplest and the hardest skill to learn.

Any captain could launch his troop at an objective, but when the trumpets called and they were needed somewhere else, no one else but the men of that troop could turn their horses and come back. Control of their passions, and enough pride in their duty to put pride in their reputations away. That was why Lord Guelerd would lose this war. His horsemen had fought bravely enough; but from what Marc had seen, they knew only how to career about at full gallop like madmen, until their horses were blown, and their formation – if there had ever been one to start with – had fallen apart, and they were easy pickings for the first Captain-of-Ten to spot them and close up his ranks and take them in flank.

The men on foot were far better soldiers, whether their weapon was the spear or the axe, and Marc's weary smile went thin and crooked at the thought of what they would have been like if anyone had taught them to stand still in ranks, rather than running about as the horsemen did. And if they were armoured, or even given shields . . . The smile was quite gone now, and he hoped fervently that Albanak-*arluth* would see this war through to its conclusion before any of the Prytenek lord's-men had that same idea.

For the present, as Lord Albanak had said, they treated war as a game; and in a game there was no reason to fight in disciplined ranks, because rushing about and striking in all directions was part of the fun. The footsoldiers had no armour because they were unimportant by comparison with the mounted nobility, and why pay good money to protect mere vassals when this was all just good sport? After all, people were killed just as frequently while hunting, and there was never a weapon drawn against them – and besides, armour would have suggested that somebody had started taking things too seriously . . .

Bayrd ar'Talvlyn had muttered something about it being all too easy to slip into the Prytenek mode of thought; he had meant in terms of being crooked, and devious, and willing to accept betrayal as commonplace, but Marc could understand exactly what his friend meant. Those excuses, and others like them, would have been trotted out a thousand times when someone forward-looking suggested change. He knew well enough, because the Alban *kailinin* could be just as hidebound by their traditions, and the lower clans were sometimes worst of all. Take his own father, for instance. As well as giving him the respect due to a Head of House, Marc loved him dearly – the two did not always go together – even when he . . .

The thought tripped up on itself and fell aside as he saw the grey horse. It was standing with head lowered, nuzzling at something on the ground, and Marc felt a sudden cramping chill in his belly as though he had swallowed ice-water. There were many horses standing like that, he only had to turn his head to see them, but even in its lamellar bard this one looked all too familiar.

'Yarak . . .?' he called, and in answer to his fears, in spite of all his hopes, the grey horse responded. It lifted its head and whinnied piteously, then returned to nudging the crumpled form on the ground at its feet. Marc had been thinking of dismounting anyway, to give his own tired horse a rest from the weight of man and armour, but now, made clumsy with haste, he scrambled from the saddle and all but fell to the ground, then ran to where the grey horse stood. As he came closer, his pace slowed. From what little he could see already, there was no longer any need of haste.

Bayrd ar'Talvlyn lay on his back, staring up at the sky, and there was blood everywhere. Marc tried to persuade himself that things looked worse than they really were, because in the last little while he had received something of an education in just how far fresh blood can spread and – hope against hope – how little of it had to be spilled to make such an appalling mess as this.

But the smashed *tsalaer* killed his hopes just as surely as whatever had shattered the armour had killed the man inside it. Black-lacquered metal scales were scattered about like leaves after an autumn storm, and others still hung loosely from their stretched and tattered lacing. As if that were not enough, he could see snapped mail-rings, telling him at once that the light mailshirt worn under the battle armour had been broken open too. There was so much blood . . . and no sign of an enemy. From the way he had seen Bayrd fight earlier, Marc would have sworn that all this blood would have come from an opponent and not from Bayrd himself.

Except that there were no other corpses for a long way around, and both of Bayrd's swords were still sheathed. Even the disdainfully dismissed axe still hung from its loop on Yarak's saddle. All that were missing was the bow – he found that a few minutes later – some arrows, and the lance. Marc didn't trouble looking for that; he had seen how it was lost, and where, almost half a mile away from where he stood. There was no point in deceiving himself any further, and as he stared down at the body, he knew that he couldn't bring himself to tell Mevn.

Not yet.

He began to understand what the older *kailinin* meant when they warned their younger comrades against becoming friends with anyone still of an age to go into battle. More certain than drink or women, that was the surest way to lose a friend. It explained why the senior warriors seemed somewhat distant, and why they never warmed to anyone whether blood-clan, family or merely allies of the House. The habits of a long, friendless maturity had become impossible to break so late in life. He gulped as the grief thickened in his throat, and tried to swallow what could not be swallowed. Marc ar'Dru had never known before that there were other pains than those of wounds, other aches than those of a long day in the saddle, and he did not know how to cure what was hurting now.

At least Bayrd was out of pain. It would have been ghastly beyond imagining if he had suffered such a wound as this and not died of it quickly, for no surgeon of the Alban people, and none of any other country that Marc knew, could do anything to patch up such a wound as must lie within the armour. If the great rip in the *tsalaer* bore true witness, Bayrd ar'Talvlyn had been all but cut in two – and the only healer left to him would have been the small red dagger riding at his belt. Putting the *tsepan* to its proper use was the responsibility of the first man to find him. That man would have been Marc ar'Dru, and Marc didn't know if he could have done it.

Yesterday he hadn't known if he could ever kill another man at all, but when that other man had an axe and no such qualms concerning him, then loosing the arrow or thrusting the spear came easier. But to do that to a friend, even a friend in agony?

No . . .

Now that the need for it was past, he reached out for the *tsepan* anyway. It would be a keepsake, something for House ar'Dru to remember its friend by – because Marc didn't want to remember him like this, lying here like a lobster cracked open by a clumsy cook. He would go back to the camp and send out a House retainer to straighten Bayrd's limbs, wash the blood away, and make the body look presentable. Then he and Mevn would come out together and bring Bayrd home with more respect and honour than he might receive from his own clan.

The *tsepan* was tightly buckled to the weapon-belt, so tightly that tugging wouldn't move it, and even though Marc didn't want to go any closer to the horrid gap in Bayrd's side, he forced himself to stoop and start picking at the straps.

'Not . . . yet.' The sound of a voice where no other voice should have been cost Marc his balance, almost his senses, and for a few heart-stopping seconds seemed to have his sanity already.

'I don't . . . don't need that . . . courtesy. Not . . . just yet.'

It was Bayrd without a doubt, though the voice was weak and hoarse. Marc scrambled backwards on hands and heels, and when he clambered hastily to his feet his sword was out already. Ugly legends filled his mind, tales to frighten children after dark; stories of the *traugarin*, the walking corpses. He had loved such stories when he was a child, even though they kept him wide awake and trembling late into the night and turned his dreams to nightmares when he slept. But they had been just stories.

Now he wasn't so sure.

'Water . . .' said Bayrd.

'What?'

'Thirsty . . . I'm very thirsty.'

To his credit, Marc steadied up enough to put his sword away and fetch the waterbottle he could see on Yarak's saddle. But he still shuddered when he saw that it too was spattered with great drops of still-wet blood. When he came back, Bayrd was fumbling with the fastenings of his helmet, almost fighting with them, such was his haste to be out of it. When the warmask came free, Marc could see that Bayrd's face had an unhealthy grey pallor; but it was not the face of a corpse. He had looked at enough of those already today to know the difference when he saw it. A little colour was already seeping back around Bayrd's mouth and below his shadowed eyes, and in any case, Marc doubted any corpse could swear like that.

'May he wander cold through the Nine Hot Hells,' ar'Talvlyn muttered, swigging more water and spitting it out as if clearing a

94

foul taste from his mouth. The foul taste, Marc saw, had stained
the water rusty brown, but his voice was already stronger than it
had been. 'The bastard came right out of nowhere! Mad sort of
way to attack, if you ask me.'

Marc did not ask. He could think of very little that he wanted to
say right now.

'I would have had him too, if he hadn't scared the horse . . .'

'Had him? Had *who* . . .? Bayrd-*ain*, what are you talking
about?' And he too must be feeling better, Marc reflected soberly,
if he was already snapping at the friend whose death he had so
recently been mourning.

'The wonder of it is that I'm talking at all.' Bayrd took a long,
long drink, then poured some water into his cupped hand and
scrubbed it onto his face and neck. 'God, that's better. Him. The
one with the axe. Over – *ow!*' He raised one arm to point over to
the left, but winced and cut the gesture short. Marc followed the
line of his arm, but saw nothing. This was the place where the first
rank of Alban horsemen had broken through, at such a speed that
they had ridden on a little way before they turned. There was
nothing to see except the feathered shafts of expended arrows and
a few hoofprints, his and Bayrd's horse, Bayrd himself – and of
course, the blood.

He almost demanded to know what game was being played, but
held his tongue. There was something about Bayrd's mood that
suggested such a question would not be taken kindly; any more
than, after this afternoon, the suggestion of playing the Prytenek
game and treating war as sport would have been greeted with
anything but contempt by an Alban clan-lord. Bayrd was looking
at him, staring at him as if he were trying to read what Marc was
thinking, and defying him to put what was on his mind into words.
Bayrd had always been what Mevn called a great 'looker', putting
more into a long moment's silent consideration than many people
gained from a quarter-hour of chatter; and what with the bright
grey eyes in the pallid grey face, the intensity of that stare was
disturbing.

'I mustn't have hit him as hard as I thought,' he said decisively.
'Obviously he got away. I'm lucky he didn't come back and cut my
throat.'

Marc raised one finger – wait one minute – and walked off to fetch his own horse. Two members of his Ten began to ride slowly towards him, but he waved them away. 'Everything's all right!' he shouted. 'I'll deal with things here. Just get yourselves out to the crest of yonder hills and establish a picket-line before this happens all over again!'

He hoped that they would attribute the shakiness of his voice to after-battle nerves – but even if they didn't, it was his place to issue orders and theirs to obey them. Both warriors raised their arms in salute, then wheeled about and cantered away again. Marc ar'Dru watched them out of sight before he took another step.

When Marc came back, he was leading his horse by the reins and walking rather more slowly than seemed necessary. Bayrd was sitting upright with one leg curled beneath him, leaning on the other knee. His *tsalaer* was off, its four lamellar panels on the ground beside him, and his mailshirt was no more than a collapsed heap of interlocked steel rings, surprisingly small and just as surprisingly heavy for its size. He glanced up at the sound of Marc's approach, as if expecting the younger man to say something.

He did not. There was a frown notched between his eyebrows and a look of intense concentration about him, as if he had been thinking hard all the way to his horse and even harder all the way back; and now he had decided to keep quiet until the subject changed to one he knew.

As if the present matter was a subject Bayrd ar'Talvlyn was familiar with. He leaned sideways very slowly, his breath catching in little gasps of – not pain any more, just discomfort; sharp, annoying stabs up under the ribs, like a stitch brought on by running too hard. As he leaned over, a slash torn through the tunic of his leathers yawned wide, then wider still. The shirt beneath was similarly ripped, but the skin under all was totally unharmed. Bayrd ran nervously probing fingers from just above his navel around to the small of his back, and felt nothing wrong. Yet he had seen – or *thought* he had seen . . .

This was ridiculous. He couldn't have imagined something which hadn't even grazed him and yet had done *that* to his armour and clothing. And then there was the blood. It had come from somewhere, and from the lassitude and the occasional spells of giddiness, it must have come from him.

It was what had happened afterwards that he would have liked to witness, but all his senses had been swamped by the shock of that one axe-blow. Smell and taste had both been clogged with the metallic saltiness of blood; he had felt nothing after the first thud of the ground against his back; all he could remember hearing was the hammer of his own heart; and the blue-white flare as the sun fell from the sky had taken effective care of eyesight. Something had shut him in a cage whose walls were his own perceptions, and had kept him imprisoned there until it had done – what . . .?

The *what* was easy, and the *how* he felt uncomfortably close to understanding; but the *why* was more of a mystery than all the other questions put together.

'We have to talk,' said Marc at last.

'About my fortunate escape?'

'Save that excuse for those who don't know you as well as I do. That . . . that was no "fortunate escape", at least not unless you look at fortune – good or bad – in a very different way than I do. And I know that you don't.' He looked at Bayrd, then bent down to the mailshirt and rummaged amongst the jumbled links until he found where the shoulders began. With a slight effort he lifted it and let it hang there while he studied the long, slightly curving gash that ran from almost centre front to almost centre back. Then he straightened the *tsalaer* and looked at where the scales had given way; plucked at a piece of lacing and examined how both the heavy, braided silk and the leather thongs had both been cleanly severed by a sharp cutting edge. Finally he walked right around Bayrd, staring at him the whole time.

'You didn't escape anything,' he said. 'You were dead – or at least you should have been. Bayrd-*ain*, my good friend, before someone with the authority to twist the information out of you asks it, tell me. What is going on?'

Bayrd rubbed at his side again, still not able to believe what his fingers told him: that the skin was whole, that there was no enormous wound, no blood, no pain. That he was alive and completely untouched. There wasn't even a scar. 'I think,' he began – then hesitated, considering and discarding one phrase after another until only the blunt truth remained. 'I think that I'm a sorcerer.'

'You're a . . . No. Not *you*. Not an ar'Talvlyn. Tell me the truth.'

'That is the truth. I think. Because I can't think of any other explanation.'

'But you're –'

'A warrior, yes. An Alban, yes. Of *kailin* rank, yes. What else should I be, or not be, that would rule against it?'

'But you have to study books, learn spells, do all sorts of –'

'This is sorcery, Marc. Not the Art Magic.' It was a weighty sort of declaration, but Bayrd tried to speak the words as he could best remember *Hospodar* Skarpeya speaking them to him.

'Is there a difference?'

'Apparently there is. You can choose to be a wizard: study the Art Magic, become expert at it, read the books, speak the spells, draw the circles . . . But for sorcery, you have to have the Talent. And if you have the Talent, then sorcery will find you. It seems I have the Talent.'

'But why now? Why here?'

'Father of Fires in the Pit!' Bayrd slammed his fist angrily into the ground beside him. 'If I knew that, don't you think I'd tell you? Don't you think I'd feel a great deal happier than I do? It's happened. That's all I know. It's part of me. As much a part, as impossible to lose as . . . as . . .' he held his left hand open between them, fingers spread wide. 'As much a part of me as this, and just as hard to lose. Harder. I can at least cut the hand off.'

'So what, er –' Marc squatted down on his haunches, picked up a twig and began to draw complicated abstract patterns on an area of exposed sandy soil between the tussocks of coarse grass, '– what can you do . . . ?'

'Not die of fatal wounds,' said Bayrd flatly. 'I think that's an impressive enough trick to start with.'

'But this, this difference between sorcery and magic. Where did you hear about that? How did you hear about it? Who told you? Not an Alban, surely?'

'I shouldn't think so, no. It was Skarpeya.'

That name produced more of a reaction than any of Bayrd's own revelations, so much so that he wasn't sure whether to be relieved or irritated by it.

'*Skarpeya?* You mean –'

'– I mean Skarpeya. The *Hospodar* at King Daykin's court in Kalitzim. Unless you know any other Skarpeyas I might have met?' It was a pointless sarcasm, and Bayrd regretted it at once.

'But he was a wizard. Albans don't speak to –'

'He still is a wizard, to the best of my knowledge. But he's also a very good judge of horseflesh, and we spoke far more about that. Your Ten were drilling while we talked. He was greatly impressed.'

'Avert!' said Marc hastily, making the sign to do so. 'Save us from the praises of such as that one!'

'From such as me, as well? Your Captain-of-One-Thousand?'

'I didn't mean that.'

'No? The difference is hard to see. Marc-*ain*, I can still be your friend. Yours – and Mevn's. Or I can be no more than your commander. The three of us have known each other long enough for . . . No, dammit. I outrank you, but I won't order you, or guide you. The choice is yours, my friend. Say the word.'

Marc looked at him for a long time in silence before he spoke, and when he did so at last it was in the awkward formal speech of Old High Alban; a language made more uncomfortable still in Bayrd's ears by its similarity to the language of Lord Gelert of Prytenon.

'Bayrd-*an* Talvalin,' he said, 'you have been friend to House ar'Dru these four years past, and as the Chosen Son of House ar'Dru I speak for all. Whether you should grow away from us or rise above us or be made different in ways we do not know, you are still friend to House ar'Dru – until you choose to have the friendship end. I speak for my father, and for all my kin, but most especially I speak for my sister Mevn who was dear to you.'

Bayrd bowed, just slightly; a token of esteem between equals, and between friends. 'And is dear still,' he said.

The swirling, vicious little battle was over; to a certain extent Bayrd's uncomfortable secrecy was over; and when they returned to the camp it seemed that the duel was over too. The red and white ar'Diskan banners had been lowered from where they had fluttered so possessively above a stretch of empty beach, and now formed the canopy above a bed. On the bed, still in his armour, lay Lord Serej ar'Diskan, and it was a bed he would never leave again.

'My father died an hour ago,' said Gerin ar'Diskan, a man stocky and dark-visaged as his father but who, even despite his loss, appeared a good deal more cheerful. Perhaps, thought Bayrd unworthily, because his long black hair had newly been bound up in the three braids. 'I am the clan-lord now.' Marc and Bayrd would have climbed immediately from their horses to give him proper obeisance, but he waved them back to their saddles. 'There will be enough time for that nonsense later,' he said.

Bayrd ar'Talvlyn felt a small thrill of astonishment at the casual use of that word. This was Serej's Chosen Son, the one picked out to succeed him, and already he seemed a much more reasonable person than his father. But then, anyone would seem more reasonable than Lord Serej ar'Diskan.

'The duel this morning,' said Lord Gerin, 'was a personal affair between my father and yourself, yes?'

'Yes, my lord.'

'Our two clans were not involved?'

'No, my lord. Words were exchanged between your lord father and myself, and, well, he was a hot-tempered man and . . .'

'I know well enough,' said Gerin. 'But since it is ill-omened to speak ill of the dead, we will speak no more at all on this matter. Although,' and again Bayrd was surprised, this time by the brief, sardonic smile which flickered across Gerin ar'Diskan's face, 'no law yet passed can enforce the way we think. Unless you intend to continue, in which case I shall name a principal from among my lord father's personal retainers, then I declare the duel and the cause of quarrel null and void.'

'There is no need to continue, my lord ar'Diskan. Your lord father is dead, and the grudge between us died with him. I salute his memory sincerely, as a clan-lord of Alba, and I say only that there are now other enemies for Alban warriors to fight besides each other.'

'That was spoken like a gentleman,' said Gerin. 'Indeed,' and he smiled again, 'it was spoken more like a gentleman than many gentlemen of my acquaintance. Though most of those are – were – my father's friends.'

That small correction told Bayrd enough. 'To give your own words back to you, my lord: it is an ill thing to speak ill of the dead, by direct words or by implication, and it brings no honour to the speaker.'

'Then keep your honour, Bayrd ar'Talvlyn. Or add to it.'

'My lord?'

'As you say yourself, we have more enemies to fight than one another. But as you have already seen . . .' Gerin ar'Diskan didn't bother to finish the sentence. It was too obvious for words. 'If Lord Guelerd leaves us alone for long enough, we will do to ourselves what he cannot, and probably do it better, unless we make more lasting alliances between the clans and families.'

'Alliances, my lord?' Bayrd was caught slightly off-balance by the apparent change of subject, because Gerin was suggesting nothing new – unless, that is, he meant –

'Alliances in the past have been between partners of equal rank,' said Gerin, *ilauem-arluth* and Clan-Lord ar'Diskan, deliberately pitching his voice loud enough for everyone to hear. 'I propose an alliance of blood and honour between the clans ar'Diskan and ar'Talvlyn.' When the murmur of astonishment died down he turned to the only member of clan ar'Talvlyn present. 'Do you agree, Bayrd-*eir*?'

'I agree that the idea is good, but – but you will need the Overlord's permission, and I don't think –'

'On this one day, set down from the old time, Overlord Albanak has no say in what I do. I am newly come into my authority as Clan-Lord ar'Diskan, and within reason I can do as I please. And I ask you, Bayrd-*eir* ar'Talvlyn, if you will be my Companion and my banner-bearer.'

Bayrd was not the only one to gasp aloud, for such a position had the same responsibilities as a Companion in a duel: in essence, to keep both sides honest. The Companion and banner-bearer of a high-clan lord was the only man or woman in hall with the right to correct the lord himself; to call his faults and failings to attention; to criticise a lack of honour or equally, the other side of the coin, to take the lord to task for being concerned with honour to the exclusion of all else.

Lord Albanak had used the term to Bayrd in jest. Now Lord ar'Diskan was offering it in reality. He wanted Bayrd to be his conscience. Such offers of preferment were not made twice. Bayrd swung from Yarak's saddle and sank gracefully down to give Second Obeisance, touching his brow to his crossed hands on the ground before him.

'I, Bayrd-*eir*, *kailin-eir ilauan* ar'Talvlyn, do become your liege man by faith and fealty, freely given and freely taken . . .' And then he stumbled, for while the first part was common to most oaths a *kailin* might be called upon to take, the rest was unfamiliar.

'In the absence of my lord father,' Gerin bowed respectfully towards the makeshift bier, 'there is no need to stand overmuch on ritual. Say what words you feel are right.'

Colouring at the honour done him, so that his complexion came almost back to normal for a few minutes, Bayrd racked his brain for fair-sounding phrases. After all the reading of old chronicles he had done in his youth, the words were there.

'To . . . To stand by your side and be your banner-bearer, to stand by your heart and be your Companion and your conscience, to stand by your honour and keep it true, and homage and true service I will bear unto you, to live and to die as you direct, against all peoples save only the clan of my own blood.'

Steel glinted as Lord Gerin drew the *tsepan* from his belt and ran the thin, triangular blade lightly across his left hand's palm. Blood oozed out and formed a long, bright trickle. He bent down and scooped a handful of sand from the beach, then trickled it onto the small wound until the blood was staunched. 'Honoured by this, I accept you. Be honoured by this: upon this blood, upon this earth, before these witnesses and beneath the Light of Heaven, your friends shall be my friends and your enemies mine also. I so swear it on my word and on my Honour.'

Everything went still and silent as Gerin ar'Diskan looked his new liegeman up and down. 'Bayrd ar'Talvlyn,' he said, 'you have been raised to *kailin-eir* of my household. So the single braid is wrong. Go see to it.'

6

Companion

LORD GERIN'S PLAN for an alliance to cement peace between two clans and thus act as an example for others to follow was a good one – in theory. But in practice, the new Clan-Lord ar'Diskan discovered all too quickly that he had left several elements out of his equation. Most immediate, most obvious, and by that very nature most easily forgotten, was that he was lord over an Alban high-clan household, with all the difficulties it could – and did – mean.

Clan ar'Diskan's resentment was immediate, general, and gathered force during the course of the next hour. They resented Bayrd ar'Talvlyn, their lord's new Companion and Bannerman, because an outblood low-clan *kailin* had been appointed to such a high position over the heads of more worthy and better-born ar'Diskan clansmen. They resented their clan-lord since he had made such a decision without consulting his own supporters, by which, of course, they meant the old, hidebound *kailinin-eir* who had supported his father before him. They resented Overlord Albanak for permitting him to do so, conveniently forgetting that Gerin had merely invoked the old tradition with which no Overlord could interfere, and if Albanak had done so, they would have resented *him* even more. And they even resented old Lord Serej for choosing to die at so inconvenient a time.

'A pretty stew, eh?' said Marc ar'Dru, under the pretence of offering Bayrd a congratulatory cup of unwatered wine. 'If this is the result of a, a . . .' he tried for the exact words, ' "an alliance of blood and honour", then what in the name of the Black Pit would a feud look like?'

'Probably much like this,' Bayrd said grimly. 'Except with more swords.' He took a long swig of the wine, deliberately insouciant for the benefit of any ar'Diskan'r warriors who might be watching, and had to fight the twist of disgust off his face. Briej white was dry and refreshing when properly chilled; drunk warm, it was little different from expensive vinegar. But warm or cold, it was strong enough – and right now the alcohol content was welcome. He felt its acidic burn right down into the pit of his stomach, and let out a long breath that distant, unfamiliar observers might have assumed was satisfaction.

Marc was neither. 'That bad?' he said.

'Worse.' Bayrd held out the cup. 'Another. Though this one's just for show.' Which meant that though he intended to drink it, he would do so at his own pace and taste, and not for mere display. He waved one hand towards the green shadows of the forested inland hills, and as if by accident sent a small arc of wine spraying from the cup in casual libation to a worthy enemy. It might have been a libation indeed, or just an accident after all. He wasn't sure. Right now, Bayrd wasn't sure of many things. 'We have Lord Gelert and his people out there, ready and willing to push us back into the sea. We have only the Light of Heaven sees how many others who might ally with him –'

'– Or against him, in hope of some sort of gain.'

'Maybe. But here, we have an Overlord who encouraged our endeavours by making certain that we couldn't leave, one clan-lord who tried to kill me earlier this morning . . .'

'I wonder if he could have managed it any better than that Prytenek axeman did.'

Even though Marc had spoken softly enough, Bayrd still shot him a warning glance that said *shut up!* as plainly as the words would have done. 'He might, or he might not. But now that one's successor is another clan-lord who might get me – or even himself – killed because he's trying to bring some peace and unity into all this mess. He was right. If Gelert stays away for long enough that we can start fighting the ones we *really* hate, all he'll need to see us off his shore will be brooms and a good high tide.'

'Then perhaps we should just have another clan war, like the old days, and get it all over and done with?' Marc ar'Dru sounded sarcastic, but not in the usual way. There was agreement in his voice as well. Safely out of involvement with all this, he had the advantage of neutrality – at least for the time being.

But if events took a turn for the worse, House ar'Dru would find

104

itself dragged into the fray, forced to choose between friends and allies who might have picked different sides. And forced to kill them, or be killed. The personal problems of an involuntary sorcerer were growing less important with every minute that passed, with every curse that was uttered, with every fist that was raised. Even though the fists were empty. At least for now.

Bayrd kept his own hand well clear of any of the weapon-hilts jutting from his belt. It would be all too easy for the armed stranger to be the spark that ignited this visibly smouldering hostility at his very presence, and at the same time all too unlikely that his restraint would serve to calm things down. People – *Alban* people – just didn't think that way.

He found himself hoping for another Prytenek attack. Not a big one, just enough to remind this crowd of once-dignified men and women that their previous lord lay dead among them, that their new live lord was trying to act wisely, and that most of all they were still stranded in unpacified enemy territory. He wanted to yell at them, to call their stupidities to notice, to do something besides just stand here being calm and dignified in the hope that it would do some good. If every Alban on this beach shared the same face and the same shoulders, he wanted to slap the one and shake the other until something like sense entered their petty little minds. He wanted . . .

Bayrd's teeth clenched and his lips stretched in a swift grimace of discomfort, but the hot, pungent heat that rose through him wasn't a wine-created belch. Although by now it was a sensation just as familiar. It was needing less and less passion to summon up the power – or summoning it was growing easier. Either way, he was Companion and banner-bearer to the Clan-Lord ar'Diskan, and he couldn't let it show. No fire, no sparks, not even healing – because there was nothing to heal, Serej ar'Diskan was far beyond the reach of any surgeon, and even if death could be turned back on itself for anyone other than himself, Bayrd was none too sure that he wanted *that* one back to life again. Neither was he sure that Serej would want such a thing himself, to owe such a debt of gratitude to the man he had so plainly despised. Except that, knowing him, it would be a debt of hatred, to know he owed his life not only to Bayrd ar'Talvlyn, but to sorcery. No. Best let him lie. He was a better man dead than he had ever been alive.

And as a respected corpse rather than a resurrected one –
Bayrd's eyes narrowed as the thought took shape – the old man
served a better purpose not just for him, but for everyone close
enough to see.

Even though his conversation with Skarpeya all those months
ago had never come around to the practicalities of sorcery and the
Art Magic, he knew what to do, not needing to think how to do it
any more than he had to think the breath into his lungs or the
blood through his veins. For the man whom everyone claimed
thought too much, it was an ironic discovery. The shapes formed
unbidden in his mind, inchoate shadows that hovered on the edge
of recognition: a rope, an outstretched hand, a hook. Other shapes
that made no sense except that they somehow represented
grasping, drawing, pulling . . .

For an instant Bayrd closed his eyes and let the pulling take
control – when it came, it was a long, steady pressure, without any
violence – then opened them again and watched it happen. The
banner-draped bed on which Serej ar'Diskan lay swayed slightly
as though brushed by a careless passer-by, even though it was of
such massive construction, a bed fit for a clan-lord, that the
passer-by would have needed a siege-ram to get any response at
all. Then without any noise or fuss, it slumped sideways and
pitched the dead man out onto the ground at his clansfolk's feet.
Serej rolled over once and lay, no longer shaded beneath the
banners raised by honourable grief, with his face upturned
accusingly to the hard blue sky and the all-seeing Light of Heaven.

The curses and the shouting and the accusations cut off like a
violently snuffed candle, and only a trickle of nervous muttering
trailed off into silence like the candle's final wisp of smoke.
Someone coughed uneasily, and the sound was shockingly loud,
drawing turned heads and anxious stares from all sides.

'Is this how the people of high-clan ar'Diskan give honour to
their worthy dead?' Bayrd ar'Talvlyn's voice was cold and quiet,
but in that appalling stillness he had no need to shout. 'The merest
independent House can show better than that. Brawling and
complaint with your last lord's body still unburnt. With it lying at
your feet.'

He took pains not to accuse them of spilling it there; since
everything else he had said was true, there was no need to add lying

and hypocrisy to his use of sorcery, and their own shame was doing more than further reproaches. Regardless of how he had felt about Serej ar'Diskan alive, the man had been a lord, and once dead he deserved some courtesy. If being untimely tumbled from his bier gained him – and more especially his son – the respect that they had not been getting, then that tumble was well-timed.

Many hands struggled the dead man awkwardly back to his proper place, too many to do other than get in each other's way, though all determined to atone in some manner for what had happened. Bayrd watched, his face expressionless, and only when Serej was once more laid out on his last bed did he raise his wine-cup to his lips, drinking once and then pouring the rest out onto the sand in a pointed final salute. As Bannerman and Companion to the new clan-lord, he had that right.

The right to be the conscience not merely of the lord, but of his whole clan.

'You are growing bold, my friend.'

Marc ar'Dru was not accusing, not blaming, simply stating a fact. His sister Mevn sat quietly, listening hard but saying not a word. She knew what he meant, because Bayrd had told her himself – and then been unsure whether to be gratified or vaguely discomfited by her lack of surprise. Formally invited to a private dinner at House ar'Dru in celebration of his new rank – which for the present meant sitting with the other two around a fire built on the sand, and the luxury of freshly shot game rather than salted rations – he had debated whether he wanted anyone other than Marc, who had found out almost by accident, to learn about what he still regarded as a guilty and dishonourable secret.

But there was a comfort in company, and this company was one he trusted with his life if necessary, so why not with his honour? Honour was always the more important: it lived on as reputation or notoriety after a *kailin*'s death, colouring the way he was remembered in the Books of Years of afterwards. If anyone was to set the matter straight, they would have to know the truth of it.

And Mevn had raised her eyebrows, and nodded, and poured more wine – red Seurandec this time, she had explained, so that the problem of chilling wouldn't arise – and that was all the astonishment she expressed. It was a relief, and at the same time it was somewhat disappointing – if disappointment was quite the word he wanted, and Bayrd wasn't sure that it was. At least she had been suitably delighted at his advancement, and even managed to restrain herself from more than a single finger-wagging observation that she had been right about him all along. That was real, that mattered where his honour was concerned, and so far as Mevn was concerned it clearly mattered more than any amount of sorcery.

And neither of them had asked him to perform conjuring tricks after dinner.

Bayrd grinned and drank Seurandec wine. Like the other two he was savouring each sip with the air of someone uncertain of where the next would come from. The attitude was entirely correct. All the ships had been burnt save those of the Ship-Clans, and every man and woman aboard them was out of favour. Though the Pryteneks presumably imported wine of their own, they would hardly sell it to the people who had invaded them. And King Daykin of Kalitz was severely out of pocket to the tune of a treasure-barge and its entire cargo, thus unlikely to countenance trade with his thieving ex-employees. For all that, Bayrd was feeling more at ease than he had done for some time.

'Bold?' he said. 'I thought I was being very circumspect and subtle.'

'Oh, you were,' said Marc. 'At least, to someone who didn't know you better. But I've known you for four years, and . . .' He stared at the contents of his wine-cup for a few seconds, as if the dark liquid was a page on which he could read . . . something. Then he shuddered visibly and drained the cup in a single long draught. 'And suddenly you were different.'

'Different?' asked Mevn. 'How?'

'Changed. Another man, and yet the same. But . . . He was harder. Colder. More –'

'– Powerful?'

'Menacing.'

'I didn't feel menacing,' protested Bayrd, slightly embarrassed at the way this examination of his character had slipped into the third person without so much as a by-your-leave; as if he wasn't there any more. 'I felt angry at how stupid they were being, given all that had happened, but –'

'You looked willing to hurt someone,' said Marc flatly. 'Or to do something you had decided, whether there would be hurt involved or not. You looked as if you didn't care. And even when you were fighting, against Lord Serej and then against the Pryteneks, you didn't look like that. As I say: changed.'

Mevn gazed thoughtfully at them both; at her brother the young gallant with his fashionably flowing locks, and at her ex-lover, whose face had become shuttered against scrutiny in a way it had never been before. 'There may be a lot of changes needed before this business is all over,' she said at last. 'And this change of yours may be one we'll all live to be glad of.'

Bayrd glanced at her and then looked away. 'I'm not sure how to take that.'

'Then take it as meant: well. And have some more wine. We've already opened the flask, and you know it won't keep when the seal's been broken.' She smiled mischievously. 'If it's going to be a while before we drink any more of this particular vintage, then I'd rather it was consumed by . . . Let's just say an influential friend of the family, and leave it at that.'

Bayrd had counted short: the Albans had been thirteen thousand and some odd when they left Kalitz, and he had estimated eleven thousand had survived the journey. It was nearer twelve and a half; and he was able to see how twelve and a half thousand people could, at need, eat into the edge of a forest like flame into dry grass. That need was strong here: to clear the land and build a place in which they could live like human beings, rather than merely scratch out an existence along the shoreline like so many wading birds.

Though many initially suffered intestinal disorders from eating too much meat and not enough vegetables until they became accustomed to identifying the half-forgotten wild varieties of greenstuff again, at least no one starved. The woodland was astonishingly rich in game, birds and beasts together, and the rivers were thick with fish. Though it surprised them at the time, later knowledge explained the reason why – and one more reason why Gelert had been so angry to find them here. They had landed on the seaward side of a province-wide game preserve.

The axes had been ringing in the woods for weeks, and still there had been no sign of Gelert and his men since that first encounter in the sandhills near the shore. Because of that, the Prytenek lord had lost whatever chance he might have had to rid his land of this invasion, and the land itself was being pulled out bit by bit from between his fingers. With every stroke of an axe-blade, with every crash of a newly-felled tree, with every clank of an adze as it shaped and squared the joints of the great fortresses that thirty generations of campaigning had taught the Albans how to build, Gelert's grasp was slipping.

For more than half a thousand years, whether fighting on their own behalf or in the pay of others, the techniques of becoming secure in hostile territory had been raised almost to an art. First, the picket-line that ensured against surprise attack; then the study of terrain: where to find water, food, fodder for the horses, where would be best for defence, where for attack, where for ambush – and where for the building of walls to keep the enemy at bay. These new fortifications were not merely the ditch-faced ramparts topped with a palisade that had been flung up so hastily along the beach. With such an ample supply of timber as the nearby woods had provided – they had taken to calling it the Forest of Guelerd, not knowing just how correct their use of that name might be, and not caring – both imagination and years of practice could be put to use.

Some were simple, squat and purposeful, their walls built of a double or triple thickness of logs with rammed earth packed between; others, perhaps echoing a more high-flown architecture, sprouted towers of lesser or greater height at intervals along their perimeters. But each and every one was another nail securing Alban possession of the land they held. With the exception of the very highmost of the high-clan lords, who merely directed, everyone worked. Men and women stood watch together, wielded felling-axes and shaping tools together, and even the children scurried to and fro with sheaves of willow-withies or baskets of mud with which to plaster those same withies once they had been woven together into wall-panels. Well fed and well motivated, untroubled by the raids which all had been expecting and which never happened, they prospered.

And with prosperity came rivalry.

At first it might be no more than an amiable race between

neighbouring clans to see which of them would be first to complete their fortress, or which could add more splendid features than the other – perhaps a taller tower to be their lord's citadel, or water run from a convenient river so that a dry ditch became a moated defence. By Bayrd ar'Talvlyn's reckoning, the amiability lasted just over a month. Clan ar'Kelayr was the first to take exception, declaring in open council that when clan ar'Menez began taking the great logs down from their fortress walls and facing the flint and rubble packing with stone and mortar, it was less in defence against the Pryteneks than as a threat against their fellow Albans and, by its very permanence, a claim set on the land on which the fortress stood.

It was only a matter of time before this, and the competition both for the best building materials and the best building land, led right back to where such discussions always seemed to end: two groups of *kailinin* snarling at each other to the exclusion of all else. Even the common enemy, when that enemy was so obliging as to let himself be forgotten.

But two days later there was a reminder of his presence, when a hunting-party came galloping back from the deep woods. There were three empty saddles and two more nearly so, their riders pierced with arrows, swaying and barely conscious. The Prytenek lords'-men who had ambushed them came swirling in a loose gaggle like fog passing between the trees, reined in to study the fortress which was their quarry's refuge – then shot half a dozen fire-arrows at the timber ramparts just to see what would happen.

And the day after that, everyone who had protested against the ar'Menez'r use of stone walls were building such walls of their own. For a time at least, the clan-strife fell silent again.

That the Pryteneks had known what to expect, and had thus come prepared with incendiary materials suitable for firing wooden buildings, suggested that their spies were still able to creep unseen through the Alban pickets. That they had come back at all suggested that whatever had drawn Lord Gelert's attention away from his new and unwanted neighbours was now no longer a concern. Bayrd, seconded by Gerin ar'Diskan, believed that he had been trying to make an alliance with the various other Prytenek and Elthanek lords against whom he had been making inter-mittent war, and that the alliance had come to nothing. At least, for the time being. Gelert's reputation was probably such that none of them would have believed him had he told them it was raining and they had been getting wet, though how long that fortunate state of affairs might last was anyone's guess. But the forest was no longer as safe as it had been.

If it had ever been truly safe at all.

There were no more battles, if that first skirmish in the hills could be dignified with the term. Instead there were ambushes, like that which had slaughtered the hunting-party, and silent stalking among the shadows of the trees, and sniping with arrows and slingstones and thrown spears, and covert murders with knife and with cord and with hatchet. It began and it did not end, either in open conflict or in reasoned discussion of terms. Lord Gelert and his people had found a new sport.

The Albans, plainsfolk for all the generations of their memory, and still so even though they had spent so many years in the cities of Drosul and Kalitz, were at a severe disadvantage for the first few months, months when the summer waxed and waned and died in the glories of such an autumn as they had never seen before. The pines remained unchanging, sombre green, but the birch and maple, the oak and lime and chestnut, flared gold and red and orange as the first frosts bit and their leaves died.

Careless Albans died too, the ones who failed to react at once to a sound where no sound should be, the ones who stared instead of ducking out of sight, the ones who wandered that little bit too far from the bowshot's-width of cleared ground that surrounded their clan's stronghold. Not many died at any one time – there were no great massacres worthy of a song or a story or a special entry in the Books of Years – but they died in a steady stream, flaring red at throat or chest or belly where a harder edge than frost had bitten them.

Without honour, without glory, without even a visible enemy for the most part, it was a filthy little war.

Taught in that hard school, educated by brutal tutors, they learned not to forget but to set aside the years upon years of drilled formation, the tactics of a set-piece battle where the general moved his units with the precision of carved pieces on a gaming-board. They learned instead what it meant to fight in the forest. The despised hatchet became as worthy a weapon as the *taiken* longsword; a mailshirt and uncovered ears attuned to the noises of the woodland became more important than the splendour of *tsalaer* and plumed helmet; and the bow came into its own, whether it was the short cased weapon every *kailin* wore on his weapon-belt, or the classic seven-foot asymmetrical Great-bow of older times with its long, heavy arrows.

Bayrd nailed a man to a tree with one of those, on a fine still winter's day at a range later paced out at three hundred and twenty yards. He had been behind a thick-boled elm when his target emerged from the shelter of a birch and paused there for a few seconds too long. This was the first Prytenek he had seen in four weeks, for all that there had been a murder every two or three days of those weeks, and because of that he did not intend to miss. This Prytenek's intention had also been more than just sightseeing, if the cord in his belt was any indication. It was a cord with a wooden handle at each end and a thick knot at its midpoint, just where it could best crush against a throat, and as Bayrd ran the ugly thing through his fingers he wondered just how many throats it had crushed in its time.

The Prytenek was unable to say. Bayrd's lucky long-range arrow had hit him above one eyebrow at a steep descending angle, popping the eyeball messily out of its pocket, and whatever havoc it had wreaked inside the man's skull had left him incapable of speech – or breath, or even bleeding more copiously than the matching thin trickles from entry and exit points. Before the ar'Diskan retainers who had accompanied Bayrd could bring the arrow back, they had been forced to lever the Pryteneck's head away from the split slender treetrunk with a pry-bar. Had it not been a particularly good, straight, well-fletched arrow, Bayrd would have been inclined to leave it in place as a warning to any other unpleasant skulking assassins with garotting-nooses in their belts.

Furtive noises, stealthy movements, patient waiting and an occasional choked-off scream. That was the war in the woods. And as the winter crawled on, and firewood was bought with blood, it became worse even than that.

'The common people of this country don't hate us,' said Goel ar'Diskan, in a tone that invited anyone to dispute his opinion – if they dared.

None did. There were drifts of snow outside, three and four and even five feet deep, but the fire was warm, the food had been good, and this was as close to a proper evening in hall as Bayrd or any of the others could remember for a long time. What if it lacked music, except for the mother's voice somewhere in the warm shadows as she crooned a lullaby to her baby, and what if the place smelt of the singed tallow that fuelled its lamps instead of herb-scented oil or honeyed beeswax? It was home, of a sort; a home in the Land. A part of Alba. If old Goel wanted a disagreement just so that he could bring down the full weight of his years and accumulated wisdom in defence of whatever theory he was riding tonight, he could go somewhere else and do it. The people in this hall just wanted to sit by the fire.

It had needed eight men this afternoon, eight men with bows, to guard four so that they could gather sufficient wood for a single day. Bayrd had thought it hardly a task suited to a clan-lord's Companion and Bannerman, but none of his other duties within the fortress walls had been as urgent as ensuring that there was fuel to cook and keep warm. Of course, they had seen no one.

And equally of course, if they had skimped on the guards then not one of the fuelling party would have come back alive.

That was the way of it, this first winter of the forest war. He drank hot spruce-beer flavoured with honey and spices of dubious provenance – the stores of wine were long since gone – and wondered idly how many more winters like this there would be. How long before someone lost patience, or made a mistake, or saw sense. At least in a real war, and he grinned to himself at his wide personal familiarity with the subject, it was all over and done with in the course of a few battles. Either you won or you lost; either you or the enemy couldn't or wouldn't continue; but it wasn't like this, going on and on with never an end to the killing in sight.

'I said, the common people don't hate us at all,' persisted Goel ar'Diskan.

'Uncle, I don't disagree with you,' said Lord Gerin. 'Nobody does. That's why you can't start an argument about it.'

Whether clan-lord or not, Goel gave his nephew an exasperated look. 'What makes you think I want an argument?'

Gerin touched one hand to brow and chest in a salute that ran with easy grace into a shrug. 'Mostly previous experience, I think.'

A quiet chuckle ran around the hall, the sound of listeners grateful that someone of high enough rank to do so had said what they had all been thinking. Goel's view of a scholarly dialogue on any subject was that he proposed, someone else expressed any view whatsoever, whether it was agreement, disagreement or no more than an observation on the state of the weather, and then he lectured them at whatever length he had been intending all along. Sometimes the old man took the hint of their heavy silence, but in the seven months that Bayrd ar'Talvlyn had been Bannerman to Clan-Lord ar'Diskan, that had been the exception rather than the rule.

'Sir, on what do you base this assumption?' he asked, and as Goel swung round on him, he heard the same people who had chuckled now groan in sympathy. 'And from where do you gain your information?'

'Hah! It needs the *hlensyarl* Companion to show courtesy to an old man. Disgrace to the rest of you.'

Bayrd bowed slightly. Though he didn't much care for that Droselan borrowing 'outlander', having heard it too many times before, the rest of Goel's words added up to more of a compliment than an insult. 'Sir, no discredit to the rest. They have doubtless heard your views many times, while I . . . I am as you say: outclan, unfamiliar – and curious.'

'As well as a damned smooth diplomat,' muttered Marc ar'Dru from behind him. Ar'Dru and as many of the rest of Bayrd's Thousand as wished to had come with him when he became clan ar'Diskan's chiefmost retainer, and had proved their loyalty to their new House more than once. Several of them had died in the proving.

Marc had escaped lightly enough, even though he had lost some of his perfect good looks in favour of a not-too-badly broken nose and a scar running through his left eyebrow. The combination gave him a sleepy, cynical air that had kept his social calendar for most of the winter months filled with the attentions of various admirers of both sexes. If Bayrd remembered correctly, he was currently in the throes of what gossip suggested was a torrid romance with Vitya ar'Diskan, the clan-lord's second-from-youngest niece. Or had that been last week? It was hard to keep track any more.

Though Bayrd was still outwardly unmarked, inwardly he was more and more inclined to question everything he heard, and especially everything he was told. Hence his interest, however mild, in Goel's utterances about the Prytenek peasantry.

'I base the assumption on the differing ways in which we and the Prytenek lords'-men conduct war,' said the old man. 'Consider: we do not raid indiscriminately, and they do, even among their own people. We do not seek out and murder non-combatants, and they do — also even among their own people, and especially if they suspect any form of collaboration. They —'

'Collaboration, sir? Pryteneks working with us?' Bayrd glanced from side to side and saw the nods of approval at his interruption of so sweeping a statement. 'Sir, I've neither seen nor heard of such a thing.'

'Just so!' said Goel ar'Diskan contentedly. 'Nor will you. They're too afraid of their own lords. But since we have not yet been starved into submission or retreat, then rather than admit their inept blockade is a failure, those lords prefer to believe that we are receiving some sort of assistance. And where else but from their own people? So they . . . persuade them otherwise.'

'Your sources, sir?'

Goel hesitated for a moment, long enough for Bayrd to raise one dubious eyebrow at the old man and wonder what differences lay between his answer and the truth. 'Personal observation,' he said finally. 'The reports of scouting parties. The condition of some villages which are known not to have been approached by our Alban warriors, but which none the less have been ravaged by armed men. All for nothing. Though the ordinary vassals won't help us, they won't hinder us either. This war is none of their concern, except that we the enemy are inclined to treat them more fairly than their own side. And Guelerd, unless he's completely blind, can see — Can see . . .'

Goel ar'Diskan's voice trailed off, and a vaguely puzzled expression crossed his face while he stared into thin air as if he, like Lord Gelert, could see something peculiar. Then he stood up so suddenly that his chair crashed over backwards and his mug of beer splashed hissing into the fireplace. Goel paid no heed to the mess. He blinked, shaking his head, then uttered a small, moaning cry, clutched at his temples with both hands and toppled sideways to the floor.

Both Bayrd and Marc had seen several people fall that way before, held in what the older folk called The Grip of the Father of Fires. Some had been paralysed, or lost their faculties for a greater or lesser time, before death or recovery released them from their prison of crippled flesh. Others, perhaps the luckiest of all, had been quickly, cleanly dead before their soul-flown bodies hit the ground.

Goel ar'Diskan fell like that.

And more than that. Though many of the other people in the hall ran uselessly to Goel's aid, Bayrd did not. Instead the clan-lord's Companion and Bannerman clenched his teeth against the stabbing pains behind his eyes and the sudden gurgling nausea rising past the good food and ale in his belly, and stared at the slumped body in the vain hope that he had not seen what his aching eyes were telling him was there.

In the instant that the old man had cried out, in the moment just before his hands went to his head, sizzling tongues of vivid green flame had jetted from ears and nose and mouth. The flames had eaten him: his brain, his mind, all that he was. Bayrd had seen the light go out of Goel's eyes like the flame of a snuffed candle, and knew it would be a long time before the sight would cease to haunt his dreams. The flames had eaten his life as easily and speedily as a leaf dropped into a furnace. Everything had been consumed in that single whirl of emerald fire, and nothing had fallen down save empty meat. Now only coils of grey smoke dwelt in the charred holes of its skull where once organs of sense had given appreciation of the world, and a thick stench of burning clogged the air.

But Bayrd ar'Talvlyn could say nothing. From their very actions, no one else had seen it, heard it – or smelt it – and the explanations, if they were even believed, would be worse for the living than what had happened to the dead.

And as always, the first question was not *how?* but *why?*

Goel ar'Diskan had been an old man, past his fighting years except perhaps for a last stand in a burning, conquered citadel. He had been – *Forgive me*, thought Bayrd – of no use any more. So why had he died? *How* had he died? That it had been through sorcery or the Art Magic was plain enough for those with the eyes to see it, and as Bayrd looked from face to face in clan ar'Diskan's hall, he could see a scattering of other people hastily schooling their features to display acceptable shock and grief, for all that they had shown other emotions and understandings a few seconds before. Even though they were high-clan and would die before admitting it to such as him, Bayrd was not alone.

And from the fleeting look that Marc ar'Dru shot at him, he had seen it too.

'So blatant,' said Mevn later that same night. 'And why the old man? Why not someone more important, like Clan-Lord Gerin himself?'

Bayrd rolled over in the big bed they had started sharing again, even if only on a mutually agreed intermittent basis. And tonight they wanted to share: warmth, closeness, and another living body. Anything rather than the thought of the dead body growing cold and stiff on a bench downstairs, a bandage of the red and white clan Colours across its eyes to bind the soul within, and candles set at head and feet to keep the dark at bay until it went into the last brightness of the funeral fire. There were candles here too, making the room smell sweetly of last autumn's honey. Bayrd had exercised a Bannerman's privilege, and refused to take *no* for an answer.

'Whoever did that was trying for the clan-lord,' he said, 'and they missed. You can do the same thing with an arrow. Hit, or miss. It's easy.'

'You don't miss.'

'And you don't leave off harping on it.' Bayrd smiled a bleak smile all the same, because that shot had done his reputation nothing but good. 'At such a long range it was more luck than anything else.'

'Like magic.'

'No. At least, I don't think so. If they – whoever *they* might be – had known more about Gerin, they might have struck him just as dead as his uncle.' And if Gerin had known anything at all about sorcery or the Art, he would have been lying downstairs between the candles as well. Goel's slight hesitation when pressed on his sources of information had left suggestions in Bayrd's memory,

118

and that abrupt stab of pain through his own head as the old man died had confirmed it. Goel had possessed a little of the Talent; not enough for him to recognise it, not enough in a man of his great age to save him when someone else, somewhere else, reached out to snuff the flame of his life. What Bayrd had felt was the wind of the blow going by. It had come as close as that.

'And –' he pulled away from his private thoughts and held his hand up quickly as Mevn opened her mouth for more questions, '– I don't know what they needed to know. Skarpeya could tell you.'

'But nobody talked to Skarpeya. Except you.'

'Except me. And what good did it do? My own blood-clan wouldn't speak a civil word for almost half a year.'

'I did. Marc did.'

'And more than that.' Bayrd pulled the furred bed-covers down enough to kiss her lightly between the breasts. 'Both of you. Much more.' He kissed her again, lingering more until Mevn sighed a long, shivering breath and pushed the covers further away and wound her fingers in his unbraided long hair, guiding his head and his mouth and his tongue and his lips to just where she wanted them.

'You can't choose your family, *kailin-eir* my lord,' she murmured, shifting languidly in the bed. 'But you can choose your friends. And, and – Oh, oh, yes. . . ! And more than friends. Yes. Yes . . . oh, much more indeed – !'

'Bayrd-*ain*?' It was Marc's voice, muffled somewhat by an inch of still-seasoning timber. 'Excuse me, Bayrd?' His knuckles rapped against the door and the mood in the bedroom shattered, seeming almost to tinkle like thin ice as it fell away to nothing.

Bayrd blinked at Mevn along the length of her body, sweetly curved and glistening and golden in the light of the candles, and squirmed up enough to rest his chin in her navel. 'I think you should be aware,' he said, 'that I intend to kill your brother. Right now, and slowly.'

'No.' He raised his eyebrows until they vanished in the tangle of dark hair hanging down over his forehead, and pushed up like a cat against the hand which stroked those tousles back to better look him in the eyes. 'I said no,' Mevn repeated, and gave him a crooked grin by way of explanation. 'Family prerogative. I get first chop. You can have what's left. But only after we find out what brings the idiot up here at this time of night. He deserves that much courtesy at least.'

Does he indeed? Bayrd liked young Marc well enough, but this was stretching friendship farther than it should be expected to bear. Except for the night-duty guards, and the *yscopen* priests and those of his family who stood deathwatch over Goel ar'Diskan's body, everyone in the entire citadel had gone to bed two hours ago. Whether that was to sleep, or for more energetic reasons, was their own affair; and Marc had better not have come here just to complain that Vitya ar'Diskan had thrown him out, even though knowing Marc as he did – and Vitya as he had done, just the wearing once and that quite enough – Bayrd couldn't imagine what reason even that notoriously voracious lady might have had. Otherwise the Chosen Son of House ar'Dru was likely to learn what being thrown out really meant. It was a long flight over the fortress wall, and the worst part was the abrupt stop on the ice of the frozen moat at the bottom.

'Are you decent?' called the muffled voice, sounding a bit plaintive. Bayrd muttered something irritable into the skin of Mevn's stomach, and rolled sideways onto his back. Then looked down, laughed, and rolled over again, face-down with his head cradled on his crossed arms. Staying there was the nearest thing to decency he would be able to manage for the next little while; Marc's timing was as bad as that.

Mevn patted him approvingly on the head, then snuggled down and pulled the top layers of bedclothes up around both their shoulders. 'Decent enough for you!' she snapped in that tone of voice which in the course of four years Bayrd had learned to recognise or avoid. 'Now get in here and stop waking decent people up.'

'And what,' Marc slipped hurriedly inside and shut the door behind him, 'about indecent people?'

'You don't want to know.' Bayrd studied him over one shoulder, not feeling inclined to turn over quite yet. For one thing . . . well, for another, it would put him in too good a position to throw something, and he was very much inclined to do just that. Something hard enough to make his displeasure obvious, like maybe the wrought-iron candlestick by the bed. 'This had better be good.'

'I think it is,' said Marc virtuously. 'And the clan-lord thinks so too.'

That was enough. It would be a poor banner-bearer who needed more of a summons than that to his place by the clan-lord's side, and a poor sort of Bannerman's lady who would give herself precedence over her lover's duty.

'Out!' ordered Bayrd and Mevn in perfect unison; and Marc, though he might have preferred to argue some point or other about it, got out.

There was a man on the floor in the hall. Or rather, it had been a man once. Now it was a corpse.

As Bayrd strode closer, belting his tunic and pulling back his hair and doing all the hasty things to make him look at least slightly as neat as a clan-lord's Companion should, he could see clearly enough that death had probably come as a welcome release. He was quietly grateful, to whoever had made the decision, that Marc ar'Dru had not been sent to fetch him until after whatever foulness had happened here was over – and as he saw more of what that foulness had entailed, was just as surprised that he hadn't heard at least some of its progress.

'A spy,' said Clan-Lord Gerin in terse explanation. 'Or more properly, an observer.'

'Observing what, my lord?'

'What do you think, ar'Talvlyn? You saw it too.' Overlord Albanak had been unseen in the shadows of the darkened hall until he stepped into one of the scattered pools of lamplight, but his voice rang harsh in the stillness. Rather than answer at once, Bayrd took refuge in an immediate First Obeisance that gave his face an opportunity to control itself.

'Seventeen people died tonight,' Albanak went on. 'Seventeen. Men and women, young and old. They died like Goel ar'Diskan, even though two of them were children. Three years old and eight. So what do you think, ar'Talvlyn?' he said again.

It was impossible to separate grief from anger, or those from any of the other emotions simmering in that hard voice. Outrage, definitely; despair, never. And the hope of an honest reply. . . ? Unlikely, but always possible. He decided to chance it, regardless of what other questions the answer might provoke.

'I think sorcery, Lord,' Bayrd told the floor. He was still bowed in his obeisance, and with the Overlord in his present mood, he wasn't about to get up without permission. 'One elderly gentleman might have died of a weakness of the heart, or great age, or . . . or any of the things that suddenly strike the old. But not so many in one night. And not men and women in good health. And most definitely not children.'

'I should have had more of my retainers put aside their dignity and speak to the *Hospodar* Skarpeya while there was still a chance to do so,' said Gerin ar'Diskan quietly. 'And so, Albanak-*arluth*, should you. Pride and wisdom do not always go together.' Fingers snapped, a sharp, twig-breaking noise that might have come from either the clan-lord or the Overlord, but it was Gerin who pre-empted Albanak and said, 'Bayrd-*eir*, get up.'

As Bayrd swung to his feet in the graceful knees-heels-hips flex that concluded an obeisance, he glanced once again at the messy corpse near the fireplace. Near enough, probably, that the red coals would lose none of their heat before they were rammed . . . He winced, and looked away.

'The spy also spoke of sorcery, Lord?' he said, thinking neutral thoughts and appreciating how well the stink of tallow masked whatever other smells were hanging in the air.

'Among other things. Guelerd used up three of his best wizards to do what he did tonight. This carrion –' Albanak kicked the charred, chopped body as it was being dragged away, '– was to have told him how well the magic had succeeded.'

'Except that my guards saw him, stalked him, caught him and brought him back here,' said Gerin. 'Then I sent for the Lord Albanak and his chief inquisitor, and we began asking questions.'

'Uh. Yes.' *And you were all in a hurry for answers, by the look of things.* He couldn't understand why Marc, with his notoriously queasy stomach where such cold-blooded violence was concerned, hadn't said something about it. Either he hadn't been here, or there was more to young ar'Dru than met the eye, and his squeamishness was no more than a pose. That wouldn't have surprised Bayrd at all. There was more than enough posing and pretence in the world already, and his own secrets were far from being the worst.

'This sorcery they enacted tonight. It killed three wizards in the making of it, and the spy could not say why. He wanted to, but he didn't have an answer for us.' Gerin hesitated delicately, perhaps not wanting to insult his Bannerman by imputing against his honour.

'And you wonder if *I* have an answer, my lord?' said Bayrd, quickly enough to indicate that if no offence was intended then he was willing to take none.

'You were the only one I know who spoke to Skarpeya in other than –' Now it was the Overlord Albanak's turn to hesitate, hastily reconsidering all the implications behind what he had been about to say.

'I spoke to him, rather than swore at him. Yes, Lord. We discussed horses, for the most part.'

'Horses. Not sorcery?'

There was enough suspicion at the evasive answer that Bayrd looked sidelong at Marc ar'Dru and briefly considered the possibility that he had been talking about things best kept silent. Then he dismissed it. *Confide in one*, the old adage went, *seldom in two; tell three and the whole world knows*. He had confided in two, Marc and Mevn, but he was willing to take oath that they had preserved his secret.

And yet, in Albanak's view at least, what else would a wizard have talked about? Just horses? Hardly.

'I knew about horses, Lord. He knew about magic. We, er, exchanged opinions on our individual skills.'

'And you were as interested in this as he was in the horses?'

What is this, another inquisition? 'The man was . . . He was ordinary, Lord. No claws, no fangs, and he didn't summon fire from the sky. My arm was broken and in a splint at the time. It seemed to me just then that I had suffered more harm from horses than he had from magic.'

'Answer the question.'

Bayrd drew himself up very straight. He was Bannerman and Companion to the lord of this clan, and had been so for long enough that Albanak should be well aware of it: and the respect that went with such a position. If the Overlord had forgotten, and if Gerin ar'Diskan had decided to take his own sweet time about defending him, then Bayrd had the right to remind them both that he was no longer an ordinary low-clan *kailin*.

'Of course I was interested, Lord. No. I was *fascinated*. As would you have been, had you taken the trouble to listen. Skarpeya spoke to me with courtesy, treating me as an equal rather than a subordinate vassal of the king. I returned that courtesy as a *kailin* should. As too many *kailinin* did not.'

And still do not . . .

The words hung unvoiced in the moment's nasty silence during which Bayrd could clearly hear the other two men breathing; then at long last Gerin grunted some wordless noise of approval, pleased as any other clan-lord to see his retainers behave arrogantly and with a sense of their own worth. At least when they were in the right.

Albanak cleared his throat with unnecessary force. 'Bayrd-*eir*,' he said, 'it has been a trying night, one way and another. That is not an excuse. Just a reason. I ask your pardon.'

'As I ask yours, Lord.' Bayrd bowed his head a little; acknowledgement and acceptance, but most definitely not another obeisance. 'This behaviour is unbefitting to both our ranks, and to the high-clan hall in which we stand.' He could sense Marc ar'Dru and the other men in the far shadows of that hall hiding their smiles or their outrage, and Gerin ar'Diskan felt it too. The clan-lord stepped forward hastily to ensure peace and no further incidents.

There were none. In common with so many Albans, Bayrd knew when it was best to accept passively what might often seem the foolishness of his superiors, and when he might be justified in a sharp retort; but unlike most of the others, he also knew when to stop. Honour had been upheld and face saved on all three sides, and unless Overlord Albanak had the inclination and enough free time on his hands to hold a grudge – which Bayrd doubted, on both counts – neither he nor Gerin ar'Diskan would hear anything more on the matter.

What he *did* hear was more curiosity about the Art Magic than Albanak would have allowed as entirely proper if coming from somebody else, and as the questions came with increasing rapidity from both sides, Bayrd explained as best he could. It had been easier with Marc; then he hadn't needed to take refuge in the vagueness of *Skarpeya said* and *Skarpeya told me* and *so I took Skarpeya to mean*, and then he hadn't needed to edit everything he said before he spoke the words, for fear of sounding that dangerous bit too knowledgeable.

'Though I can guess why the three Pryteneks died, Lord,' was one of the few things he could say without worrying, 'I don't know enough to say for sure. They were –' he hunted for a comparison that would make sense to the two high-clan lords, and after a moment found one that would suffice. 'They were swinging a weapon of unknown weight at an unknown number of targets. Some hit, and the targets died. Some missed, and the force of the blow had to go somewhere. So it came back on the wielders. And *they* died. But more than that I won't even guess, because I don't even know if they were sorcerers or wizards, practising the Old Magic or the High.'

And that led to yet another round of questions. The Alban words were *pestreyhar* and *purkanyath*: 'powerwielder' and 'spell-singer'. The only time Bayrd had heard any Alban use those words before was as part of a curse, and now he was sitting by his own lord's fire, in the presence of the Overlord of all Albans, drinking more honeyed spruce-beer and trying to explain the difference between the two without incriminating himself.

'As I understand it, my lords, wizardry and the Art Magic is a studied skill, while sorcery is an inborn Talent.' *There; he had actually used the proper term for it, and neither of them had noticed.* 'The sorcerer summons or directs or focuses the Old Magic of the old elements: earth and air, fire and water. Natural forces – or even his or her own personal force, for all I know.'

For all I know . . . The sound of mocking laughter hung softly at the back of his mind until he shook it aside like a cobweb.

'And the wizard?'

'Again, summoning and directing and controlling . . .' Bayrd shook his head. '*Hospodar* Skarpeya called it the High Magic; but he wasn't very forthcoming about the rest. That makes me suspect the forces and powers involved are very far from natural. Or safe, or wholesome, or particularly High, except in the way of stinking meat. I think he was referring to the summoning of demons.'

'Avert. . . !' He heard the chorus of nervous gasps running around the hall, and even in the shadowy light of dimmed lamps and banked coals, could see the flicker of hands moving in the hasty gesture to turn evil-wishing aside.

'Lord and my lord, I suspect that this is only the latest and most blatant demonstration of such power.' Heads turned towards the source of the new voice, and Marc ar'Dru gave both clan-lord and

125

Overlord a swift obeisance at being properly noticed for the first time that evening. Then he straightened up again and nodded a subtle reassurance to Bayrd that what he was about to say had no bearing on any privileged information he might hold.

'Explain,' said Albanak, intrigued.

'Lord and my lord, we have always been a quarrelsome people, but never more than now – at a time when all past chronicles set down in the Books of Years prove we are best able to put our private wrangling aside in face of the common enemy. I believe that same enemy has – somehow – been encouraging our own worst traits, in the hope that we will do to one another what Lord Guelerd and all his men have been unable to do this past half-year. That it has not worked is obvious: we are still here, and Guelerd is turning his attention to more direct means of attack.'

'The boy's words make an uncomfortable sense, Albanak-*arluth*,' said Gerin.

Albanak nodded grimly, and stared at the settling coals in the great hearth for several minutes whilst he digested this latest information. 'Is such a thing possible, Bayrd-*eir*?' he asked at last.

Bayrd shrugged. 'Yes. No. Or maybe. *Hospodar* Skarpeya could tell us better. But I for one wouldn't discount the risk just because I don't know the proper answer.'

'So and indeed. You will not be drawn on it?'

'No, Lord. Without more information, or more expert advice . . . No.'

'I had hoped you might reach that conclusion. Because I have been persuaded.'

Bayrd blinked apprehensively at the Overlord, wondering just what had slipped out without him noticing, but Albanak was not referring to any excessive knowledge of the Art Magic which he might have revealed. At least, Bayrd hoped not.

'Guelerd of Prytenon,' said the Overlord, choosing his words and phrases as carefully as Bayrd ar'Talvlyn had done, 'has set aside whatever honour he may once have had, and even that hunger for glory which the younger among my *kailinin* can well understand. He fights by stealth; by murder and now by sorcery. Thus I am persuaded, and I am doubly persuaded, that despite the strictures of our own honour we must fight fire with fire, storm with storm – and sorcery with sorcery.'

'Albanak-*arluth*, what about the other clans?' said Gerin ar'Diskan. 'What about their lords? Surely they have a say in this?'

'A say, yes. A veto, no. They have given me their oaths of allegiance, by faith and fealty freely given and received. So let them have their say tomorrow. I will have my say tonight. And it is this: if Lord Guelerd and his people have been using magic against us, and are now employing spells so powerful that they can kill on their side with the remaining force that somehow was not expended here, then we must meet them with magic. Match them with magic. Surpass them, as we do with skill at arms on the battlefield. Or we must be prepared to face the possibility of defeat. And I have not come so far to claim this land, and fought so long to hold it, only to be cast out of it by . . . by *sorcery*.'

Albanak dredged up a smile from somewhere, and to Bayrd's mind dredged was right. It was a wide, humourless skinning of teeth that would have looked as much at home on a face ten days under water. 'Or wizardry either, Bayrd-*eir*. If that's what they're using.'

'It could be both, Lord. Skarpeya told me that much. Lacking the Talent, a wizard cannot be a sorcerer; but a sorcerer can study the books and write the patterns on the ground and be a wizard as well.'

'All the more reason, then.'

'For Albans to study the Art Magic, Lord. . . ?' For all the hope rising up inside him, Bayrd didn't dare suggest the alternative: that a search be started for any who might have the Talent – and that once found, they be publicly assured that possession of the skill meant no loss of honour . . .

And neither did Albanak. 'Light of Heaven, no!' he said, with a sour little laugh. 'That would drag us down to Guelerd's level, and I wouldn't ask any decent person to demean themselves so much.'

When Bayrd glanced at him, there was sympathy in Marc ar'Dru's eyes; but it did little to take away the sting of having been slapped across the face, even though he and Marc alone in the hall knew that any blow had landed.

'These Pryteneks are a devious people,' Albanak went on as if the proposal had never been uttered. 'We've all seen that.

127

Betrayal and treachery are second nature. There is still enough Kalitzak gold left in the coffers to make a change of sides worth while, don't you think?'

Clan-Lord Gerin grinned and nodded agreement. 'Assuredly, Albanak-*arluth*. More than enough. Also an offer of honours, and protection of course. Or anonymity. That would probably come cheaper in the long run. After all, we're talking about a *sorcerer* here, rather than a real person . . .'

'How will you find a – your sorcerer? My lord.' Bayrd remembered to put in the proper honorific only as an afterthought, because suddenly there was an ugly undertone to the way the high lords were speaking that had not been present before. As though they were no longer talking to him, but at him. It implied that after all he had said, they were finding it all too easy to include him as one who was somehow 'not a real person'. There was a feeling about it as though he should be wearing a plague-sign, a badge to warn others off and keep them at a safe distance from his contagion. Bayrd hoped he might be wrong; but he could hear little enough to justify the hope.

'Find one?' Gerin glanced at him and looked him up and down in a way that Bayrd didn't care for. 'Look under a stone, perhaps!' The two lords chuckled, and were joined in their laughter by as many of the retainers in the hall who had heard or understood the joke.

Marc ar'Dru did not laugh.

'We have money and privileges to offer, Bayrd-*eir*,' said Overlord Albanak. 'All we need is someone capable of making the offer to the right, er . . . person.'

'A volunteer. Someone to go beyond the fortress line, looking for a sorcerer who's also willing to turn traitor. A dangerous task, Lord. And not especially honourable. I mean,' he was already hating himself for using their inflection on the word, 'looking for a *sorcerer* . . .'

'Bayrd-*eir*, I think that *you* could go.'

Bayrd's eyes snapped round to stare at Clan-Lord Gerin ar'Diskan so sharply that he was willing to believe they clicked in their sockets. He surely hadn't heard that. Surely not. No. 'My lord. . . ?'

'You could go. You speak their clumsy form of Alban better

than anyone else in hall – no, no false modesty. Don't deny it, I've heard you. And as my Companion and Bannerman, nobody could accuse you of any lack of honour without accusing all of clan ar'Diskan – and offering disrespect to its lord, who chose you.'

Bayrd wondered how long this plan had been taking shape in the back of Gerin's mind. Since his father Serej died? Since Bayrd's first offer of insult to the old bastard, and thus an offer of disrespect to the whole clan? How long. . . ?

Because otherwise he surely couldn't mean it.

'A good choice,' said Albanak on perfect cue, and Bayrd tried to keep a spasm of loathing off his face. 'An excellent choice. Set an honourable man to a dishonourable duty, and both earn merit. Besides which, what other *kailin* of all the clans and families and Houses knows so much about magic, or is so confident of his own good name that he would talk about it in public?'

And maybe he *could* mean it, after all. Maybe both of them could mean everything they said, every compliment, every assurance, every trust they were placing in him for the successful completion of a difficult and hazardous duty. Which didn't change the fact that he was just as likely to die hanging head-down in a tree with his guts reeled out of his belly and wrapped around the trunk, like that sentry from clan ar'Lerutz they found in the woods a month ago. It just meant that he was going to die *honourably*.

And that would make it hurt much less, he was sure . . .

7

Wanderer

RIDING HIS MARE Yarak and leading a pack-pony, Bayrd ar'Talvlyn rode out into the snow-shrouded darkness. He and the two horses were swaddled in furs and blankets, as much for camouflage as for warmth, and of the three, Yarak's temper was the foulest by only a very short margin. He had already guessed that he might be required to leave the fortress that same night. After half a year in the clan-lord's service, he had come to know that once Gerin ar'Diskan made up his mind, immediate action on that decision would be expected; no matter what it might be, and no matter how much disruption of routine – or other matters – might be involved in the execution of it.

Bayrd would have liked to make his own farewells to Mevn, but with Lord Gerin taking a personal interest in the speed of his departure, taking the time to do so was out of the question. And it would have taken time, he was sure of that. He made do with a second-hand goodbye sent through Marc ar'Dru, the verbal equivalent of a terse little note to Mevn rather than the long poem he would have preferred that they compose together. Had his best friend and his lover been other than brother and sister, he might have requested that the enforced dryness of his farewell be eased by a little enthusiasm in its delivery, but the very thought made him smile wryly. The only enthusiasm he could expect there was Marc's defence of his honour and reputation against whatever sarcastic accusations Mevn would level at his sneaking off into the night. Bayrd had listened with amusement to such arguments before, when neither of them thought he was able to overhear and the wit grew edged like knives – and he hoped he would live long enough to hear one again.

For all that it had interfered with his private life, there was a certain advantage about sneaking off by night; by dawn he would be well clear of what reports said was already being called 'the invader's country', and thus be less obviously one of those invaders. No Alban had yet ventured more than ten miles inland. At least, he recalled without much relish, none that had come back. But then, they had been obviously *intending* to come back – a hunting party, a scouting party or whatever. He, however, was striking straight towards the province of Elthan to the northwest, the province whose lord was not so far an enemy, and he was heading out and away from Erdhaven just as fast as he was able.

Erdhaven . . . It was still only the place where the ships were burnt, and where despite the best efforts of time and tide, some blackened skeletons still remained visible between the tidelines. The place where that first rough fortification had been built, a child's conceit of sand and pebbles that with the benefit of hindsight had been proof against little more than a few turns of the tide. They had named it. They had even, with a spectacular optimism that quite took the breath away, begun to build again, up beyond the line of dunes; and not this time in sand and wooden planks stripped from the ships. What wood they used now had become massive baulks of timber, whole trees lopped and trimmed and squared, and the sand and pebbles had become roughly shaped stone blocks. If the inland fortress-line protecting the beach could be built in stone, then so could the dwellings which now lined that beach. It was the first town in the new land of Alba, and the first port.

That great sweep of bay, guarded by headlands at either end of its four-mile curve, made an excellent natural harbour. It had been proven time and again by the ships of the Undeclared, still anchored there and still safe despite the autumn storms. There was already a growing admiration for their stubbornness, and their very name had in the past few months come to be spoken more as a title of honour than as the barely veiled insult it had been in the beginning. Port facilities had become a matter for immediate attention. Not to entice the Undeclared inland, of course; and if it was, neither side would be the first to admit it. If gales and blizzards hadn't done so, then certainly soft words and wooden docks would have no better chance.

There was no blizzard blowing when Bayrd left Hold ar'Diskan, even though the snow was still falling from the featureless overcast of the night sky. But the blizzard began shortly afterwards: just as soon, in fact, as he was far enough away from the gaze of eyes that might not approve of what he had done. Sitting in the middle of the night, sitting literally at – and as – its focus, Bayrd could not see or even say the storm's extent. But it was enough to fill in the tracks he and Yarak left behind, and mask his passage from eyes even more unfriendly than those of his own people. That was more than enough.

The wind shrieked and wailed and howled like a pack of wolves as it slashed past him, driving any Prytenek scouts – or indeed, thought Bayrd ruefully as the more energetic gusts pierced through even the heavy furs he wore, any self-respecting pack of wolves – under cover, managing to send ice-spicules and flakes of snow at one and the same time against his cloaked back and full into his scarf-muffled face, so that he was forced to squint his eyes almost shut. As if it wasn't difficult enough to see at night . . .

Such conditions for travel were not the most comfortable Bayrd had ever experienced, but they were certainly more comfortable than the alternative, which would end with not just ice in the back but an arrow. Even so, there might be such a thing as performing a storm-summoning *too* well. Or not; there was always the thought of that arrow out of the stillness to make him glad such stillness was in short supply.

For all that his position and rank left him very much at Gerin's beck and call, the right to privacy available to a clan-lord's Companion and Bannerman was greater and more impenetrable than anything a mere *kailin* could hope to command. Bayrd had put his new-found seclusion to good use, practising his new-found skill at sorcery alone, without tuition or guidance. He learned that it was not necessary to feel anger, or fear, or pain, or any other of the intense emotions that had triggered it in the past, in order for the focused passions to take shape within him. After that breakthrough he had progressed rapidly – if somewhat destructively. Needing to tidy up the aftermath of failed or over-effective experiments was another reason he was grateful for his various privileges.

As a self-taught sorcerer his knowledge and abilities were shockingly spotty, and there were many, many things he did not know how to do; but making a change in the weather was surprisingly simple if the ingredients were already to hand. This personal blizzard, for one: the snow was already sifting down, spun into coils and fine, twisted skeins by a light breeze filtering through the trees. It had taken only a little exertion and the forming of the proper structures in his mind, circular to linear, gentle to vigorous, to change that whirling breeze into one which blew in an unwavering straight line. After that, like a round stone rolled downhill, the weather did the rest.

Granted, sometimes the effects were localised – *very* localised indeed, sometimes no more than an arm's length away – but they were effective. He had completely stopped rain from falling on his head once; however, since it had continued to fall on his shoulders, he didn't consider that charm much of a success. A few moments of thought and a different slant on the problem had given him a better answer: the rain fell as before, but each drop split and split again until when they reached him they were little more than a fine mist that felt cool on his skin, silvered his garments, but barely made him wet at all. Since he wasn't trying to alter how much snow was falling, but simply the manner in which it fell, the little snowstorm was much easier.

Or rather, too easy. Within an hour of his interference the wind of the world had risen, the snowfall had doubled, and Bayrd's private blizzard had become the real thing. After two failed attempts to change it had left him with a splitting headache, he hunched down in his saddle and swore venomously. This storm had gone far beyond his small ability to stop, control – or do anything much, except endure . . .

After what had to be ninety miserable miles, Bayrd felt sure he was no longer at risk – at least, no longer at risk from Lord Gelert's men. The bitter weather was another matter entirely. Riding from dawn till dusk, in good conditions and with adequate changes of mount, he would have taken no more than two long days over the journey. But covering the same distance with only one horse had taken him four days, or maybe five; he had a nasty suspicion that he had lost count somewhere along the way once the blizzard closed in around him. Even that distance was no more than a guess formed in his half-frozen brain; but there had been enough breaks in the clouds before they shut off the sky again like great iron-grey doors to let him feel certain enough he was still moving north by west. Or rather, that Yarak and the tough little pack-pony were still moving northwest. *He* just happened to be along for the ride, and with each passing hour Bayrd would have far rather been anywhere else at all.

As abruptly as they had begun, the wind and the snow died away. There were a few sporadic flurries, and after that, utter peace. He had an hour, or a little less, in which to appreciate the stark beauty of the long-shadowed white landscape under the empty blue sky and its small, pale sun – and then the cold came down like a hammer. Bayrd ar'Talvlyn had thought he might have been glued to the saddle by a glaze of ice while the wind was blowing and the snow was lashing at his face, but it was nothing to the grinding chill that settled over the world now. He snarled an oath that came past the wrapping of his scarf in a smoky cloud of exhaled breath, for he was all too familiar with this sudden drop in temperature. He had felt it before, on a pointless winter campaign for Daykin of Kalitz that had won nobody any honour – even though it lost several of his Hundred their fingers and toes.

Damn Gelert. Damn the Pryteneks. Damn every sorcerer in this damned country. If they came out right now from wherever they were hiding and formed a line dressed by the left for his inspection, he would have ignored them. There was a more important concern requiring his attention than even the most honourable mission for his lord. If he didn't build some sort of shelter right now for himself and the horses, they would all freeze by sundown, and the mission could go hang.

Bayrd swung down from the saddle and stood for a few seconds to let the cramps work their way somewhat out of his muscles, his hand poised to fend off Yarak's inevitable tooth-snapping demonstration of her displeasure. Nothing happened; neither she nor the pack-pony attempted to bite, or even kick. Bayrd frowned, because when even the wicked-minded little Ferhana mare was too weary to be irritable, matters were serious indeed.

The shelter, when he finished it, had not so much been built as dug. Though the wind had scoured most of the open spaces so that only a foot or so of snow lay there, it took Bayrd only a few minutes to find where deeper drifts had built up, between the trees whose undergrowth and roots had served to catch the snow and hold it. There was a shovel among the bits and pieces of gear in the pony's pack, a necessary piece of equipment for various tactical as well as hygienic reasons, and with it gripped in both his gauntleted hands, Bayrd went boring into the largest snowbank like a hot coal.

There was no point in trying sorcery on it. For one thing, he didn't know what to do, and anyway, simply creating a hole in the drift without packing its walls tight would have caused the whole thing to collapse, and so defeat his entire purpose of making some sort of enclosed shelter. The second reason was more personal. He had no wish to kill himself.

Those two attempts at stopping or diverting the blizzard had frightened him more than he cared to admit. The headache they had caused had lingered for hours, spreading sluggishly like a syrup distilled from pure pain down from his temples, where a proper headache belonged, into all the bones of his skull until everything hurt. Everything: his eyes, his teeth, his skin, the very hair on his scalp. Until even the passage of breath through mouth and nose burned like fire. The grating agony had faded at last, but it had left Bayrd more wary and respectful of sorcery – and those who practised it properly – than he had ever been before. That might well have been how the three Prytenek wizards had died, pressured by Lord Gelert or his vassals into extending their powers further than their bodies could bear. And it had killed them.

Bayrd had shivered at the thought of how close he might have come to that, and for once had not tried to explain to himself that it was just because of the cold.

The place was a cave of sorts when he was done, walls and much of the roof of packed snow reinforced with the same lattice of hastily plaited twigs and small branches as made up its door. That lattice was glazed now with ice, because the snow behind and around it had begun to melt in the heat of a small, hastily lit fire, before giving up and simply freezing all over again.

The drift had been as big as some of the houses Bayrd had lived in, and even the hollow he had carved in it was bigger than the home he shared with Mahaut during their brief marriage – though that had been rather better furnished. This boasted a fireplace at least – an untidy if functional jumble of thick logs, earth and grubbed-up rocks, everything he could find to get the fire itself up off the snow that would otherwise have drowned it in meltwater before it was properly lit. For the rest, his shelter had two chairs that looked remarkably like saddles, a bed made of furs and blankets and the padded bards which had been keeping his horses warm, and for pets the two horses themselves, as eager to get close to the fire as any pair of house-cats.

'Snug, eh?' said Bayrd, threading a piece of smoked but mercifully not salted meat onto a skewer of green wood. Snow was already melting in a small bronze kettle by the fire, and he was ready to persuade himself that the place was almost comfortable. Yarak thought otherwise, for though the pack-pony ignored him, the mare put her ears back and showed him her teeth. 'Oh. Well, pardon me, madam. You're used to better, of course.'

She was, too. And so was he. There had been enough little luxuries in Hold ar'Diskan that he had grown entirely too used to them, and now that the luxuries were gone, he realised how much he had come to regard them as a right rather than a token of his lord's favour. He had been getting soft. Bayrd thought about that, then grinned at himself and his pretensions. It wasn't as if he had ever been hard and tough in the first place. He liked his comforts as well as the next man or woman, but typically Alban, felt it more heroic – pronounced 'stupid' – not to admit such weakness. Well, when all this was over he was going to indulge himself, and anybody else who could appreciate it. 'Yes, even you.'

Yarak snorted, and nibbled disdainfully at the fodder he had gathered them from under the blanket of snow, not even grateful that Bayrd had found it himself this time instead of letting both horses forage for themselves as usual.

'I'm talking to a horse,' he muttered, shaking his head. 'Talking as if I'm expecting sensible answers. And I'm talking to myself. Ar'Talvlyn, this winter has frosted your brain.'

Just as the meat began to toast and fill the air with a savoury smell, Bayrd's head jerked up and out of the beginning of a cold-wearied doze. His brain might have been frosted beyond all use, but not his ears. Even through the background sizzle of his dinner, they still knew the difference between the various small, crisp noises of an icebound forest and the footfalls of . . . something . . . approaching through the crusted snow.

There was an arrow nocked on the string of his short bow before he came up out of his cross-legged seat by the fire, though because of the strange ringing stillness of the snow-muted woods, he didn't yet know where to aim it. The sound of those feet seemed to come from all around him. It was somehow unnatural, a high, ringing crunch unlike the heavy, plodding sound he had made as he moved. As if they were the feet of a creature both larger and lighter and more stealthy than seemed reasonable.

Sudden nightmarish images of snow-devils flitted through his mind, stories from childhood and from more than childhood. Legends from the time when *ar Ayelbann'r kozh*, the ancient Albans, lived on the open steppes. The old ones had forgotten more about harsh winters and the beings those winters conjured forth than every generation after them had ever known. Despite the cold, Bayrd could feel himself sweating, in a way he had never done even during the exertion of digging out the shelter. That had been a glow, loosening the knots in his muscles, filling him with the warm satisfaction of actually doing something after so long in the saddle.

This . . . This was clammy, liquid terror.

As much as anything else, it was a terror of being caught in this enclosed space of his own making like a beast in a trap. Bayrd held the arrow in place on the bow with the thumb of one hand and with the other scooped up his *taipan* shortsword, ramming it sheath and all through the belt of his tunic, then dived for the door. It went down under him and he felt his feet slip sideways on the ice which filmed it, so that instead of coming out in a poised combat crouch, he emerged rolling like a shot rabbit in a cloud of snow and little, tinkling crystals of ice.

The bow went one way, the arrow another, and in a spasm of sheer panic at having been so suddenly disarmed, Bayrd scrabbled wildly around his belt for the *taipan* that the tumble had sent sliding underneath him. He found the hilt at last, and its curved blade came free with a scrape of steel. Coming up onto one knee as best he could and wiping snow from his eyes even though they were still half-blinded by the sudden sunlight after the warm dimness of his cave, Bayrd levelled the shortsword in warning towards where he thought the footsteps had last been.

They had stopped.

As his vision cleared, Bayrd could see a silhouette backlit against the brilliance – but not where he had expected it, and already far too close. The outline was bulky, misshapen, and huge; a head again taller than he was, and its own head rising to three tapering horns that was like nothing human or even animal that Bayrd ar'Talvlyn had ever seen. Frantically he threw himself around to face it, trying to get his balance, get his back against a tree – trying to do something structured and defensive, rather than just sprawl on the ground like the rankest amateur swordsman taken unawares. Then he blinked as that final wild squirm took him into a pool of shade and out of the full dazzling light of the sun, blinked again in sheer embarrassment, and with a sheepish grin lowered the *taipan*'s blade until it rested in the snow.

The big man with the frost-covered beard who stared down at him looked very relieved at that; though certainly no more relieved than Bayrd was feeling right now. Bulky and misshapen the stranger might be, but without the sun in his eyes, Bayrd could see why. The bulk came from his furs, the weird distortion in his shape from the twenty or so dead snow-hares tied in two bundles and hung from his shoulders, and the horns that had so shockingly altered the shape of his head were nothing more than the upturned ear-flaps and conical peak of a tall fur hat. For the rest, he was tall enough, but not so much as had seemed at first. There were wide rectangular pads of woven osiers strapped to the soles of his heavy boots, and they prevented him from sinking as far into the snow as he would have done otherwise, and when he moved, shifting his weight uneasily from one foot to the other, they also produced that strange high ringing on the frozen crust which had so startled the Alban when he first heard it approaching.

'Uh,' said Bayrd, swallowing hard. 'Good day and hunting to you.'

It wasn't a very original conversational opening, but until his nerves stopped jangling it was the best he could manage. He glanced at the sword, no longer poised for action but still drawn, still a menace, and caught the other man looking at it too. Thinking the same thing, almost certainly, and he armed only with whatever had killed all those dead hares. Against a *taipan*, never mind against the heavier weapons, whatever it was couldn't be much of a threat – and anyway, even if it was, the fellow had already chosen not to use it. There had been plenty of chances earlier, and he had not taken them, which indicated that the three braids of the distinctive *kailin-eir*'s hairstyle might mean nothing to him. For that, if for nothing else, Bayrd was willing to trust the man. He fumbled briefly for the scabbard, found it, and put the blade away.

The hunter's name was Jord Koutlan. At least, he claimed he was a hunter, though Bayrd privately suspected that 'poacher' would be closer to the mark. Either definition had been obvious from the burden of freshly caught game, and since the hares had all been snared, not shot, Bayrd had been in even less danger than he had at first thought. Even without the carefully shaped sentences in Old Alban, Koutlan's name alone made his ancestry clear.

But there was something Bayrd still didn't fully understand. Even though they were sharing the fire, the shelter, and the toasted smoked meat – Koutlan even contributed one of the hares – the hunter still seemed ill at ease and reluctant to say more than courtesy required he must. And all this despite Bayrd's having made all the proper signs of peace, made it plain that he was no threat and just a curious traveller from foreign parts, and most of all had made it plain that he could both speak and understand the man's language, for the love of the Light of Heaven!

Besides his own not-so-wasted afternoons of long ago puzzling his way through the old Books of Years, Bayrd had the Archivists of both ar'Talvlyn and ar'Diskan to thank for that. Once his interest was known to be genuine – rather than the all too common pose of erudition – one of the old men had even taken him to where his own private treasures were stored, amid the clan's gold and plate, and had shown him an ancient wood and leather trunk that looked strangely out of place among the plundered magnificence of Gerin ar'Diskan's ancestral triumphs. When the Year-Keeper unlocked and flung open its lid, Bayrd began to understand why all of his calling looked so thin and ragged. None of them had brought wealth out of Kalitz and Drosul, not even a wardrobe of new clothes. But they had brought their lives, and the work of their lives, and the lives that had gone before them, all written down on parchment.

Arranged in neat leatherbound rows in the trunk, were books. *Ylvern Vlethanek'r an-Diskan*, the clan and Household Books of

Years, but for more years than Bayrd could count. How far back they went, he didn't know. This one trunk was crammed three layers deep, and the writing in each book was tiny. His mind tried and failed to encompass how much history lay here, and in other trunks and boxes in other halls among-the clan-holds of all Alba.

He remembered how the old *hanan-vlethanek* had pulled out one book and opened it at random. The date, in a jagged diminutive of the normal script, related to events – and Bayrd had paused for a few seconds of hasty mental arithmetic – four hundred and thirty-seven years ago. Then the old man withdrew another book, this one only sixty years old. Two generations past. And another: seven generations. Almost two and a half centuries. He had shown how the lettering differed, changing from angular to rounded, from flowing to crabbed, and always there were the diacritical marks to show how the words were spoken aloud. Or had *been* spoken; as he silently rehearsed the sentences in his mind, Bayrd ar'Talvlyn had heard the echo of voices long ago, of men and women long since dust.

It had been an eerie sensation.

With that still tickling at the back of his mind, Bayrd began to listen more closely to the way Jord Koutlan was speaking – at least, when he managed to persuade the big man to utter more than his grudging two or three words at a time. The pieces began slotting into place. It was not so much that each could understand what the other said at all, but that they were speaking different dialects to do it. Jord spoke in a welter of elision and abbreviation and elaboration and just plain mispronunciation, slurring some words and giving unfamiliar emphasis to others, while Bayrd . . .

Bayrd spoke the language as he had learned it from the books, in the stilted, formal speech of the Archives, the high-born – in the mode and manner of High Lord Gelert and his kind, so that the abyss of rank and birth and title yawned between them from the very first. That was not enough in itself. But a stranger whose first words had been in the Lord-speech might have friendships in high places, and in token of such friendship might report back to them about any misdemeanours he had witnessed. Poaching, for one. Jord Koutlan's wariness told Bayrd more than enough about the fearful way in which the Pryteneks regarded their overlords, and it implied that old Goel ar'Diskan had been right in everything he said.

It was that same wariness which saw him – reluctantly – invited to spend a night or two in Koutlan's village. There was an undertone in the way the invitation was made that suggested the big hunter was almost as frightened by the prospect of Bayrd's acceptance as by whatever reason he might have had for a refusal. Better by far not to have made the offer in the first place – except that then this friend of the High Lords, who spoke like them and probably with them, would have taken offence. It was an ugly dilemma, and rather than any real kindness it was what had prompted Jord Koutlan's hospitality. It was an attempt at the nearest thing to a bribe that he dared to offer; warmth and comfort and someone else's food and drink, in the hope that his guest might forget a certain matter of dead game-animals when he next came to speak to his lordly friends. Bayrd shrugged and didn't waste his breath trying to explain that he knew none of the High Lords and had no desire to speak to any of them. There was little point, because there was no hope of being believed.

Bayrd had already formed an impression of what he would find when they reached the village. He was expecting to see a settlement like all the others trying to survive a tyrannical overlord: a poor, frightened place, a huddle of nothing more than huts, crouched in the middle of a clearing scraped from the forest. A place unable to maintain itself in good repair because of the continuous cycle of raid and counter-raid that Gelert and his noble opponents regarded as their sporting due. A place as heavily defended as it dared to be.

And he was wrong on all three counts.

The village – he never learned its name – was no collection of hovels, and if the woodland had indeed been cleared to make room for the houses, not a stick of that clearance had been wasted. He found himself gazing at a neat group of sturdy timber buildings, their walls built from whole logs carefully jointed together at the corners and any spaces caulked with clay, their roofs – where the snow had melted near the fireplace smoke-holes – of thatch or split wooden shingles. But one thing was missing.

He could see no defences.

Even in a peaceful country, a forest-built village like this needed a fence of sorts to keep wild creatures out and domestic animals in. Bayrd knew well enough that Prytenon had not been so peaceful, even before the coming of the Albans. There were other, more dangerous things needing to be kept at bay than deer or wolves or the occasional sounder of wild boar. That meant a deep ditch with the spoil piled into a rampart, and a timber stockade or maybe even a dry-stone wall at the top. But this place was wide open.

As all the ugly implications struck home, Bayrd showed his teeth in a small, silent snarl of disgust. Lord Gelert evidently permitted nothing to get in the way of his entertainment. The Alban was to learn that Gelert was not the only lord with such a notion, but his first sight of vulnerability by decree was as repellent as any of the more brutal excesses he had seen in King Daykin's service. Raids by the lords'-men of one side or the other plainly weren't frequent enough to ravage the land, because he knew well enough what that looked like; so it could only mean that they weren't *allowed* to be too frequent. The sport had to show some profit, after all. The village's small, solid prosperity took on a new light. It was a tethered goat being fattened up for the butcher, and once it was fat enough to be a worthwhile target . . .

Bayrd spat sourness from his mouth onto the snow, but like Jord Koutlan, thought it best to keep his opinions to himself.

As he walked Yarak out of the forest, Bayrd could see the villagers as they watched his approach – and the terror in their eyes when he pulled his hood back from his head. The source of that terror was obvious. Though Jord Koutlan had never dared to mention it, the triple-braid formal hairstyle of an Alban *kailin-eir* must have looked ominously similar to the many small braids worn by Gelert and his Prytenek lord's-men. Though his chilled and aching body cried out for the comfort of even a day out of the cold, Bayrd did not stay longer than to find new fodder for the horses. Even someone less observant or imaginative than he would have been hard put to remain in a place like this, where his very presence caused a palpable aura of fear to hang in the air like smoke everywhere he went.

Their gratitude when he asked for directions to the next village north was just as tangible, even though they tried to hide it even more than the fear in case, again, he should take offence at their eagerness to be rid of him. That, as much as anything else, stuck in Bayrd's throat. He had long harboured unpleasant thoughts concerning the High Lords of this country, whatever province they might hail from, and now those thoughts had begun to take on solid form. The form of an axe, or a sword, or a hard-shot arrow. Bayrd had begun to grow angry, and it was the slow, deep anger that an ar'Talvlyn could hold closer to his heart than any lover. What he would do with that anger, and when, and even against whom, was not something that concerned him now. He would know, when the time came. He would know . . .

He went from village to village after that first one, and almost from hand to hand like a too-hot plate around a dinner-table, and for the first three villages he was escorted by Koutlan himself. It was another generous gesture – or would have appeared so to the casual observer. What Bayrd saw was the man making quite certain of where he went and who he saw and spoke to until he was far enough away to do no harm.

Jord Koutlan and his folk might have been glad to see the back of him, but the further north and west he went – and the more he learned how to moderate that frightening hauteur in his speech – the more eager the people were to see him. And especially, to hear him. They had heard of Albans, the people from across the sea, but they had never seen one. Heaven alone knew what they had heard from their own lords, or what they had been expecting from the rumours of war that had filtered down from the high places; but at least they seemed to find him more or less acceptable. Certainly he was neither seen nor treated as an invader and an enemy.

What they saw instead was just a foreign traveller, if so rare a creature was ever 'just' anything. Bayrd was much sought after as a source of news from the outside world, and still more so when it became known that he could speak without need of an interpreter. Granted, he spoke oddly, sometimes with the rounded, dignified phrases of the High Lords and their retainers, and sometimes – as if trying too hard to be a peasant – short and slangy; but then he was young, and the young were always known to be notoriously slipshod in their speech.

Bayrd was rather surprised, and not especially pleased, when in one village all the children old enough to understand were brought into the headman's cottage by twos and threes so that they could look at him and remember for afterwards. The annoyance came when he heard how they were remembering not Bayrd ar'Talvlyn, *kailin-eir*, Bannerman and clan-lord's Companion. They were remembering 'The man from the Empire'. Where that Empire was, the village headman didn't know, and not even the most carefully worded questions could tell him until Bayrd realised the truth behind the situation, and grinned ruefully at his own short-sightedness. This small, land-locked, isolated community, who had never seen the sea but only heard of it as an element in stories, could not conceive of anything else they had not seen without adding one or more of those legendary characteristics. The land across the sea *had* to be an Empire. It was so big, and had so many people living in it, that it couldn't be anything less.

Now was the wrong time to start explaining Droselan politics; these people had enough difficulty with their own uncaring local lords without trying to comprehend the convoluted mental workings of someone like King Daykin of Kalitz. And as for that one – or indeed any of his contemporaries – at the head of an empire . . .

Only good manners and the knowledge that he would have to account for it kept Bayrd from laughing aloud. Kalitz and the other small domains had only just stopped fighting amongst themselves, and the thought of a Droselan Empire was nothing more than a bad joke.

King Daykin; king indeed. For all his high-sounding titles, of which 'king' was only one, he was little more than the foremost brigand among other brigands, a little warlord with delusions of his own grandeur, his importance in the great scheme of things. And they had helped make him what he was: Bayrd's people, the Albans, with all their concern over personal honour, had helped raise that paltry despot. They had, Bayrd now suspected, helped bring to Kalitz and to as many of the surrounding lands as Daykin's small army could reach, the same petty tyrannies as this country suffered. Force, and the threat of force; the usual policy of minds too small to comprehend that ruling a people might require something more than just the behaviour of a thug at the head of other thugs.

They gave him food and lodging in exchange for his news, and the new songs and stories he could tell them – those told twice and sometimes three times while Bayrd watched his words, even more important than the face of the 'man from the Empire', being committed to memory. Those words, those stories and songs, would be remembered when he was a shadowy figure in the dim past, a mysterious stranger who had passed by on his own private business that was of no account save only that it brought him here. The words might even last long enough to see a Droselan Empire after all; but that would take more years than Bayrd cared to think about.

Granted, his lodging was sometimes no more than a pile of straw shaped into a mattress by the blanket over it; more often it was a pallet unrolled near the fire, and once or twice a room of his very own, even if the family who offered it had to put themselves to some inconvenient sleeping rearrangements. But once the offer was made, they would not hear his objections. Unlike Jord Koutlan's village, these Pryteneks – or had he travelled far enough north for them to be Elthans now? – were a truly hospitable people, made more so because that hospitality was all they could give him. They were not poor, at least not the way Bayrd thought of poverty as he had seen it in Vlekh and Yuvan, while the Kalitzak armies rolled to and fro in search of supremacy. But nor were they wealthy. They seemed not to go hungry, and in the deep winter of a country at war, that was as much as any could hope for.

The food they gave him was winter fare: meat and fish all treated the same way, dried or salted or smoked. Military rations by any other name. Bayrd grinned crookedly at that, like a man greeting an old friend he is not entirely glad to see again so soon. They were cooked with beans, or lentils, or . . . any of the other things that would keep. It usually meant things that were also more or less tasteless. Except, of course, for the ever-present salt. Despite the hares that Jord Koutlan had been carrying, there was never any game, and Bayrd soon learned why – and why the big hunter had been so frightened to be caught red-handed. The lesser lords of this land were granted their hunting-rights by the higher, those to whom they owed allegiance, and both high and low guarded those rights with all the jealousy Bayrd had seen in Kalitz – and even more ferocity. A man caught carrying game, or a woman caught cooking it, would be tied wrist and ankle to four horses and ripped apart. There was no referral of the sentence to any higher authority, and no appeal. With that knowledge as a sharp sauce for his meals, Bayrd ar'Talvlyn chewed on the dried, smoked, salted meat, and did his best to like it.

The drink was better. Sometimes it was milk, from goats or more rarely cows; in other places it might be odd herbal decoctions, hot or cold, with alcohol brewed or distilled in, or just as often not. But Bayrd preferred their ale; any ale, all ales, the many beers of different styles of brewing. He had all but forgotten how much he enjoyed it, because the better part of a year had passed since he had last tasted any.

Instead of ale from Kalitz, the Albans had brought wine: the great hogsheads of costly vintages had already been in the harbours, and sometimes still in the holds, of the ships they had 'borrowed' from King Daykin. It was not just more easily transported, but every soldier knew that it could be cut several times with water before the flavour was seriously affected. Not so with beer; and to drink beer one first had to plant grain crops. The Albans had been busy with other matters than farming since they reached Gelert's domain . . .

Of all the beers, his favourite was a brew he was given in that same village which believed he came from the Empire over the sea. Whether it was wheat beer or white beer he was never sure either then or later; the old man who told him the name slurred his words even worse than Bayrd himself, and after the third time of asking had left him no wiser and was beginning to make him look foolish, he gave up and accepted it for what it was. Which was thin, pale blond stuff, sharp as buttermilk and just as refreshing, but the villagers didn't drink it like that. Instead, for extra flavour they mixed in the juice of wild raspberries which had been boiled until it thickened into syrup, or for health a green essence of sweet woodruff, the herb called 'wood-master'. Either way – and had he not reminded himself that there might be little enough for the brewers themselves come the spring – Bayrd knew he could have consumed many happy mugfuls and never become drunk; he could almost see the alcohol burn off as he talked, and talked, and never tired of talking, any more than his listeners tired of hearing him.

'We are the earth, and of the earth, and bring forth all that grows upon the earth,' said Youenn Kloatr, the headman of Redmer.

There was a shy pride in the way the words were spoken; shy, and very understated, almost as if the man was afraid that what he said might be taken in the wrong way. 'It is our skill which grows the food we eat; and our toil in the cold rain, and our sweat in the hot sun.'

'And the lords?' prompted Bayrd gently. 'High Lord Gelert of Prytenon, maybe?' He had been living in the village for five days, long enough that they had come to trust him a little. There was also the advantage that since he was now in High Lord Yakez's province of Elthan, what was said about any neighbouring lord was less likely to be guarded by the fear of reprisals.

'The lords . . .' Youenn looked sidelong at him, twisting thoughtfully at the ends of his iron-grey moustache. 'The lords and their vassals defend us. Against other lords and *their* vassals. It doesn't matter whether they are here or not: the cattle are stolen, the crops are burned, the women and boys are raped, and . . . And one raiding-party of lords'-men looks very like another. It doesn't matter if it's in reprisal for a raid, or to provoke a raid, or –'

'Or your own lord Benart, giving himself reason to go raiding into another lord's domain?' Youenn looked shocked, but it was a mechanical expression, the shock of a man who had already considered that possibility for himself and not dared to give credence to his suspicions. 'One raiding-party looks very much like another: you said so yourself.'

'They wouldn't raid Lord Benart's own . . .'

'No?' said Bayrd sardonically. 'If his neighbours gave up raiding for a couple of seasons, and did nothing to provoke him, then what use would your lord have for so many warriors to "defend" his territory and give him such prestige? Youenn Kloatr, I've kept my eyes and ears open. My people may be the invaders in this country, but the ordinary folk have less hatred for us than for their own overlords. Why would that be, do you think? Unless I'm right.'

The headman turned slightly to stare him full in the face, came to some conclusion about what he read from Bayrd's expression, and abruptly abandoned the nervous editing of his opinion into something that would make acceptable repetition. 'Very well, Ayelban'r. I agree. You are right. All the lords, theirs, ours, anyone's – even yours, deny it if you dare – are the boots which tread upon the land, knowing they will have its support beneath them.' Youenn took a long drink of his beer, but looked better for having relieved his feelings to a neutral observer.

And we are just another boot, thought Bayrd. *Whether the Albans tread more lightly or not makes no difference to him. He doesn't really care. Because he knows we can't tread more heavily than the High Lords like Gelert and Yakez have already done.*

For all of that, Redmer was better off than most of the villages he had seen, because the local Lord Benart's retainers had not come raiding for supplies. The reason, as Youenn told him, watching with bright eyes for his reaction, was because they were so close to the haunted castle. Bayrd stumbled over that word for a few seconds, until the headman elaborated for his benefit. 'The strong place on the hill. Dunarat. Lord Ared's Hold, they called it in the old time. Over by the Forest of Baylen.'

'Oh, a fortress. Why didn't you . . .' He waved the quibble away. 'Never mind. Ared's hold by the woods. Dunn'ar'h'ath.' Bayrd sounded the word out to himself as if testing its flavour. 'All that in four syllables. Or three, the way you pronounce it. Your language has been rubbed a little smooth since then.'

'And it will be rubbed down still more in times to come,' said Youenn simply. 'That's the way of things. Time is like water on stone, and wears things away as it passes – and the young are always more hasty than the old, in the way they speak as much as in everything else. But the Old Speech serves to remind us of what has been. I look at a rock on the ground, and I see the mountain it was. I speak of Dunarat, and I see the great fortress that once stood on the hill.'

'In your time? Your father's?'

'How old do you think I look, *margh-arlut*' horsemaster horselord?' Bayrd grinned at the title, rather liking it, and at the way the headman tried to sound scandalised though his eyes were twinkling. 'Just because you're a mere child, anyone older must be an ancient . . .'

He prepared each of them another drink; this time it wasn't strong, sweet black winter beer splashed with cheerful abandon into the big turned-wood mazers, but a carefully measured dollop of something clear and syrupy and honey-smelling into small red clayware cups. Bayrd knew what to expect even before the fire exploded on the back of his throat – though he had not expected quite so much of it.

'Honey, and I think herbs,' he said after a few seconds, and the aspirated 'h' sound came out as a wheezy squeak each time. 'But the rest . . . The rest has to be metal polish and lamp-oil. *Lit* lamp-oil at that.'

'Heh. You like it. Good. Keeps the cold out, eh?' Youenn poured another, which, as is usual with roughly distilled alcohol, went down a good deal more smoothly. 'Not all the grain goes into beer and bread. Some we use to honour the Father of Fires.'

'Father, Tesh and the Maiden,' said Bayrd automatically, dipping a finger into the honeyfire and flicking a drop towards the hearth, where it flared briefly and made a smell like singed sugar. The habit had become ingrained while he lived in the barracks at Kalitz, and whether he believed or not, it was simple courtesy to any who did. One more proof, if he needed any more, that these people had passed through Drosul and Vlekh. 'And the Light of Heaven.'

'The honey for that,' said Youenn Kloatr. 'Think how much the bees work in the summer, under Her Light. And we can taste that light, that summer heat, and smell those flowers – even now, with the snow on the ground. Drink, and be glad of it.'

Bayrd did, and was.

'You said Dunarat was on the hill,' he said some time later, circling the conversation back towards his own points of interest. 'Which hill? I saw nothing.'

'Out yonder.'

Bayrd turned his head to follow the line of the outstretched arm, then walked to the door of the cottage and peered out, wincing slightly as the cold outside air bit at his nose and ears. Not all the black beer and honeyfire in the world was anything more than illusory protection against a winter evening. Though the day and the light were dying, it was still bright enough that he could see the snow-covered bulk of the hill overlooking Redmer village, but apart from that huge empty curve against the skyline, he saw nothing 'yonder', and said so.

'Of course not.' Youenn managed to imply he was an idiot for thinking any such thing, even though it probably came from youth and inexperience of the wicked world rather than solid bone

149

between the ears, and all without being so rude as to let the implication take more form than a quirked eyebrow. 'It's *haunted*. You think we would live so close to a haunted place?'

'But the lords'-men think –'

'They *think*, horselord. And we help them.' The headman twirled his moustache again and gave Bayrd a charming grin, one that managed to combine every possible variant of satisfaction with a plain hint of what he thought of people who believed everything they were told. 'Thinking is not their best skill.'

'Then where –'

'A day. Maybe closer. Much closer on a horse. They ride horses, so they think,' again that roguish leer, 'that it's just as close for us. And if not, if they ask why we fear something a full day's journey away, why then,' Youenn Kloatr shrugged expressively, 'we tell them how all the village had to move because the haunting was too bad for us. And they leave us alone.'

'Friend Youenn, I like the way your mind works. I really do. Now tell me truthfully, just you and me: how haunted is it really?'

The headman looked at him thoughtfully, debating perhaps how many lies, exaggerations and just plain damn good stories he could foist off on a guest in the course of a single evening. Then he shrugged. 'Go find out, if you must know. I – all of us here – sleep better for *not* knowing. Its presence keeps the lords'-men away, and helps us keep our corn and pigs and all the rest right here, where we can use them rather than Lord Benart. So it can't be such a bad haunting after all. Can it?'

'I, er, I suppose not.'

It might also be the sort of place where a man looking for that sort of person could find a sorcerer; or where the man looking for a sorcerer might be able to ask about such matters aloud. If he was going to summon up enough courage to actually ask questions, and it was high time he did something of the sort, Bayrd had already decided that this worldly, cynical chieftain might be the best man with which to start. At least, once he had been to the haunted citadel and come back again. If he came back.

That could well prove to be the greatest challenge of all.

8

Arrowsong

BAYRD AR'TALVLYN SAT quietly and gazed at the headman of Redmer while thoughts ticked through his head like water dripping on rock. 'How did Ared's fortress of Dunarat come to be haunted in the first place?' he said eventually, and then, trying to keep the question thrilling-story light, added, 'Was it unrequited love or suicide? Or something as simple as sudden death or bloody murder?'

'Neither,' said Youenn, and from the sound of him he wasn't at all convinced about how light Bayrd wanted the information. He sipped reflectively at his honeyfire, then topped up his cup with the nonchalance of a man well accustomed to the sweetly wicked stuff. 'Or maybe both.'

And that, thought Bayrd, *tells me exactly nothing more than I didn't already know.*

The Elthanek headman looked up suddenly and gave his guest a lopsided grin. 'It depends, horselord,' he said, 'on your point of view.'

Bayrd shook his head, not so much in denial as like a fist-fighter clearing the effect of an unexpected punch. 'My view is that you've got someone here who has never heard this tale before, and thus doesn't know the places where you can effectively be asked to hurry it up.' Youenn said nothing, but he smiled, shrugged, and offered Bayrd more honeyfire. The Alban looked at it, at his cup, licked his lips and produced a matching shrug. 'Why not,' he said. 'So long as you get around to answering the question eventually – and so long as I can still remember what the answer was. Or the question, come to that.'

'It's an old story, Ayelban'r. Very old.'

'Aren't they all,' said Bayrd drily. 'Harder to disprove that way.'

'Come now, look at your horse.'

'Once more for that one, please?' Bayrd eyed the headman, then glanced accusingly at the cup of honeyfire as if the liquor had started to affect his hearing as well as his pleasantly sweet-seared throat. 'What has a Ferhana mare to do with hauntings?'

'Nothing to do with the haunting, but plenty to do with the story. The best horses and the best dogs – and the best people too, I suppose – all have long pedigrees. Why not the best stories as well?'

Bayrd considered that; there was logic in it, of the skewed sort he had grown familiar with both in Kalitz and here in his dealings with Overlord Albanak. 'Why not, I suppose,' he conceded, tasting the honeyfire and finding its flavour and slow, sweet burn even more insidiously appealing. 'You were saying. . . ?'

'That once, long, long ago, Lord Ared built himself a fine citadel on the hill overlooking the lake –'

'Now just wait. I'm not that drunk. You said it overlooked the *woods*.'

'It does,' said Youenn, giving him a gently reproving look. 'Lake and forest both. You haven't seen it yet, or you wouldn't wonder so much. The one runs along the shoreline of the other. May I get on. . . ?'

'Don't let me stop you.'

Youenn Kloatr drew breath to say something on that very subject, but took time to study his words from all sides before he spoke and after that thought better of saying anything at all. There might be a guest in the headman's house, and a guest who was reacting well to scholarly teasing, but that guest had brought in an excessive number of weapons and none of them looked as though they were meant just for show. Best not to push too hard.

'He built,' Youenn resumed, 'a fortress overlooking the lake and the great Forest of Baylen. He built it well, and he built it strong, a great hold for his children to inherit – for he was a man newly married, and a man who married for love in the face of every opposition from his linefather and his family and his House. Thus he had determined to have many fine children, and raise them with obligation owed to none save himself alone, and thus put to censure all those who disparaged him and his name.'

'I sympathise with the man,' muttered Bayrd into his cup; then he raised it in silent salute, and emptied it with a single sharp flick of his wrist, and filled it to brimming again. Youenn paused and studied him thoughtfully, then without comment resumed his story.

'The old tales say that it was in Ared's mind,' he said, 'that if his family and his House did not accept his wife then he would discard them – as was the right of a lord in the ancient time – and with them their name and all the history of high deeds that went with that name, and make his own new name and line more famous still. Hence the splendour of his castle.'

'Fortress.'

'Fortress. Whatever. Horselord, if you want to travel in Elthan, then learn all our words and not just the old ones from the old books. The Lord Ared had gained much favour in the wars – no, the wars aren't mentioned; they're in a different story – and much wealth and support from all the other Houses who had grown angry to see one of such high renown disdained by his own line. He used this support, and almost all his own wealth, and regardless of the obstacles laid in his way by those who should have known better, Lord Ared built Dunarat. When it was built and the great banners of blue and white flowed from its towers –'

Bayrd's head jerked up at that, though he managed to disguise the movement as a near-sneeze. Youenn Kloatr might be well enough disposed, but there were still some things that were none of his concern. This was one of them. Blue and white, with their thin piping of black, had been the ar'Talvlyn clan Colours for almost half a thousand years, and to hear them mentioned here and now, in such a tale . . . Bayrd felt himself shiver slightly, and took another hasty swallow of honeyfire to kill whatever chill had caused it.

'– There were feasts and banquets to celebrate its completion, great hunts in the forest both for sport and to bring more meat for the feast-fires, and races both of men and horses along the shore and men and boats across the waters of the lake –'

'Boats? And racing?'

'You have not seen Baylen's lake, horselord.' Youenn's lean left hand described a sinuous line across the rough-hewn tabletop. 'A long lake, mostly straight between the knolls of the wooded hills, well shaped for racing – and for those who would gamble on the outcome of the races. The people of the ancient time were mighty gamblers, men and women who would wager on the flight of birds and the fall of snowflakes and –'

'– Two flies walking up a wall. Yes. I know the sort.' Bayrd gave the headman a tight little smile, back on familiar territory again and glad of it. 'If you keep the right wrong company, Youenn Kloatr, you'll find that times have changed very little.'

'Just so. Then you can guess how fortunes were made and lost and made again, in races between men, or boats, or horses, or trained birds; in feats of strength or skill or simple bloody-minded daring.'

That hasn't changed either, thought Bayrd. *Sooner lose your life, among some people, than refuse an offered wager.* He had seen it happen; not to the death, at least not quite, but certainly once to the barrack infirmary in Kalitzim, back when he was still just a Captain-of-Ten. That was the time one of his Ten, young Iskar ar'Joren, had bet that he could snatch a bag of twenty gold crowns from the stop-bar of a tripped catapult before its throwing-arm slammed up to squash them. On one of the big, ponderous siege-machines, he would have won – but this was a battlefield bombardment petrary, a small thing of iron-braced oak and cedar, as highly strung as a blood mare and with an action once the trigger was tripped that was as fast as a striking snake. Ar'Joren lost; he lost both the bet and his hand halfway to the elbow, though he got to keep the coins. Even though the surgeon-commander had been able to pry all twenty of the flattened precious-metal discs from the mess of pulped meat and shattered bone, and even after they had been carefully scrubbed clean, nobody else seemed to want them any more . . .

'Do your lords still gamble?' he said, to take his mind off unpleasant memories.

'On the outcome of hunts and the outcome of wars,' said Youenn. 'On the number of cattle seized in a raid and on the number of . . .' He faltered and stared at his drink, the image of a man whose mouth had run that little bit too fast for his mind to keep up.

On the number of kills, said a voice at the back of Bayrd's mind, too tactful to say so aloud. 'I understand,' he said, wishing that he didn't. If war was a sport for the great lords, for Gelert and Yakez and Benart and the rest, then the easiest way that they could measure their success was in the number of corpses laid out at the end of a busy sporting day. Even if the Alban clan-lords and Heads of House made war savagely, in the manner of the harsh battles from across the sea, they did so to get it over with and finished, rather than to keep it going on and on for their own entertainment. War was not entertaining.

'Lord Ared's time was long before that of the present lords, of course,' said Bayrd, shifting the subject away from what they both brooded on with the deliberate clumsiness of an awkward servant clearing a table.

'So the story goes.'

'And he gambled too?'

'You will find out just how much he gambled, and for what stakes.' Youenn pulled up a quick small smile from somewhere, one that suggested his spirit was less quenched than it might have been. 'At least, you will if I am ever allowed to get that far into the story. Ayelban'r horselord, there's more beer in the keg. It's a good brew; you said so yourself. So fill the jug and busy your mouth with that rather than questions. Just leave your ears free to listen.'

'That means no loud belching?' Bayrd glanced over his shoulder to return the smile as he went to the beer-barrel, considering that there was a story of his own to Youenn Kloatr. The man spoke with far more authority than any other headman the Alban had encountered in his travels, and with a better command of language than most of them as well. But that story would be one for much later. Any further interruptions and Youenn might just give up in disgust and talk about unimportant things whose sense wouldn't suffer by the constant butting in of an inquisitive stranger. And Bayrd wanted to hear about Dunarat-hold. He suspected he *needed* to hear about it. The best way to hear was to shut up and listen. So he shut up.

And listened . . .

The feasting had gone on for most of the day; feasting and drinking and dancing and music, people falling into the lake and occasionally falling out of their clothes. That was appropriate enough, in its own way. Elyan, Ared's lady wife, had told him only that morning that she was certain their first child was already on the way. It had been a last, wild string to their bow; that if all else failed, then they could marry with the grudging blessing of either side or both just so that the child would not be born without a family or line, and thus have to earn its own good name. Ironic, in its way, now that they were *all* without family or line or House.

Except for the house that reared above them on the hill.

That one had no history, not yet, save for the history of the land that dwelt dreaming in the worked stone of its grey bones; but it would make a history of its own. No fortress so magnificent would be just a home for the many generations of the lords who dwelt there. It would see years of peace, and it would see battles and sieges and triumphant victories, and always its great walls would be inviolate, unbreached by fire or foe or treachery.

The great blue and white banners rippled softly in the warm summer air, eighty feet and more of the finest imported silk hanging from the battlements, their fabric sifted with spices and sweet oils so that every time they moved leisurely in the passing breeze, it was scented by their heavy caress.

Lord Ared filled his cup, saluted his wife and the child within her that would surely be a son, raised the great stemmed bowl of gold and crystal high above his head and for the hundredth time that day bade all his friends be welcome. Some were of such rank that no one could say what they might or might not do; but others had defied their own lords and Heads of House to be here, had lost respect and honour to prove by their presence under the Light of Heaven and in the eyes of the world that they thought him worthy of just such honour and respect.

'Ye have faced a challenge worse than battle to be here!' he cried in a voice that carried from the forest to the lake-shore and came slapping back from the silk-shrouded towers of his great hold. 'Ye have given defiance to all those who have defied me! All of ye have laid your honour at my feet to show ye judge me worthy of it – and so do I judge all of ye! Take up thy honour again, take it up, I say. And ask me any task within my power, within my rank, within –' and he laughed at the thought, splashing wine from the cup so that it spattered in great garnet drops like blood across the ground at his feet, and soaked in too, as quickly and irrevocably as blood, '– within what little wealth remains to me after the building of Dunarat. Ask me what I may do to repay ye, one and all, and I will do it though it take me to the last generation of my line yet unbegun . . . *Ask. . . !*'

There was no reply save silence. The rashness of such a vow had taken all their breath away. To pledge himself: why, that was only fair, and what any man of honour had every right to do when his friends were deserving such a token of esteem. But to pledge the unborn, to set aside an obligation for them that might be as heavy and more long-lived than any shirt of mail, that was far from fair, and very far from honour.

Lord Ared looked at them, at the silent faces and the wide eyes, and perhaps a chill of premonition, a hint that he might have been just too rash after all, chilled the wine-heat in his blood enough for sense to take its place. He drank from the cup and looked quickly at what remained within, as though the dark red of the wine had become for that brief moment the dark red of another and more vital fluid.

'I am not drunk,' he said, half to himself. 'I meant what I said. They gave their honour in trust to me, and what else could I do but . . .'

He turned the cup over in a single movement, so that the wine flowed out and drained away without a trace into the thirsty soil. After that the moment passed; but for the rest of the day Lord Ared drank white wine instead of red, and mixed that half and half with water so that it did no more than quench his thirst. He and Lady Elyan his wife were glad of it, and his foolish words were forgotten.

There were more wagers that night in the great hall of Dunarat-hold, wagers that would have seemed foolish even to children had it not been for the large sums of money staked against their outcome. Warrior-lords whose dignity on other days would never have permitted such behaviour, thought nothing of laying a hundred marks of silver against their being able to hop on one leg right around a laden table, upsetting none of the dishes whilst all the time drinking a great beaker of wine without spilling any. Others balanced on their hands while their friends counted piled-up plates onto the soles of their feet. Others, younger and stronger, engaged each other in such feats of strength as trying to lift chairs with people sitting in them, or leaping across a table, or two tables, or leaping the length rather than the breadth of a table. The conclusion of all those wagers was invariably signalled by a crash and slithering of fragments, the whoops of merriment from those who had not landed in the fire or whose arms and legs had not been broken in the fall, and the yells from those who had. Winning or losing, it all sounded just the same.

They began calling to Lord Ared, asking him how he would wager and how much and on what, it being the custom and sporting gesture for the lord who gave a feast to be for that one night as foolish as the most drunken of his guests. They called on him as much to show how they had forgotten his rash words of that afternoon, when he had pledged what had not been his to promise, and had offered to give up what was not yet his to have and hold.

Lord Ared chose not to wager, but instead to offer a prize in a contest. He was a great owner and breeder of horses, and the herds he possessed were his own, rather than the property of family or House. Thus they were his to dispose of as he saw fit – and one of his best Andarran mares was in foal to a fine blood stallion. He and his stable-master were the only ones who knew of it, and so he thought it would be a fine joke to offer nothing specific as the prize, only the newest thing that might be found in the fortress on this day next year . . .

'I know this tale,' said Bayrd with a grim smile, 'and you were right. It's an old one.' When Youenn gave him an odd look, he flicked one hand in a dismissive gesture. 'Oh, I haven't heard this *particular* story before. But the way events are beginning to fall into place is familiar enough. Your Lord Ared has forgotten about his wife, hasn't he? And the child she carries? Idiot.'

'As you say.' Youenn Kloatr wasn't annoyed by the interruption; if anything he was amused by it. 'The stories don't change, any more than the stupidities of young men with too much to drink.'

If that was a jab aimed at him, Bayrd let it go by without comment and took another mouthful of the black beer. 'What was the contest?' he wanted to know. 'What did Ared want in exchange for the . . . the newest thing in the fortress?'

'He wanted a sword.'

'Just a sword?'

Youenn grinned at him. 'No, horselord, not *just* a sword. This is a story, not a history. He wanted the finest sword in the world.'

'Oh, *that*,' said Bayrd. 'And how would he know it when he found it? A written certificate from the finest swordsmith? Or would he be willing to settle for something a little less superlative?'

'Do your Ayelbann storytellers have all this trouble?'

'No. Usually they'd have left by now, or thrown something. But I have an enquiring mind. I like to know things.'

'Your problem, if it is a problem, is that you think too much.'

Bayrd raised his eyebrows at the old, old insult – if indeed it really was just an insult any more. *Once is an insult*, the saying went, *twice is an opinion, three times might be the truth*. And three hundred times, from as many different people – what was that? The thought hovered briefly, but led nowhere. 'Maybe so,' he said. 'Or as you like to put it, maybe not. But right now I'm thinking about the sword. What about it?'

Youenn studied him a moment, then shrugged dismissively. 'The sword was brought, and given, and accepted by Lord Ared before he knew that the newest thing within his walls was no longer just a colt. His child, his first-born, his son, was the prize, and it was a prize that his honour and his own sworn word required that he give up, for all that he offered everything else that he possessed if only the infant was left with him. Those offers were refused. The prize was taken from the fortress, and Lord Ared and his wife both slew themselves for rage and grief. They say their spirits walk the ruins still.' The headman sat back in his chair and took a drink of honeyfire, then looked Bayrd up and down. 'There, horselord,' he said. 'Is that telling short enough for your impulsive ears?'

Bayrd grimaced slightly. That had been an unmistakable rap across the knuckles for his impatience. 'Too short,' he said. 'Too short by half.'

'Strange. I thought you were in a hurry to know what had happened. Now you do, and now you say I was too quick about it.'

'There's hurry and there's indecent haste. And that was haste indeed. But no matter; it tells me what I wanted to know, more or less.' He raised his mazer of beer in a sketchy half-salute, to the storyteller and the story he had told – and to the dead, if they had ever been alive and more than just characters in an old, grim tale from long ago. 'So Lord Ared killed himself. And his wife too . . . Is suicide a custom of the Prytenek people?'

'No. Nor of the folk of Elthan, either.' Youenn was pointed in his correction of Bayrd's geographic error. 'But who can say what a man will do when he has been so completely tricked, so totally betrayed?'

Who can say indeed? Until it happens? Bayrd ar'Talvlyn drank his beer and kept his thought to himself. 'And what happened after that?'

'The fortress was abandoned. Dunarat was eight years in the building, but its existence was no more than another year before the long, long dying that took a hundred years and more. No one cared to live in it after what had happened, and as time went by it was picked to pieces by those who could see better uses for good, worked stone than just letting it crumble into dust.' Youenn laughed shortly. 'Why waste it, after all. Parts of many villages are made of that fortress. Parts of this village too, I'm sure.'

Bayrd looked quizzically at the headman. 'Are you? Sure, I mean?'

Youenn shook his head. 'No,' he said, 'I'm not. Nor have I any great desire to be so. I said before, this is a story. Nothing else. Stories are meant to be *just* stories, no matter how much meaning and accuracy you try to fit into them. They are fictions. Entertainments. Tales for a winter evening, like this one. That way we who live too near them can be assured of sleep at night.'

'And the haunting? When did that begin? As soon as it was convenient to keep the lord's-men away, perhaps?'

'Something like that.'

'So what you're telling me –' Youenn shook his head again, this time in deliberate denial of everything he had said, '– or *not* telling me, is that the fortress of Dunarat is haunted just as much or as little as you need it to be.'

'Ayelban'r horselord, if a place can be haunted by the feeling of misfortune that hangs around it, then Dunarat is haunted indeed.'

'By the dead lord and his lady? By the lost child?'

'By all of them, and maybe by none of them. And perhaps only by the sorcerer who made the sword that began it all. Or claimed he made it. After so long, and so many retellings, who can say what really happened any more?'

Bayrd held his breath to control the little gasp of triumph it so wanted to be, and let it out easily between his teeth. 'A sorcerer, eh?' he said, interested – but not too much. 'You didn't mention any sorcerer to me.'

'*Margh-arlut*', you gave me little time and opportunity to mention anything but the barest bones. And now you want to put the flesh back onto them. This is a backwards way to learn anything.' For the first time there was an edge of annoyance, even of accusation, in Youenn Kloatr's voice.

'But I still want to learn it, and I ask you to help me do so.' Bayrd bowed his head, not bothering with any of the formal obeisances that the headman wouldn't recognise but going straight to a simple gesture of respect. 'I ask politely. And I offer you an apology for my hastiness.'

'The apology is accepted, horselord. Not that there was any real need for it, but – but I appreciate your courtesy. I would never have received any such thing from our own Lord Benart, or his men.'

'I had guessed that much for myself,' said Bayrd with a wry smile. 'Just as I guess that Lord Ared's son returns as a grown man and a great hero.'

'Now there you would be wrong,' said Youenn, doing a poor job of hiding his satisfaction at finally seeing Bayrd make a mistake in his all-too-learned commentary on the story.

'But usually –'

'Usually, yes. In a story with a happy ending. I never claimed that this was one of those stories. Because it isn't.' The headman considered his small cup and the severely depleted flask of honeyfire, then changed his mind and poured himself some beer instead. 'Oh, there are some storytellers who make links to other tales for the sake of that happy ending – and the sake of their pay for the night – but no. The child was never seen again. Nor the wizard who took him away.'

'Tell me about the wizard,' said Bayrd, setting aside for the time being his curiosity about how the word had changed, as if unlike the Alban language, the Elthan dialect made no difference between them. 'And tell me about the sword.'

'Yes,' said Youenn, his eyes shifting sidelong to where Bayrd's pile of gear and weapons were stacked by the wall, 'you'd be interested in that, I think. More than sorcery, at least.'

Bayrd nodded at him, and chose not to correct the error.

The sorcerer had not been at the feast Lord Ared gave for Dunarat-hold's completion, or if he had, none had seen him there. Thus afterwards, when all was over, there was a deal of antagonism about how he had learned of the Lord's contest and its vaguely-worded prize. There was still more bitterness that he should have learned of the mare whose foal was meant to be the prize, and of the Lady Elyan's pregnancy – both deep and well-kept secrets, for their own separate reasons. Someone, it was claimed, had told him, and all forgot that because he was a sorcerer there had been no need for anyone to tell him anything at all. Workers in the Art Magic have their own ways of learning what they wish to know, and few of those ways are revealed to ordinary men. But whether he had been there the year before or not, when the anniversary of that feast and that rash oath came round, he was there without a doubt. And the sword was with him.

Lord Ared had required the best sword in the world. What the sorcerer gave him was a sword he claimed was better than the best, for the metal of which it had been forged came from beyond the world. That was starsteel, the black iron that fell from the sky on clear frosty nights. The quick-eyed could see it fall, could watch the long white scratch of its passage across the starry dark, as though a star itself had come adrift from the great vault of Heaven.

Lord Ared accepted it at once, giving the judgment in its favour and the prize as well, and – until the truth was learned of what that over-hasty acceptance had lost him – there were none among his vassals or retainers or supporters of equal rank who thought their lord and friend was wrong. It was a superb weapon, double-edged and straight-bladed, a shape which at once set it apart from the long curved cutting-swords carried by the warriors of Lord Ared's day. That blade was polished bright, but no polished surface could ever quite conceal the darkness of the steel from which it had been made, so that it gleamed grey as smoke. As befitted something of such rarity and beauty, it was a named-blade. Though the newer custom was for the sword's owner to name it as he claimed it, the sorcerer had claimed an older privilege, where the right to name the blade went to the man who had created it. And to honour the shadow in the depths of the bright steel, he had called it Greylady . . .

Bayrd ar'Talvlyn stared down at the puddle of beer and at the wooden mazer spinning slowly in the middle of it, then raised apologetic eyes to meet Youenn Kloatr's questioning gaze.

'I think,' said the headman, 'that you might have had enough to drink by now.' He bent over, stopped the still-turning cup with one finger and picked it up, then glanced thoughtfully at Bayrd's face, noting the sudden pallor that was the wrong colour for a drunk. 'Or was it something else? Something I said, perhaps?'

Bayrd nodded. 'Yes,' he said, 'it was. "Greylady".' As Youenn raised his bushy eyebrows, the Alban scrubbed his hands against his face and tried to sort out the sudden tumble of questions and doubts that had spilled through his brain like dice from a shaker. 'Greylady,' he said at last, 'is the Overlord's sword. Albanak's sword. It always has been. It's as much a part of him as his own name.'

'Since the name is a title that doesn't mean anything but "Landmaster",' Youenn pointed out, 'and he obviously doesn't have a name of his own, you aren't saying much.'

'You don't understand. Greylady is –'

'The Overlord's sword. Yes. I understand. I understood when I heard you the first time.'

'But it's been the same sword for hundreds of years. It's a badge of rank. Like a mace. Or the sceptre that the outlander kings carry, that's no more than a civilised mace anyway. And even the shape is old; out of date. Archaic. A sword from the Old Time.'

'Perhaps it was a name taken from the story I've been telling you – no, trying to tell you – all afternoon?'

'No. It couldn't be, because that isn't one of our stories. Not even with the names and places changed. I'd know otherwise. I'd have heard or read it already.'

'Oh, would you indeed,' Youenn began to say. Then he closed his teeth around a sharp rebuke against unnecessary boasting, and considered instead the way Bayrd had been talking with such authority about the elements and common features of the construction of old tales. 'Well, maybe you would at that. But don't you think it odd that your Overlord Landmaster has a sword of the old shape, while the Greylady in the story is so plainly described as a modern blade. That was the description I was taught to remember when I heard the tale for the first time. As modern as, as –' he pointed towards Bayrd's *taiken*, laid across the top of the rest of his gear as though put there deliberately to guard it, '– as modern as that.'

Youenn looked at the wooden mazer in his hands, decided it wasn't dusty enough to make any difference, and refilled it with beer from the jug. 'Here,' he said, pushing it towards Bayrd. 'I thought at first you'd drunk too much. Now I'm beginning to suspect you haven't drunk enough, not if you want to get any sleep. And since you're planning to ride up to the fortress tomorrow –'

'I'm going tonight. At once.'

The headman blinked at Bayrd's declaration, studied the younger man's face, then shrugged. 'As you wish,' he said simply. 'But you'll freeze. And then what good will you be to whoever sent you here?' Youenn met the Alban's startled eyes with a bland, humourless smile of his own, the smile of a man who has suspected something for a long time without finding the right time or place in which to voice those suspicions – and who has found them entirely justified after all. 'Because you were sent, weren't you? And not just to admire the winter landscape.'

Bayrd considered and discarded a dozen excuses in half that many seconds. 'I prefer summer,' he said non-commitally.

'So do I. But as headman of this village, my duty requires me to stay in it whatever happens. Your duty, of course, requires you to go wherever your lord commands. But not tonight. Wait until morning at least. Otherwise you *will* freeze, I promise you.'

'I said I was going now. I meant it. I want to see Dunarat.'

'Horselord,' said Youenn in a voice of infinite patience, 'look outside. It's almost fully night. Dark, you see. Or rather, don't see. There's little to look at in the dark as it is, and there's no moon. Even with a clear sky it won't be any lighter by the time you reach the ruins.'

'I'll see enough,' said Bayrd obstinately. 'And anyway, by the time I get there it should be almost dawn. The days are short enough that I can't waste them in travelling.'

'Father of Fires, but you're a stubborn one, aren't you. Stubborn enough to get yourself killed, if you're not very careful. What was it your lord wanted you to do, anyway? – I mean, after the cold and the wolves and the bears are done with you, somebody should still know why you were sent here.'

Youenn put his head on one side, a quizzical little gesture like an inquisitive sparrow. Bayrd found it incongruous, and said as much. 'Looking peculiar is safe enough, Ayelban'r,' Youenn retorted. 'Acting peculiar, especially in this weather – now there's another matter entirely. But might you be here to offer your people's services to Benart or High Lord Yakez – against Gelert, that is, especially since he's refused you?'

'I doubt my people would thank me for that,' said Bayrd. 'We've been sickened of foreign employers.' He weighed his options for a few more seconds, then gave up on the elaborate pretence he had successfully maintained in Redmer for the best part of a week. 'What they *would* thank me for is if I came back with a wizard willing to help us.' He grinned sourly. 'Against Gelert, that is.'

Youenn gazed at him in silence, twirling the tips of his grey moustache until they stood out to either side of his nose like the curved horns of a wild ox. 'And why would you be wanting a wizard, pray?'

'Because –' and Bayrd told him.

About the old folk and the young, the frail and the healthy, those who might be expected to die after many years and those whose brief lives had been riven from them, all because of what Gelert of Prytenon and his sorcerers had been doing. He left out only his own very private involvement in the subject. That, like so much else, was none of Youenn Kloatr's business – but unlike the various other matters that had fallen into the same category, Bayrd doubted he would hear much in the way of comfort after telling the headman about it. He seemed unconcerned enough about talk of sorcery and the Art Magic but that could be only because it was safely distanced from him, something romantic in one of his stories or something reprehensible practised by the High Lord of a safely-distant enemy province. To actually have a sorcerer sitting under his roof and drinking his beer, even an unwilling and involuntary one, might put a rather different complexion on things. Bayrd had no great desire to find out one way or the other.

All of what he wanted to find out lay in the tumbled ruins of Dunarat-hold on the far hill, where it overlooked the forest and the lake; the one place in all his travelling that had a sorcerer associated with its name . . .

Bayrd reined in, staring up the long slope towards the hunched, angular mass of masonry that crouched on top of it like some sleeping beast from legend, and he felt a small shiver run through him that raised the fine hair at the nape of his neck. For all the drifted snow that lay across the ground, his long ride through the night had been a journey into blackness; but silhouetted as they were against the sky that was now slowly paling to a distant dawn, the tumbled ruins of the haunted citadel were blacker still.

He grinned bravado at the darkness and exhaled a smug breath that drifted smokily away from his face. He had been right, and Youenn Kloatr had been wrong. There had been no wolves and no bears. Though he had heard small nervous rustlings and seen starlight reflected back from curious eyes in the deep shadows, the only other living creature he had seen was a single startled white owl, which had solemnly hooted its annoyance at him for spoiling the hunting by daring to be abroad at a time when all sensible men were fast asleep in bed.

But there had always been the cold. Youenn had been all too right about that at least. Neither he nor the horses had frozen – though it had been a close-run race, that contest between Bayrd and the cold, and the energy he had expended in fighting it had left him drained and weary. But the fight had been successful, sending a faint, far glow running through the marrow of his bones, just enough to keep the worst of the deadly chill at bay.

It had not been a spell, at least not as his scant knowledge of sorcery recognised the term; instead the meagre warmth had been conjured up from little more than his own bloody-minded determination. But it had suffused both himself and the two horses with a heat as fleeting and as often repeated as the rubbing of hands, at least for long enough that they had reached the shelter of the fortress walls where he was able to build a small fire.

For fear of what it might do if he over-extended himself, Bayrd had been wary, almost miserly, in that expenditure of power. There were memories of things suddenly catching fire to make him careful, and memories of agonising blisters when the summoned heat exploded on the wrong side of the skin of his pointing fingertips. None of the three had been as warm or as comfortable as they might have wished, even under the swathing of furs and quilted blankets. But they had remained unfrozen, and that was the most important thing. Shelter and fire and a little food would do the rest; that, and sleep.

The remnants of the fortress walls had slumped together with the passage of years and the removal of the smaller masonry, until all that remained were the huge fieldstones of the lowest run, roughly shaped blocks that with the foundations had supported the weight of all the rest. They had been of no use to even the most ambitious villager, for each one was almost as big as Youenn's cottage in Redmer, and the headman's home had been large in comparison with all the rest. With the loss of the iron clamps that had held them together – mortar had not been enough for such a weight, and according to Youenn the villagers had mined them as thoroughly as any seam beneath the ground – they had collapsed against each other into a jumble of caves and tunnels and small, near-windproof shelters. Bayrd was grateful for that at least. He had no energy left for digging in the drifted snow. What he wanted was the real heat of a fire, and the superficial comfort of a saddle-blanket spread across the rocks, and most of all he wanted to lie down. Even food could wait. If the remnants of the walls had not fallen flat in all this time, he was willing to trust that they would stay upright for just a little longer.

Having managed against the odds to make the journey from Redmer to Dunarat, and with all of the coming short winter's day at his disposal for an exploration of the site – though exploring for *what* was still a question without a satisfactory answer – Bayrd felt secure in the prospect of a few hours snuggled in a corner with his eyes closed. The brightness of the sun on the snow would dazzle him awake in good time, as it had always done before when he was sleeping rough. Once his small fire was well lit, he banked it with the thickest logs that he could find and then, secure in the knowledge that he and the two horses were as comfortable as he could make them, he rolled up in his blanket and fell instantly asleep.

It was not the sun that woke him, but the sound of voices drifting down the breeze. Bayrd ar'Talvlyn might have been weary to the point of exhaustion when he closed his eyes, but no *kailin* who hoped to see the sunrise had ever slept through night-noises where no noise should be. It was an art ingrained only through long practice, and Bayrd had practised often enough on pointless campaigns for other people's lords that he was good at it. His hand had closed on the hilt of his *taipan* shortsword even before he was fully awake; but the blade stayed in its scabbard. The scrape of steel drawn in a hurry in the stillness of the night not only carried an unfortunate distance, but if ever heard once in the proper context was impossible to forget, much less mistake for something else.

A single quick glance satisfied him that the fire was making hardly any smoke, and the few small threads of grey that coiled up from the embers were dispersing on the wind that blew gently from the source of the voices. Bayrd took a few necessary seconds to give both horses their nose-bags; it was no guarantee of silence, but at least it gave them something else to do besides whinny after him when he slipped quietly out between the massive rocks.

This was something else for Youenn Kloatr to be wrong about, thought Bayrd as he snaked through the jumbled boulders to a vantage-point behind and halfway to the top of one of the largest. It looked and sounded as though someone's retainers were less impressed by the tales of haunting than the headman thought, and Bayrd hoped Youenn's assumptions wouldn't someday backfire on him. There were eight of them – no, nine; he revised the count upwards as another man entered his line of sight. This last was still hitching at the fastenings of his breeches, and making little progress at it.

Bayrd would have smiled, except that he could see why the man was having difficulties – and it wasn't much reason for amusement. He, and seven of the others, wore full armour underneath their furs, the elaborate harness of mail-linked plates he had seen before on Lord Gelert of Prytenon. Eight in armour, and one in travelling-leathers. Then the leather-clad person turned, and he revised his figures yet again. Eight armoured men – and one woman.

What they were doing here was anybody's guess, and what *she* was doing in such company he couldn't begin to imagine. She moved, and was dressed, in a style superior to the ordinary peasants he had seen before – except perhaps for Youenn Kloatr, but then the headman of Redmer was something of a mystery in more ways than just that. Both her voice and her gestures were those of someone giving peremptory commands, and the warriors seemed, though reluctantly and with no great haste, to be doing as they were bidden. For the most part their behaviour towards her appeared to be a rough-and-ready courtesy, though even at this distance he could see that the roughness took considerable precedence. Bayrd was sure that they were not her personal guard, and that they resented being ordered about by this female. He began to wonder what power or title she had that held their truculence in check – and why it was that her escort was composed of men of rank.

Their armour had told him that much. They were of higher status than the axemen he had encountered before, warriors perhaps of some lord's retinue. There perhaps lay the seeds of their resentment, although there had to be more to it than that. They were certainly well enough equipped to do anybody honour as an escort; then Bayrd shook his head. If anything they were far *too* well equipped, more heavily armed than necessary for men travelling in – presumably – friendly or at least allied territory. As he dubiously eyed the plates and mail-mesh of their armour, the heavy cutting-spears they carried, the axes and maces shoved through their belts and the long swords hanging by their sides, he became uncomfortably aware that by comparison he was almost naked.

The *taipan* was at his belt, as was his *tsepan* dirk – though that was no weapon for a fight. Neither of them were. The shortsword was horribly inadequate, and the dirk was a joke. Everything else was back in the shelter under the ruined walls, just waiting to be discovered if one of the horses chanced to neigh a protest at eating all the grain in its feed-bag, or if the small wind changed and blew the smoke and smell of his fire in the wrong direction. Bayrd slithered silently back down the rocks and hurried off to do something about it.

Encased in his own armour for the first time in several weeks, he immediately felt more secure – even if the odds of eight or possibly even nine to one made that security illusory at best. It was just a precautionary measure in case he was discovered, because Bayrd did not intend to get himself into a fight without good reason, especially with the odds so heavily weighted against him; and if he could avoid any reason at all, be it good, bad or indifferent, so much the better. Gerin ar'Diskan and the Overlord had not sent him here to fight, but to watch, to learn, and to come back safely with his gathered knowledge.

With the fire extinguished and spare furs wrapped with strips of blanketing around the horses' hoofs to deaden their sound, he led them cautiously towards the shadow of the trees and safety. Those trees were huddled as close to the ruins as their roots could find soil to support them, and he was grateful that whatever had happened in Dunarat – whether Youenn's story, or something more historically accurate and boring – had taken place so long ago. Otherwise, in common with every other fortress he had ever seen, those trees would have been cleared back from the walls for a distance of one, two or even more bowshots. With the prevailing weather conditions of a fine, clear morning, there was no chance of his inadequate skill at sorcery creating a sudden fall of snow or even a convenient mist, and the prospect of crossing half a mile of open, snowclad country while still hoping to pass the gaze of eighteen eyes unseen was one he preferred not to consider.

Once in the friendly shadows, Bayrd tethered the packhorse so far into the depths of the wood that any risk of accidental discovery was academic at best – though if worst came to worst and he didn't come back, a determined search by the men who had . . . had prevented his return, would find the animal easily enough. He mounted Yarak, checked the weapons hung around his belt and saddle, then turned the mare's head back towards the fortress. Bayrd still had no intention of going looking for a fight; but after all he had been told about this place and how reluctant Lord Benart's people were to approach it, he was curious to learn what had changed their minds. If nothing else, he owed Youenn and the entire village of Redmer a sizable debt of gratitude for their hospitality, and a timely warning that their supposed supernatural defence was a defence no longer would go some little way towards repaying it.

Swinging around so that he would be approaching the place where he had last seen the intruders from straight out of the deep forest with the shadows at his back, Bayrd guided Yarak carefully through the trees as close as he dared before dismounting within sound of the voices and carefully setting hobbles round the mare's front legs. He hooked the cased shortbow and its arrow-crammed quiver to his belt, set one arrow to the string, then eased forward on the yielding crispness of snow and long-dead leaves. He moved with all the delicacy learned during the brutal weeks of the woodland war in and around Gelert's Forest, where a single sound out of place, a single missed step, would end in any number of particularly foul, protracted ways to die.

It didn't matter that the voices were rising in argument, making enough noise of their own to cover any he might make. He knew well enough how such a reliance could betray, with a sudden, unexpected silence falling at the one instant when it could do most harm. Bayrd set down his booted feet as though the surface under them was not just vegetation and a crust of frozen water, but blown eggshells filled with red-hot coals – and even then, there were times when his tread was dangerously heavy.

Finally Bayrd could go no further. There was only the lightest screening of bushes and undergrowth between him and the enemy warriors – for they were the enemy, and would remain so until they had proved otherwise. He was certain that the scored, open area beyond was where past generations of peasant stonemasons had done their thieving from the vast quarry that had been the fortress of Dunarat, and the last had been recent enough that the encroaching forest had not yet recovered the broken ground. Not that there was need to risk taking another step; he could hear as well from where he stood. Bayrd relaxed the half-drawn bow-string – though most certainly he didn't return the arrow to its quiver – and rested his armoured weight against the comfortably-broad bole of an elm tree to listen to what was being said.

They hated being here. There was no good reason to be here. And anyway, it felt wrong. . . Bayrd grinned harshly at that, knowing the sound of unadmitted fear when he heard it. He heard their accents, too, and it watered down his grin to an unpleasant smile, because despite where they were all standing, not all of them were Elthanek and entitled to be here at all. Four were, as was the woman.

But the others were Prytenek, of High Lord Gelert's own household. There had not been enough difference in the patterns of their armour for him to notice anything amiss, but the voices were unmistakable. Bayrd ar'Talvlyn leaned back against his tree and stared at nothing, trying to imagine what threat had brought these two old enemies together. From the first thought to the last, his answer remained the same.

Albans. Invaders. His own people.

And that answer told him something else he had kept restrained at the back of his mind during all the long, cold weeks of absence. In all that time without contact, without information except the unreliable rumours of war passed on to him by peasants who were more concerned to hear what *he* might have to say, one question had been nagging at him. And now he knew. Sorcery or not, the war was going in the Albans' favour. They were not merely holding, they were winning, pushing Gelert back until he had been forced to turn for help to the very lord, the very province, he had hoped to defeat with Alban assistance. Until it all went sour . . .

Bayrd fought down the great whooping laugh of delight that came surging up inside him. This might even mean that his own mission no longer had any significance; that he could come home with honour and fight in a clean war that had no need to resort to the Art Magic – and that he could perhaps even forget all the things that had begun to happen to him since he first stepped onto the beach at Dunakr.

Except – the reality of the situation was like a dousing with cold water – that he could do nothing of the sort. Without the direct instructions of his lord to the contrary, Bayrd's last orders still held good. Find a wizard or a sorcerer. Find out if he will help us. Bring him back. That was all; no room for flexibility, question, or debate. Do it.

'*Purkanth'yen tarlekh!*' roared a voice. Hard on the heels of the shout came a sound as unmistakable in its way as steel leaving a scabbard. A slapped face sounded much the same in any language. And this language had just called someone a sorcerous bitch.

Bring him back. Or bring *her* . . .

Bayrd ar'Talvlyn had old-fashioned ideas about the mistreatment of women, or indeed anyone outnumbered and outweighed. He didn't permit it. And at the same time he couldn't intervene in

172

this; it wasn't his fight. Whatever was going on wasn't even his business, except so far as it might tell him things that were. But inside the layered gloves of mail and fur and leather his knuckles were white against the skin as his fingers clamped around the grip of the bow. Trying to persuade himself to follow the road of duty, sense and silence rather than that of honourable, suicidal interference, he listened again to what was being said.

'. . . and Lord Yakez told you to help us,' said the first voice, its Prytenek accent thick with anger and what might have been poorly suppressed fright at what had just been done – and maybe also *where* it had been done. 'He even made a formal promise to the High Lord Gelert that you would help us. So we brought you here. Now *help* us!' There was the high flat crack of another slap.

'I can't help you,' said the woman's voice. 'Not here. Look at the place. How long since any of the lords, or any of their so-courageous warriors, came up here? It's been destroyed. Taken to pieces. And any trace of sorcery is long gone too.'

'It's haunted, wizard.' That was another Elthanek accent, heavier than the woman's. 'Everyone knows that. You know that. It's your business to know it. The ghosts must have done this, because nobody comes near it. Even the closest village is a full day's distance. So use the haunting, and let's get out of here!'

Bayrd grinned again, though this time, with too many teeth on show and not enough humour baring them, it was nearer to being a snarl. At least Youenn and the villagers of Redmer was still safe after all.

'You can't "use" a haunting like that, if this place is even haunted at all – which I doubt.' For all that she had been slapped at least twice, and hard if the sound was anything to go by, the woman's voice was calm and reasonable. 'No matter what it looks like, it's not a proper magic. You might as well put white wine in a lamp and expect it to burn just because it's a liquid with the same colour as oil.'

From his hiding-place, Bayrd nodded approval. The argument was a sensible one. Now if they would just pay her the attention that her good sense deserved, and go away. But she had already put a dangerous doubt into their minds – if they had been listening – about whether the ruins were truly haunted or not. The risk, if the lord's-men had heard enough for it to take root in their minds, was not to Bayrd, but to his friends in Redmer village. If a simple warrior said 'haunted' but a wizard said 'not', it was easy enough to see who would be believed, at least on that subject.

He unclipped the arrow's sinew-wrapped horn nock from the string – the whole thing cleverly designed to hold a chosen arrow in place even at full gallop – and examined its wicked leaf-shaped steel head while at the same time an equally wicked idea took shape inside his own head. He slipped the arrow back into its quiver, and carefully selected another. This one looked, was, and most important of all, *sounded* different. The bulb that took the place of an ordinary arrowhead was made of wood, or metal, or even unglazed pottery, but each was pierced and channelled in a different way to produce a different sound.

They were called various things, depending on what that sound might be: whistlers, warblers, singers, and screamers – but depending on how they were used, their function was always the same, as signals, or to frighten horses. In the proper circumstances Bayrd hoped that this one might successfully frighten men as well. Any one of the half-dozen he carried as part of the quiver's normal complement of missiles might serve to chase the doubts away, if shot at the right time out of the black depths of the forest. There was only one hazard: if any of the Pryteneks had heard such an arrow put to use before, perhaps down in the 'invader's country', then the only thing Bayrd would have done was to reveal his all-too-human presence.

Decisions, decisions . . .

He risked a peek out from behind the tree. Until one or another of the warriors spoke, it was impossible to be sure which of them was Elthanek and which from Gelert's household; but even at this distance he could make an educated guess. The Elthaneks, those who knew how haunted Dunarat was supposed to be, were the ones who looked scared. At least the warriors did. The Elthanek wizard, and the other four Prytenek lord's-men, just looked angry. The woman wore the marks of those two slaps plainly on her right cheek, bright red hand-prints that seemed almost to glow against the pallor of her furious face, and as he rolled the screamer-tipped arrow to and fro between his fingers, Bayrd somehow didn't think that she would try to dissuade anyone who jumped to the wrong conclusions about any eerie sounds that might surprise them.

He made up his mind, and fitted the screamer arrow to his bowstring, then rummaged briefly among the bristling feathered shafts and extracted two more arrows, these with singer tips. He clipped them next to the first, and made sure with a judicious plucking of the string that all three were held securely enough by their springy nocks. The result of loosing them off all together would win him no prizes for bowmanship, nor break any records – even though the unfamiliar strain might well break the string. Prompted by which thought, he hurriedly made certain there was a spare in its beeswaxed container at the back of the bow-case. But the record for flight and distance he was hoping to achieve had nothing, or at least not much, to do with the arrows, and a great deal to do with the quartet of sweating, nervous Elthanek warriors.

Fading back towards where he had left Yarak, Bayrd unhobbled her and swung easily up into the saddle. For all the cold, he too was sweating, and inside the cage of his ribs his heart was thumping with unnecessary vigour. Kneeing the little mare forward, he guided her slightly to one side so that if anybody chanced to look in the right – or for him, wrong – direction, they would be usefully illuminated by the newly-risen sun, while it would be at his back and shining full into their eyes so that he and the rising arrows would be lost in the glare. Bayrd knew it would be a long time before he managed to forget his first shocking encounter with the hunter Jord Koutlan, and the way the big man had looked even bigger with the blinding light of morning behind him. If he was spotted, he wanted all the advantages that he could find.

But with care and good luck, those precautions wouldn't be necessary. If all went well, at least four and hopefully all eight of the warriors would be interested in only one direction, that taken by their own horses along the shortest route away from the most definitely haunted ruins of Dunarat. Still sheltered by the trees, if only just, Bayrd rose just enough in his stirrups to make sure that he could still see where the warriors and their tame wizard were standing. Then he took a long, deep breath, and drew the bowstring back, and loosed the arrows in a long, high arc straight up and over their heads.

Even Bayrd was shocked by the eldritch triple wail as the arrows shot upwards – and he at least had been expecting it. To those taken unawares and unfamiliar with the sound's more natural origin, or all too ready with an alternate explanation for its source, the arrowsong could have been little short of hellish. There were masculine yells, both deep and shrill, and a single female scream, hastily stifled. Bayrd guessed that was either because the wizard had guessed what she was hearing, or because her sorcerous training had given her more control over herself than most of the warriors, and showing fear in front of them was a worse thing than the fear itself.

Some of the other shouting was not stifled. Instead those voices receded in a clattering of hoofs, cut through by the harshly bellowed demands that they stand still or come back. Bayrd risked another craning through the branches, and a swift count of the remaining opposition. Then he flopped back into Yarak's saddle and swore venomously under his breath. Only three had run away, two of the Elthaneks and a single one of Gelert's men. The others had drawn into a tight half-circle with the ruined fortress at their backs and the woman wizard securely in the middle. After what he had heard and seen already, it looked to Bayrd's jaundiced eye less for her protection than to prevent her escape – and he was still outnumbered.

A swift hot surge of anger that heralded the release of power welled up inside him, but he fought it down again. Maybe the wizard *was* being forced to help the lord's-men against her will, or maybe not; but there was little point in fighting fire with fire when he had the equivalent of a small oil-lamp and the woman yonder might have something like a furnace at her command. But then he saw just how willing she really was, and how highly Gelert's men regarded their allies.

The largest of the Pryteneks, and the man Bayrd would most have laid money on as the source of those two slaps, broke out of the circle and made his way back into the broken labyrinth of tumbled stone that had been Dunarat-hold. When he came back, one of the arrows was clutched in his armoured fist. Either he had seen it fall, or he had heard it. That didn't matter. He shook it under the wizard's nose and said something Bayrd didn't hear, then turned to face the forest, snapped it in two and threw the pieces on the ground, where he spat on them.

'Alban,' he shouted. 'Alban, we know you're there! The trick didn't work, Alban, did it? We're still here. How much did this treacherous sow pay you to "haunt" the fortress for her, Alban? Was it enough to pay for what we'll do to you?' His axe jerked free of his belt, and he laid the flat of the blade under where the wizard's breasts swelled against her travelling-leathers. 'Is it enough for you to watch what we can do to her. . . ?'

It wasn't his fight; it wasn't his business; Lord Gelert's thug didn't know where he was, because he was shouting his threats at a completely wrong part of the forest. So Bayrd wasn't entirely sure why he was suddenly sitting astride Yarak squarely in the middle of the old approach-road, with the sun throwing his shadow huge and black down to the old citadel and another arrow in his bow and bloody murder in his heart. *Too many stories*, said the accusing little voice at the back of his mind. *Too many heroes.* Except that after what he had just heard, he knew that there could never be too many heroes; that there were more often not enough.

'Let her go,' he said, knowing his voice would carry well enough without the need to shout. 'Let her go, and I might let you live.'

There was a spatter of laughter among the lord's-men, and a quick muttered discussion before one of the warriors Bayrd had marked as Elthanek stepped forward, twirling his cutting-spear. 'I defy you,' the man called. 'I defy you, and I challenge you to fight me with any weapon that you choose! I am Lerent Skarayz, and I ha*Akh –!*'

Bayrd's bow thumped once. The spear, still twirling dramatically, clattered on the frozen ground as a single broad-bladed, heavy arrow slammed the rest of the formal defiance back into the Elthanek warrior's mouth and out through the back of his head in a spatter of blood and spinal fluid. Lerent Skarayz dropped without another word.

'I am the *kailin-eir* Bayrd ar'Talvlyn; I choose my bow; and I have no more time for challenges.'

It might have been outrage at his conduct, or the sudden horrid realisation that none of them had missile weapons, but three of the lord's-men lowered spear or drew sword and charged at Bayrd. Only one remained; the big man with the axe had not taken its blade from the wizard's breast, but he had shifted his position just enough to leave her at more risk from a long-range arrow than himself.

Bayrd had seen him move, and put his second arrow instead through a Prytenek warrior's kneecap before the man who had hoped to run on it was properly in his stride. Suddenly the odds that had seemed so weighted against him were much more in favour, and as the wounded man collapsed shrieking, Yarak was well into a stride of her own. Had they been proper horsemen, rather than fighters on foot who simply travelled on horseback, the two remaining warriors might have seen something to avoid in the malevolent way the small grey mare came for them.

They did not: something obviously a war-horse, like a huge frothing red-eyed stallion, might have concerned them, but it was beneath their notice to be afraid of mere transport. Until that 'transport' sidestepped the thrust of a spear with all the neatness of a dancer, snapped her huge square teeth at the face of the man who held it so that he went staggering back off-balance from the unexpected attack, then sent him flying with a vicious, liver-bursting double kick that his armour didn't do a thing to stop.

As he dropped out of the saddle with longsword in one hand and axe in the other, it struck Bayrd that for all the loud talk he had overheard, none of his assailants had ever been to the 'invader's country'. They knew nothing about Alban cavalry tactics, or even that a well-trained horse was more than just an animal, a mount and a mobile archery platform. It was a biting battering-ram six times the weight of a man, it was propped up on four war-hammers, and it knew how to use every one of those weapons to murderous effect.

Nor had they encountered the less formal variants of *taiken* play, as practised – not very well – by the late and unlamented Lord Serej ar'Diskan. The last but one of the Pryteneks skidded slightly in the churned snow, then lunged at Bayrd with the curved blade of his cutting-spear. It was taken by the longsword in a simple block that twisted half around into a far from simple parry guiding the spearpoint into the ground, and then its braced shaft snapped under a quick downward chop from the axe.

The lord's-man snarled something through his clenched teeth then used what remained of his spear as a quarterstaff, bringing it up and around in a solid swing against the flat of Bayrd's sword. Few swords forged could take that sort of punishment, and this was no exception. The blade snapped off a handspan above the hilt.

Without taking a single lethal second to gape at the damage, Bayrd dropped the useless chunk of metal and swung his axe twice. It had a clipped-crescent blade backed by a four-inch triangular pick, and the first swing brought it up backwards and under the skirts of the Prytenek's armour to bury that pick in his groin. The man's mouth and eyes went wide with shock at the impact, but his agonised screech as the pick wrenched free was barely begun when the axeblade came whirring around in a long, merciful stroke through the side of his neck and the sound was cut off at its source.

Bayrd ar'Talvlyn shook blood from his face. It was hardly adequate, but there was no point in attempting to wipe himself clean through the narrow trefoil opening of the warmask, and he still needed to see what had become of the unaware cause of this carnage. A thought wandered idly through his jangling brain. *The first wizard you found . . . but if she had been a man, would you have gone to this trouble? You don't even know if she's pretty . . .*

There was no sensible answer to that. He might, or he might not. A man could have defended himself – and then his head snapped around at a sound like the crack of a monstrous whip.

The Elthanek woman and the lord's-man who had been threatening her with the axe were still where he had last seen them. But there had been some small, subtle changes of posture. That axe now dangled harmlessly by the warrior's side, and he was leaning back against one of the great rocks of the old fortress walls. The woman's hand was pressed flat against his chest, where before she had never dared to move a muscle.

And then she took her hand away, shaking it as though it stung, and Lord Gelert's man fell flat on his face. At least, most of him fell. There was a handprint on the rock where he had been leaning. Punched into the stone, steaming in the cold air and beginning to dribble unpleasantly, the handprint was a thick, glistening cross-section of the warrior's chest; armour plates, the leather beneath, and the flesh, blood and bone beneath that, each separate layer already peeling apart under its own weight. As he walked closer and saw better what that print was, Bayrd winced inwardly and allowed that this woman at least had needed no hero at all.

'Bayrd ar'Talvlyn, you called yourself.' She gave him a speculative glance as she washed her fingers in a handful of snow. 'Thank you. I think.'

'Lady, I . . .'

'Call me Eskra. Most people do.'

'Lady Eskra, my lord – my overlord desires me to ask . . .'

Eskra looked him up and down, her expression unreadable. 'Your lord has a proposal for me?' she asked finally. 'Another one. Well. At least you're an Alban. That makes a change. I might be asked what *I* think for once.' She finished with the snow, looked at it, curled her lip in faint disgust and dropped it to the ground. 'This proposal. Can it wait?'

'Er, yes. Probably.'

'Good.' And she stalked off as though there weren't five dead or noisily wounded men strewn around her. Given what they had threatened to do to her, Bayrd doubted if she cared. He watched her go, and swallowed nervously. The nerves were not because he had just seen what a wizard could do, but because his hands were sweating inside their armoured gloves, and a peculiar sensation had started churning in his blood. It was a feeling he recognised, and had hoped – though never dared to dream – that he would feel again. Least of all here and now. The last and only time had been on the day he met his second wife for the first time. The only day in all his life when all the carefully learned cynical controls had lost their grip. The only day he ever fell in love.

Until now.

Bayrd shook his head and licked dry, crusted lips with a tongue that was equally dry. *Of all the things that might have happened!* he thought, trying to be wryly amused about it and not succeeding any better than the last time, *this is the only one I never expected. Never rehearsed. Never even considered . . .*

Bayrd looked at the drying blood on his hands, and shuddered. Of all the courtship displays he might have made, why did it have to be this one? Saving a lady's life sounded very good in the old tales, but somehow they always managed to skim past the grim details of what that saving might involve for those she was saved *from*. He walked back to Yarak and patted the mare's nose, stared at the distant snow as though hoping its unblemished whiteness concealed some sort of answer, and finally put Albanak's and Lord Gerin's proposal out of his mind for the next few hours. Because if Eskra was agreeable, and he could summon up enough nerve, he might well make her a proposal of his own . . .

9

Shadows

ESKRA CAME BACK a few minutes later. There was a square satchel of scuffed brown leather slung over one shoulder, and she was leading the string of six remaining horses that Bayrd had guessed were tethered somewhere nearby. 'These are yours,' she said, indicating them with a nod of her head. 'You won them. And you deserve them.' She hesitated, colouring a little. 'You saved my life.'

Blushes or not, it was something of an improvement on the cool 'Thank you. I think' of their first exchange. Bayrd suspected she was unaccustomed to thanking anyone for favours or kindnesses, however minor; for the simple reason that she seldom received any. It might have been because she was a woman, or because she was a wizard, or maybe for both reasons. The attitudes of the Prytenek and Elthanek warrior aristocracy – or the thugs who passed for them – was a mystery which he had no especial desire to unravel.

'I didn't,' he said. 'If that one had decided to kill you, I was too far away to do anything about it.'

'All right. You distracted him. The distraction let me deal with him. That saved my life. Therefore *you* saved my life. Or do you want to argue some more?' There wasn't the grin he might have expected from Mevn, or even the flicker of annoyance that was the other side of that coin. Eskra didn't seem to care one way or the other. She knew she was right.

'Point taken,' said Bayrd, offering her a small salute. 'I agree. The conclusion is proved.'

'Good. Now. What next . . .?'

Bayrd shrugged. 'Food,' he said. 'And fire. I'm cold. Unless you've something else to do?' Dammit, but that laconic briskness was infectious.

Eskra stared at him for long enough that he began to wonder what she might be thinking; but then she nodded. 'Food is good. Fire too.' Her gaze shifted past Bayrd's shoulder to where the man with the shattered kneecap still wailed out in the snow, and she pointed with one open hand towards the lord's-man. 'And some quiet.'

Hoping that the movement wasn't obvious, but not especially concerned one way or the other, Bayrd leaned out of the way. He didn't look around as her hand closed to a fist, even when the wailing stopped as abruptly as if . . . As if a hand had closed around the Prytenek's throat and choked the sound to silence.

'He wouldn't have walked again,' said Eskra. Her voice revealed nothing of what went on in her mind. 'And the crows would have had his eyes by evening. Another day of life was no kindness.' She gave Bayrd's *tsepan* a thoughtful look, as though wondering why he hadn't put the weapon to its proper use, then shrugged and strode away without another word.

It was his arrow that had crippled the man, and it was his obligation – and if necessary that of his *tsepan* dirk – to see him out of distress one way or the other. Eskra's lack of comment was a courtesy he didn't really deserve, and it was one he wouldn't have received from any Alban *kailin* of his own rank. They would have taken pains, and maybe some malicious delight, in pointing out the duty he had owed, and would have gone on to say more about the woman and sorcerer who had done what Bayrd ar'Talvlyn could not.

Quite apart from her ruthless streak, and the fluttering inside him that Mahaut had joked about and called 'the cudgel', because even though it might feel like a butterfly's wings or the touch of a feather, it was as hard to ignore as the stroke of a stick, Bayrd found himself starting to like her. That was the thing: there was liking, and loving, and lusting, and they were three different facets of any relationship that a sensible man or woman soon learned to recognise – and to keep separate, if necessary. He had learned that through experience, and was fortunate so little of it had been bitter.

Bayrd had liked Lorey, his first wife, and still liked her now; but he had never loved her. Their arranged marriage-of-alliance had been too cold-blooded for that. He had loved Mahaut, and had liked simply being in her company; the lust between them had been a pleasant extra that waxed and waned with their moods. With Mevn ar'Dru it was liking and lust, with no love involved to muddy the water. There was not, and had never been, any long-term commitment. When she married, or he married again, they would still remain as good friends as they were now.

While Eskra . . .

Eskra was a sorcerer, or a wizard, or both; he would find out the proper definition eventually. Eskra was all business when she wanted to be, or when, such as now, she was covering for the sort of fright and shakiness that her pride wouldn't allow her to show. She was also lethal when she had to be, and Bayrd had only to listen to the sudden silence, or turn his head and look at the hand-printed rock beside the old fortress gate, to gain plenty of evidence for that.

There was a birdlike quality to the quickness of her speech and movement, and to the sharp delicacy of her features; but she was no sparrow. Instead, she was like a hawk Bayrd had once seen, a kestrel, all red-brown plumage and sharp bright eyes. Eskra was just the same, her own dark red-brown hair clipped short around her ears in a style that said little about Elthanek fashions for women, but a great deal about her own practical turn of mind. The hawk's eyes had been black and hot, hers were blue and cool, but the intensity of their regard remained the same. She had the same way of looking at things, or more unnervingly, at people, as Bayrd's long-dead grandfather, who the family had said would have stared through a rock rather than take the trouble to walk round it. Her nose was not that of the hawk she resembled in so many other respects, being short and straight instead of hooked – Bayrd was to learn she had a habit of sighting down the bridge of it as though taking aim with a crossbow – and her mouth was small, with lips more thin than full and well-suited to the short, sharp manner of her speech.

Eskra was no great beauty in the accepted meaning of sensual face and long legs and curved figure, but there was a mind like a razor in there, and a glamour that hung about her in the oldest and truest sense of the word. She looked, and sounded, and behaved like what she was: a wielder of Power.

184

'You didn't come here to just look for me,' said Eskra bluntly, between licking the grease of a grilled strip of bacon off her fingers. 'So why?'

The bacon had been smoked a deep russet – as well as dried and salted, which Bayrd had suggested to Youenn Kloatr was somewhat excessive – and it smelt very good. What smelt and tasted even better, despite the faint flavour of turpentine it had acquired from a winter of dining on pine-needles, was the white woodgrouse he had shot on the way back from recovering his packhorse. It had been a fluke, he being more likely to miss than to hit such a target, but Bayrd had no intention of admitting it. He was out to impress, and if keeping his mouth shut about how lucky that snap-shot had been would further his cause, he was going to be as quiet as a newly filled-in grave. Between them, the grouse and the bacon gave him the excuse for a few extra seconds of nibbling and chewing before he had to come up with an answer to Eskra's question.

She wasn't quite that patient. 'Your lord's proposal,' the sharp voice rapped. 'What did he want? Intelligence? Information? Or a traitor?'

That was when a scrap of bacon went the wrong way down Bayrd's throat. He had already manfully stifled his chuckle at the concept of some of the Alban lords sending their trusted emissaries out to gather intelligence. Why look in foreign lands for what's so hard to find at home . . .? But that mention of a traitor was less funny, and far too close to his original instructions: not just to find a sorcerer, but one who was willing to betray his own people for the sake of offered gold and power and privilege.

Well, he had found the sorcerer at least, even though *he* had turned out to be *she* – and his unexpected personal involvement was making further discussion of the less creditable parts of the mission stick in his throat even worse than the bacon had done. Bayrd ar'Talvlyn could speak three languages, or four if the various older dialects of Alban spoken in this country were counted as something separate – but not one of all of them used 'traitor' in other than its pejorative sense. He finished choking on the bacon and his problems, and took a careful swallow of the strong black beer that Youenn Kloatr of Redmer had pressed on him. 'The Overlord Albanak,' he began formally, and saw the usual small smile that the name prompted in a speaker of Old Alban, 'required me to find a sorcerer . . .'

'Yes. I was thinking it might be that. Or something like. Your Landmaster and his people alone are a thorn in Lord Gelert's backside. So a way to poison the thorn makes sense.' She leaned forward and wrenched a leg off the roasted wood-grouse, then waved it at Bayrd like a truncheon of office. 'Have you Albans no Talented ones among you? Are you too honourable for it? Or just too honourable to *admit* it?'

Eskra sank her white teeth into the rich dark meat and stripped it from the bone in three or four neat bites. She chewed thoughtfully, swallowed, drank beer, and eyed Bayrd over the rim of the horn cup. 'And what makes Albans so different? The rest of the world has its sorcerers. Why not you? Did you kill them all?'

She tilted the cup and drained it, but when she lowered it again her eyes were still fixed on Bayrd's face in one of those long looks that could mean half a dozen things, depending on how guilty he was feeling. 'You now. You're good at killing. I watched you. But you don't like it.' Was that a commendation or a criticism? There was nothing in her tone to let him know one way or the other.

It was a compliment.

'The lord's-men like it. They like it too much. And now they can't stop. It would make them look weak if they did. So they kill their enemies. And each other. And the peasants who grow their food. All for glory. All to show how brave they are. So let them kill everyone. Let them eat glory and courage. And then let's see how fat they get!'

Eskra threw the cleaned bone into the fire; but Bayrd's eyes were quick enough to see that it was burning with a hot white flame well before it hit the embers. He watched it sizzle for a few seconds, then looked up and said, 'I don't want a traitor.' *I want you.* 'I want – that is, my lord wants . . . We need someone to help us. Gelert is –'

'Is using the Art Magic against you. I was told. And it isn't working. Which is why they brought me here.'

'Isn't *working*?' Bayrd's voice went shrill, and he laughed hollowly. He had been there, that first night. He had seen with his own eyes how it hadn't worked on Goel ar'Diskan. 'If it isn't working, how did Gelert's sorcery kill seventeen people the first

186

time it was used? I saw one of them die. He was an old man, but some of the others –'

'Were children. Yes. I was told that too. And I also know that Gelert killed three of his wizards to do it. To miss every important target. I call that a poor exchange.'

'Poor, is it?'

'Yes. Their parents can replace the children in less than a year. But the wizards . . . Not so easy.'

'That is the most ruthless –'

'– Piece of good sense that you've heard for a while. Understand me. Gelert is losing this war. Not even the wizards can help him. And anyway he keeps killing them.' Bayrd stared at her. 'Oh yes. Because of impatience. Demands for results. And then rage when results aren't forthcoming. There are no wizards left in his service.' Then Eskra hesitated, and her thin lips curved in a mirthless smile. 'Not quite true. There is one. If you can call it service. But young Kalarr's safe enough.'

'Why?'

'Because the precocious brat is Gelert's son.'

'Precocious?' Bayrd frowned a little. 'How old is he?'

'Twelve years. No. Thirteen. Old enough at least – and skilled enough – to have earned his nickname. "Spellwreaker". Except that he prefers the old form: cu Ruruc.'

'And Gelert tolerates a wizard as his own son?' Eskra looked at Bayrd sharply, hearing at first only the meaning of what he said; but her look softened as her ears detected the faint wistfulness which underlay the words.

'The child was a sorcerer first. Born with the Talent. And yes. He is tolerated. Or was. Now . . . Now he is feared.'

'At thirteen years old?' said Bayrd, grinning slightly.

'Save your amusement until after you meet him,' snapped Eskra. 'Then laugh. If you can. He is a red serpent, that one. He deserves to die.'

'At thirteen years old?' Bayrd repeated, and this time he wasn't smiling. Eskra met his stare without flinching, and nodded.

'At birth,' she said. Then her eyes narrowed. 'And give me no moralising about the right to live and the right to die. One day Kalarr cu Ruruc will trouble this unhappy world. And you will know the truth of what I say. For the little good it will have done.'

She looked away, and when she turned back it was as if the subject had never been discussed. 'But this is the sole exception. No others will go anywhere near him. So you and your lord don't need me as he does.' *I do*, thought Bayrd. *But not as a wizard*. 'And he won't have me. Not again. Not after . . . this attempt at a so-called alliance. Do you still want to listen? Or would you rather take refuge in your affectation of outrage? Your choice.'

Her abruptness was the verbal equivalent of, if not quite a slap in the face – there had been too much of that already this morning – then certainly a good shaking, and it jolted him back to sense. There was the same chilly logic about it as he had heard a hundred times during tactical discussions before battle, even though in his case none of those battles had ever come to anything. He had never objected to it then, even though some of the opinions expressed by his fellow *kailinin* had been even more callous and unfeeling. It was just that . . .

Reluctantly, Bayrd smiled. It was just that here was the second sorcerer he had ever – knowingly – spoken to in his life, and she was as different to the first as it was possible to be. Never mind that Eskra was a slight and definitely pretty woman, while *Hospodar* Skarpeya had been a huge and hearty man with a beard like a bramble bush, who gave an impression of being almost as broad as he was tall or at least of expanding to fill all the available space around him. But the way they each had addressed him was more disparate even than that. Eskra said no more than was absolutely necessary for her meaning to be clear, while Skarpeya had littered the landscape with words as though he were a tree in autumn and they were his leaves. Granted, one tended to be told much more than the simple answer to a question, which was something unlikely to happen where Eskra's guarded speech was concerned, but there had been times during his single long conversation with Skarpeya when Bayrd had wished himself elsewhere.

'Something amusing you? Good. It's about time. So listen. And learn something. Your Landmaster sent you to find a sorcerer. You found a wizard instead. Me. Does the difference concern him?'

'No,' said Bayrd. 'Albanak-*arluth* didn't know there was a difference at all, until –' He hesitated, and Eskra pounced on it at once.

'Until? Until someone explained it to him. Until you did. Yes?'

'Yes.' Bayrd said it reluctantly, not sure how much that simple agreement might sound like a confession to knowledge he wasn't supposed to have. Confession or not, Eskra approved.

'So there's at least a trace of intelligence you don't need to find out in the wilds.' *So she noticed that as well*, Bayrd thought. *What else have I let slip?* 'And you? Did you want a wizard or a sorcerer? Does it matter?'

'I said no.' There might have been something more defensive in his tone than he had intended, another piece for whatever she was constructing, because Eskra gave him a swift and rather knowing smile. 'That is, if one can help us as well as the other, then it doesn't really matter.' He gave her a long look full of wide-eyed innocence. 'Does it?'

'You might be surprised. Yes. You might indeed. The question's moot anyway. You don't have a sorcerer. A wizard will have to do.' She slapped the heavy leather satchel resting by her side, and grinned cheerfully. Bayrd had already noticed that since she had recovered the bag earlier on, she never let it further away than she could comfortably reach, moving it whenever she moved, treating it, in fact, as any honourable *kailin* might treat his swords and especially his *tsepan* dagger.

'Your books?' he ventured, doing his best to keep the raw edge of curiosity out of his voice; but again, from the way that Eskra looked at him and raised her narrow eyebrows, that best was not quite good enough.

'My books. Interested? And I thought Albans had no time for the Art Magic.'

'They're books, and I like books,' said Bayrd with dignity. 'The subject doesn't matter. And I'm not under my Overlord's eye out here, so I can find time for whatever I please.'

'Is that so?' Eskra grinned at him again, her eyes glittering, so that Bayrd felt certain that she had read all the subtexts of that simple statement and found entertainment in every one of them. 'Then we might expand your awareness somewhat. But not now. I'd like to leave this place.'

'Because of the haunting?'

'Haunting? Stories! There's no haunting here. And if there was, it wouldn't disturb me. The dead are dead. It's the living that are dangerous. And three of them got away. Remember?'

'I'd hoped to frighten all of them away – but the ones who ran are probably still running.'

'Running home. Benart's hold at Tauren is about a long day's ride away. At the rate they were going they'll be there by nightfall. If they don't run into a patrol first. Either way,' Eskra stretched luxuriously, reluctant to leave the warmth of the fire, 'by noon tomorrow this place will be crawling with lord's-men. Looking for me. And whoever did that piece of skilful butchery outside. So gather up your arrows. No sense in advertising you were here. Or who you are.'

'So there's nothing to the old tale after all?' Bayrd was disappointed. Youenn Kloatr had sounded so convincing that he was prepared for almost anything. He smiled inwardly. Prepared, at least, for everything except what had really happened. 'No Lord Ared, no stolen child, no wizard –'

'Ah. Now your presence makes some sense. As much as mine, anyway. How much more than nothing do you want there to be?'

'I want to know, that's all. We write down our history; we don't turn it into tales for children.'

'So everything in the Alban clan Archives is true.' Eskra covered her mouth with one hand, but her eyes twinkled at him. 'Now that I'd like to see. I really would.' She cleared her throat, probably of any remaining tendency to laugh out loud. 'And if you worry about children's stories taking the edge off history, don't. I've heard some so-called children's tales that would scare any child I know out of sleeping for a year. But you really want to know about Ared and this fortress?' Bayrd nodded. 'Then give me some more beer. Not much. We should go soon. But this won't take long.'

It didn't. Even though Eskra's speech was expanding a little from her usual staccato phrases, it didn't take long at all. Ared had been a local lord, like Benart, or like Gerin ar'Diskan and all the other clan-lords Bayrd knew. He owed fealty and service for his lands to a provincial High Lord, one of Gelert's or Yakez's ancestors, but he was fortunate to marry into influence and wealth. Lady Elyan's father was the High Lord's chief henchman, rich, powerful, with influence at court and in hall. Ared was elevated in rank, granted more land, and given permission to build himself a fortress; all thanks to his father-in-law, who would not have tolerated his daughter living in anything less. They had a child – but that was when everything fell apart.

Ared refused to acknowledge it, claiming that his calculations proved – 'Whatever *that* means,' said Eskra – the child had been conceived during his absence at the High Lord's citadel. He dismissed insistence that the baby was born prematurely as no more than an excuse to cover Elyan's betrayal of his honour, and finally, in a fit of red rage, flung the infant to its death from the walls of Dunarat. Mad with grief and in blind terror of worse, Elyan jumped after it. Her father called down blood-feud, for the insult to his family as much as the murder, and after a battle and a short siege, watched as Lord Ared was flung from the same walls as his wife and child. After that the fortress was pulled down and Ared's very name struck from the chronicles and abolished.

Bayrd sat in silence for a long while after she had finished, staring at the dying fire and thinking his own thoughts. 'I preferred the story,' he said at last. 'It might not have been true, and it might not have had a happy ending, but at least it wasn't as black as that.'

'Believe what you like,' said Eskra, and there was less sharpness in her voice than usual. 'That history might be no more true than the story. It might not have turned out that way at all. Or it might have been changed in someone's favour. Not every Archivist is an Alban who writes only truth.'

'Ha-ha,' said Bayrd sarcastically, but not very. At least he had found his wizard – and something more besides. All that remained was to deal with the convoluted bargaining and persuasion both cases were likely to involve. Then his teeth shut with an audible click and the expression which crossed his face – before he controlled it – was as clear as anything written down in an Archive. And probably more truthful as well. 'Say that again . . ?'

'I said: "Of course there *is* still the sword".'

'The sword is real? The sword from the story?'

'Real enough. Your version has it made by a wizard. But wizards aren't usually swordsmiths. I should know. My version has Ared stealing it from one of the old grave-mounds.'

'Your version would.' Bayrd tried a small sneer that didn't work properly. He was still too intrigued by what she had said, and also slanted towards optimistic belief by the empty scabbard hanging from his own weaponbelt. Besides, there were weapons and artifacts highly regarded by clan-lords of excellent repute – Gerin ar'Diskan was one – whose provenance would not bear too much close scrutiny. Clan ar'Talvlyn themselves had various small golden bits and pieces which, though they came from the distant past, were not quite the family legacy they were claimed to be. Scorn for others didn't go very far in such circumstances.

'High Lord Gelert of Prytenon –' even though the words weren't shaped well for that sort of delivery, Eskra still contrived to spit most of them, – 'knows your version better. We weren't here just for the haunting. Though I think that was in his mind as well.' She waved one hand casually at the ruins surrounding them, the tumbled stones, the snow, and the desolation. 'If he thinks that ghosts did this, made one hold abandoned, then they might do the same to the Albans. Their fortresses are plaguing his province. But I never did learn what he planned for the sword when we found it. Cutting his toenails, perhaps. Now let's go.'

'No. Not yet.'

'I'd much prefer not to be here when Benart's men come back.'

'You said *when*, not *if*. About the sword. About finding it.'

'Ah. The sword.' She gave him an indulgent smile that from anyone else would have set his teeth on edge. 'You Albans and your weapons. After no more than half a year in this country you're already –'

'Lady, my own sword was broken. Saving your life, remember? So if there's a replacement here, I mean to find it before we leave.'

'There's no magic in it.'

'I don't want magic, I don't need magic – at least, not magic like that. But I want and I need a new sword, or even an old one, and Greylady will –'

'Who?'

'Greylady. It's the sword's name.'

'No it isn'.'

'Yes it . . .' For a moment they hovered on the brink of a farcical argument, until Bayrd bit down on the usual response and changed it to, 'Well, that's what I heard,' instead.

'You must mean Isileth.'

Bayrd eyed her thoughtfully. 'No I don't,' he said, and there was the merest malicious hint of an invitation to mischief riding his choice of the words.

'If it's the sword from your story, then I'm sorry to correct you, but without any doubt, yes it is,' Eskra replied, taking refuge from the obvious in a longer sentence than she usually allowed past her lips. 'The blade's name is Isileth. Starsteel. Even the story got that part right. Think about it. Then tell me I'm wrong. If you dare.'

Bayrd thought about it, and didn't dare. The sword in the story, Greylady, had a name appropriate to high rank – or at least, aspirations that way. The historical name was more appropriate: *Isil-aleth*, 'iron of Heaven', 'starsteel'. Most of the named-blades of any lineage were like that, simple titles, descriptions of origin or function rather than anything more grandiose. They needed nothing more. Serej ar'Diskan's *taiken* Lethayr was just 'noble-steel', *aleth-eir*, and even the best known sword of all the old Alban legends, Erwan ar'Matan's blade Kelet, the name that every child had given to his favourite weed-slashing stick at one time or another, was called nothing more imposing than 'sharp-edge'. The legends lay in what was done by the sharp edge, the noble steel, and the men and women who wielded them, down all the long years from the forge.

Bayrd puzzled briefly over the coincidence of the Landmaster of Alba, and some possibly fictional character in a dubious and gloomy tale, sharing the same name for their sword; then he dismissed it as no more than another of those insertions made by a travelling storyman, adding something a little more up-to-date and authentic to his next telling of an unlikely yarn.

'Where is it?' he said eventually.

Eskra extended one long index finger and pointed it straight down. 'In the crypt beneath the old high citadel. Where else? Whether you believe the chronicles or the stories, after all the death around this place no one would be rash enough to take it away. Are you sure you want to?'

'Yes. Even if I had another choice.'

'Which you don't.'

'Exactly. Shall we go?'

'To the crypt?'

'Where else?'

'A girl can always hope. Even when it's a waste of time . . .'

*

She knew where to find the entrance to the crypt so easily that Bayrd almost asked her how; and how many times she had been up to Dunarat's ruins before the coercion of an armed escort forced her back this latest time. But he kept his mouth shut. For all her declarations of how safe and deserted the place was, she moved with a wariness that made Bayrd glad he had thought to bring his shortsword and his axe.

'Here,' she said, pointing. At first and even second glance, the place she indicated looked no different to any other cavern made by the fallen blocks of masonry lying beside or on top of one another. There were hundreds and maybe thousands of those scattered across the all too spacious site of the old fortress. How Eskra had ever found it, how she had even known the location of the citadel and thus where to start to look, was just one more mystery that only another wizard could understand. As an untrained and very amateur sorcerer, Bayrd didn't even try. Instead, when he peered at and into the cavern, he could even see where the sunlight reflected from the melt-shiny slab of solid stone that formed its rearmost wall. The place was only slighly deeper than the shelter they had just left, a shelter which last night had just been big enough for Bayrd and his gear and two horses. But then Eskra stooped, rummaged beneath the snow until she came up with a pebble, and lobbed it in a lazy underarm beneath the arch of stones and into the small cave. It curved only slightly in the air before coming down again, but just where sense suggested they would hear the clatter of its impact on the ground, it vanished without a sound.

The clatter, when it came that deceptive instant later, was hollower and more distant than it should have been, repeating and diminishing at short intervals in the unmistakable rhythm of something bouncing down a flight of steps, until it stopped or dropped beyond the range of hearing and the silence fell again.

'This isn't the funerary entrance,' said Eskra by way of explanation. 'Far too steep and narrow for people carrying a coffined body. The proper gate is out there somewhere. Choked by the roots of trees by now. Or collapsed completely. No-one knows exactly where. Even though they've been rummaging up here for a hundred years or more. Ghosts or no ghosts,' she added with a grin. 'The lure of Lord Ared's gold can be a wonderful anodyne for fear.'

'Gold, eh?'

'Forget it. There isn't any. The Old Ones were a practical people. Folk tend to forget that.' Another quick grin, the cheery flash of teeth that lit up her whole face just when he had grown accustomed to an expression of cool stillness. 'Why should they leave any treasure lying about the place? They didn't even leave the fortress standing. And enough years had passed for anything they didn't take away to have been found long since.' She unbuckled the flap of her satchel and delved inside for a moment – Bayrd could see the cloth or leatherbound spines of several elderly books – before she withdrew a wooden baton gripped firmly in one hand.

He looked at it at first with interest, and then with barely concealed disapproval. If that was a wizard's staff, it was a great deal less imposing than he had been led to expect. Instead of a great thing as tall as a spear, all cunningly graven with symbols of power – though he conceded that putting such a thing into a small satchel already crowded with books might have posed problems even to a wizard – it was just a slender, polished stave of blond wood no longer than his forearm, its only suggestion of patterning the dark brindle which ran with its grain, and an odd twist to the wood that suggested it had been spiralling around something as it grew. Eskra caught his expression and pursed her lips in feigned annoyance. 'You don't like it?' she said.

Bayrd shrugged one shoulder; it wasn't worth two. 'Let's just say I'm not impressed.'

'Tsk. Typical of a man. It's not the size that counts. It's what you can do with it.' She spoke no spell, but suddenly the little stave flared as bright and then brighter than the finest of lamps. 'Like that, for one. Now we can see where we're going.' Bayrd, still blushing from the deliberate innuendo even while he grinned inwardly at what might have prompted it, pulled the axe from his belt and moved to pass her, but Eskra waved him back. 'Very courteous and very protective,' she said. 'But I know the way. So this time at least, ladies first.'

She, and then rather too quickly the light that she carried, disappeared downwards and out of sight. Bayrd waited for a few seconds so that he wouldn't step on her heels, and then followed.

The first step, and then abruptly and all together the second, third and fourth brought home to him just how steep this staircase was, and as he fought with flailing arms to retain his balance and keep from tumbling the rest of the way to the bottom, he was heartily relieved that Eskra had gone first.

'Carefully now,' came her voice, already in so short a time well below him. 'The first few are very steep –' *Tell me something I don't know already*, though Bayrd, leaning back against the rock wall to get his breath back. '– But after that it levels out and gets easier.' *Thank you*, he thought, and grinned down into the darkness.

Once they had descended past the dangerously steep section, by which time Bayrd had come even more to appreciate the light glowing from Eskra's small spellstave, he drew level with her and looked around. 'They may have built the walls and towers above all this,' he said, 'but they can't have been digging out the cavern at the same time. It's too big. It would take more men than anyone could spare. This place must have been here already.'

'Well spotted,' said Eskra. 'It probably was. One good reason to put a fortress on top of it. The old lords of Elthan –' Bayrd couldn't help noticing that she made no mention of Prytenon or Cerenau, '– were no fools. They would take a natural feature like this one and put it to their advantage. A network of caverns like these must have been a real find.'

'A network?' said Bayrd, looking around him. Eskra's light, bright though it was, illuminated only those parts of the cave where they were standing. The rest was utter blackness.

'Yes. Network. And an extensive one. You might have guessed already.' She looked about her, and smiled slightly. 'I've been here before. This entire hill is a honeycomb. It's limestone, like most of the land around here. Right up to the Blue Mountains in the west. Good, solid rock. But that can cut it like a knife in cheese.' She gestured at a stream of water running down the cavern wall not far from where they stood. 'A damned slow knife and damned hard cheese. But given enough water and time it can cut, carve and hollow out the hills. Until you get somewhere like *this*.'

She raised the spellstave high overhead, and for just a few seconds its light drove away the darkness for as far as the eye could see. Moisture and crystal encrustations glittered back at them, a decoration for the walls of echoing vaults that could have served as feast-halls for hundreds. Long fangs of rock hung from the high ceilings or rose in spikes from the floor, and where they had met, and joined, and continued to grow, they reared up in sleek, gleaming columns. Wide, dark pools of water gave back the reflection over and over again, distorted now and then by slow concentric ripples from the drops that had been falling for uncounted centuries . . . until at last Eskra let the light die down and the long night return. 'And there might,' she said softly in the shadows, 'be even bigger caverns underneath the mountains.'

Bayrd digested that scrap of information in silence. Bigger than this . . .? It would be a place so vast that it could swallow half a town. Never mind building a fortress on top of it, a man could live guarded by the mountains themselves, the very walls of the world, and he could construct anything he pleased inside the caves, and never in his life run out of room.

Eskra broke into his thoughts again. 'Feel the air?' she said.

'It's cold,' said Bayrd. 'That's hard to miss.'

'And it never grows warm. This is only the second time that I've been here in winter. But I've been here in spring and the heat of high summer. It's never warmer. Never colder. A good place for storing your siege-supplies.' She snickered a wicked little laugh that ran echoing away into the dark. 'As well as your honoured relations.'

'At least it's not cold enough for the water to freeze.' Bayrd dabbled his fingers thoughtfully in the little stream without concern for what the water might do to the metal of his gauntlets.

'Just so. As I say, a gift to any fortress-builder. Somewhere for provisions, and a place where the years have carved huge cisterns filled with fresh water. Taste it – it's cold, but very good.'

Bayrd pushed his helmet back and let it hang between his shoulderblades from its straps, then leaned forward carefully to taste the water. Eskra was right, it was good; clean, fresh and sweet – although icy enough that his teeth ached from the single mouthful and his lips briefly lost all feeling. 'If Dunarat hadn't been destroyed,' he said, 'this would have been a place where fifty well-armed men could have held off an army.'

Eskra turned to him and grinned, one side of her face in shadow and the other bleached bone-white by the light beside it, the lines of her smile carved deep and black. 'Good man,' she said. 'History says one thing. The children's story says another. I suspect you'll find the truth hiding somewhere in the middle. Lord Ared was ambitious. Hence his marriage. They both agree on that, though they phrase it in different ways. He was popular and well-trusted. Otherwise no lord would ever have granted him the right to build a place like this. And then someone had second thoughts. The High Lord himself perhaps. Or one of his well-placed retainers suggested that a man with such ambition as Ared had displayed – and with a fortress that promised to be impregnable once its fortifications were complete – was too ambitious to remain alive. So they trumped up a charge and killed him.'

Bayrd nodded slowly. 'That would explain the wife and child.'

'Now you know something that I don't. It sounds nasty. But this whole subject is a nasty one. Tell me more.'

'It was a common enough practice long ago,' he began, then hesitated as he remembered an ugly incident eight years ago in Kalitzim. 'And maybe not so long ago at that. If you have reason for a blood-feud, well and good. If you have plenty of supporters willing to back you in law or in combat, even better. But when you defeat your enemy, kill his whole family down to the child that was born today. Children grow, and they learn the meaning of revenge, and you can never be secure while one of them is breathing.'

Eskra looked at him thoughtfully, and held the light a little higher as she judged his mood. Then she nodded, and smiled a little, a thin, sympathetic, understanding smile. 'And this is the man who called *me* ruthless. Truth has to be a little ruthless. Otherwise it gets softened from what people need to hear to no more than they want to hear.'

'I understand that duty well enough. When I'm not about my clan-lord's business, wandering the wilderness in wintertime looking for wizards, and hiding from lord's-men or fighting them –'

'– And rescuing young women,' added Eskra. 'I leave out almost falling down the stairs on top of them.'

'– I am Lord Gerin ar'Diskan's Bannerman and Companion.'

'I understand "bannerman" clearly enough. But the honorific form of the word "companion"? What does that mean?'

'I listen, and I don't repeat what I hear; I give him my opinions on matters where no one with anything to gain would dare; and I correct him when he can't see that he's wrong. It's an honourable duty, and one which carries much respect.'

'You tell the truth,' said Eskra with approval. 'You tell him what he needs to hear whether he wants to hear it or not. And you don't sweeten what you say. Yes?'

'More or less, yes.'

'Then if that's your honourable function, with all the rights and privileges that I presume go with it –'

'Less of those than you think,' Bayrd pointed out, though sounding cheerful enough about the fact that Eskra could surely tell how little it mattered to him.

'So. But do you tell good lies or bad lies? Or are you ever permitted to tell lies at all?'

'Truth is sometimes difficult, but preferable. Though every now and again,' he grinned quickly to cover a sudden feeling of unease at the way her line of questioning was trending, 'it can get skewed a little. Or small, unimportant parts of it fall out.'

'Good. Then tell me something. Just as you would tell it to your lord as his honoured Companion. Without skewing, even slightly, and with all the parts in place. What do your people really think of sorcery and the Art Magic? Behind any smiles of welcome, what will they really think of *me*?'

Though it was dazzling him a little, Bayrd was grateful for the brightness of the light. It turned his face to black and white; prevented any shameful blush or pallor being visible; and gave him a reason to turn his head aside while he tried to shape a truthful answer that was not also a hurtful one. This was the one question he had been secretly dreading, so much that he had forced it to the back of his mind and paid it no further heed – so that now it had taken him completely unprepared. That she had asked him how he told his lies was no help now; for all he was aware, her training in the Art Magic would let her hear a lie even before he spoke it. He wanted to say something encouraging, but he could not. His own honour, his courtesy towards Eskra, his respect for – no, dammit, his *love* for her just wouldn't let him. Better she know now. And in the event he had no need to say a word.

Eskra nodded. 'The hesitation and the silence tells me every-thing,' she said. 'I'll help your people. I'll accept the gold they offer me. And then I'll leave this country. One thing. I'll need enough to take me far away from here. My dear countrymen can be as cruel as children in the most ordinary circumstances. The way they deal with traitors and renegades . . .' she stumbled over the words, as if realising for the first time how much it now applied to her, '. . . is even less pleasant.'

'The Houses will honour you,' said Bayrd, speaking slowly and bitting off each word as though it were something solid. 'They will honour you, and the families will show you respect.'

'Easy to say. Why should they? Who will make them? You?'

'I will. My clan will. My name will.'

'How? Why? Bayrd —' it was only the second time that she had used his name, just as he awkwardly avoided using hers until granted permission to do so, '— Bayrd, why should they do these things?'

'Don't you know?'

'I know, I *think* I know. But I have to hear the words spoken aloud.'

Bayrd took a long breath in a useless attempt to ease the nervous flutter in his stomach, and swallowed down a throat gone dry. 'I offer you a name,' he said finally, 'to shield you from what fools might say. My name. My hand. My heart. All of them are yours, to accept or to refuse.'

'But not to return to you?'

'I still have my honour. But my heart is in your hands now, and it was freely given.'

The light surrounding the spellstave dimmed and wavered as her concentration shifted. How much of this she had already guessed, Bayrd didn't know. He didn't want to know. That ignorance might, just might, make a refusal hurt less. Then the light flared up again. Eskra had come to a decision.

'I refuse nothing,' she said, and though her face was impossible to read in the harsh illumination from the spellstave, her eyes were huge and glistening despite its glare. 'But I accept nothing. Yet. We have known each other for just three hours. That is not enough on which to base a lifetime. Your heart is safe in my keeping, Bayrd ar'Talvlyn. And your honour, too.' She gave him a watery little smile. 'At least now I know. That should make the same question easier to ask in the future.'

'Somewhat easier to hear, at least,' said Bayrd, forcing a weak laugh and relieved that the tremor in his chest had not communicated to his voice. She was right, of course. Light of Heaven, why was she always right! Three hours of casual and businesslike acquaintance was nothing like enough. He and Mahaut had known each other for . . . oh, three whole days, before they finally and cheerfully acknowledged what all their friends had seen as inevitable from the very start. 'Until the future, then,' he said, and gave her the cold, precise salute reserved for Commanders whose orders were unpleasant but correct.

And after that, with all distractions carefully set aside, they both went looking for the sword.

For all that she had called it the citadel's crypt, there were no graves down here, and no memorial stones or cinerary urns. Dunarat-hold had not existed long enough for anyone to be interred with ceremony, and neither grief nor anger would have permitted the Lord Ared, Elyan his wife and their child to be buried here. Mother and child would have gone home to their family vault – and Ared, like as not, would have fed the crows. If you believed the history.

So why his sword had been put down here and left, and never stolen in all those years, was a question without an answer. That made sense only if you believed the children's tale instead. A wizard-forged blade which had caused such tragedy was not a weapon any right-thinking warrior would want to carry at his side, much less entrust with the guarding of his honour and his life.

If it had been a sword of more common make, then there was no reason why it should still be here – or why it should have been concealed in the first place. No matter what the stories said, an ordinary sword was like a poorly trained horse, willing to work for whoever put it to use and recognising no one master above all the rest. The first man to take it after Ared's death would have kept it, worn it and used it – unless there was some reason why not. The only reason was in the story, not the history.

'There,' said Eskra, pointing.

'There', at first, was no more than a crack in the rock – at least until Bayrd looked a little closer. Then he saw something gleaming down in the darkness, a long bright shape that seemed to rise towards him, up through the shadows within the crevice like some slim fish coming to the surface of a murky pond. He took a wary step backwards and gave Eskra a thoughtful sidelong look. 'Did *you* hide it like this?'

She shook her head. 'Not I. This is how I found it. And how I chose to leave it.'

Bayrd stared suspiciously at the slender, glinting outline, still little more than a band of reflected light. 'I don't blame you,' he said. 'But how did you find it in the first place? It can't have been easy.'

Eskra looked at the crevice and what lay within it, then squared her shoulders, evidently deciding that there was no right way to say what she intended. 'I found it because I was searching for hidden things.' She saw the silent, sardonic question in Bayrd's eye. 'Yes. There are certain charms that can counter deliberate concealment.'

For some reason she seemed embarrassed to admit that she had used any such thing. Perhaps even among practitioners of the Art Magic, such spells were regarded as cheating. 'But why this was hidden and nothing else, I don't know. And rest assured, there's nothing else. These caverns spread for a considerable distance underneath the site of the old fortress, but I've seen them all. And they're empty. Except for the sword. Now take what you came for and let's go!'

Bayrd reached out for the sword, and it was truly a sword now, not just a gleam in the darkness. Even then he wasn't entirely convinced that he could touch it, because it still had the shimmering, insubstantial look of something reproduced by a conjurer's trick in a very non-magical half-silvered mirror. He had watched such entertainments, been the victim of such tricks and seen them played on others, and so was half-anticipating as his hand went out that his fingertips would bump against a smooth, slick surface.

They passed instead into a strange layer of chill that he could feel even through the leather and steel of his armoured gauntlet. It was like, and yet unlike, dipping his hand into another of the icy underground streams, and the feel of the sword, when his fingers closed at last around its hilt, was so ordinary as to be almost an anticlimax.

'Maybe it was hidden by the wizard who made it,' he said over his shoulder, half teasing and half serious. Eskra didn't reply. She was standing to one side, watching and waiting for something – or nothing – to happen. And nothing did.

There was no sense of it being held in place, not even by the slight grip of the sprung-metal clips that were used in the Kalitzim barracks. But there was a strange, slight, clinging resistance, as though the darkness in the crevice itself was composed of something like syrup, a pressure against which he had to pull. So Bayrd pulled, and the sword came free.

'I've heard of swords in trees, and swords in stones,' he told Eskra. 'But never before of swords in . . . honey?' That was what it had felt like. Honey, thickened by cold. He glanced down at the scabbard, almost expecting to see the glistening filaments trailing back to the fissure as they would have trailed from a spoon to the honey-jar. But the scabbard was clean, and the hilt was clean, and when he eased a handspan of it out into the light, the blade was clean as well.

It gleamed at him, with just that dark grey glimmer under the shine that the story – but not the history – had mentioned. The shape was that of a modern longsword, at least to within the last hundred years or so, and only the hilt-furniture was dated. That narrow, straight crossguard was long out of style, replaced by the deep curve which was popular now. But if this sword had been built in the way of other *taikenin* like it, that was easily changed. Bayrd examined the pommel, and found that his guess was right. It was the securing-piece which held the grip and the guard and the locking-collar at the scabbard tight and snug against the long tang.

Brief pressure on the metal holding-peg at the end of the grip, and a few quick twists of the cunningly tapped and threaded pommel, soon released all the parts of the hilt so that what Bayrd held in his hands was no longer a sword, but a scabbard with a blade in it. As he had hoped, there was writing on the tang. Most good swordsmiths signed their work, and whoever had made this was no exception.

'Forged was I of iron Heaven-born,' it read, in sweeping uncial letters so neatly indented into the unpolished steel of the tang that they looked to have been written with a pen, not carved with a chisel. 'Uelan made me,' the inscription continued. 'I am Isileth.'

'So that much is true,' he said, almost to himself. Then he turned to look at Eskra. 'The name, I mean. But the starsteel is true as well.' And that was in the story, along with the wizard, but no mention of either had been made in the more formal chronicle of events. Bayrd didn't say that aloud, but from the crooked smile on her face, there was no need of it.

'The truth of most things is somewhere in the middle,' she reminded him. 'I said so before. A little piece from here. A little piece from there. A little fact, and a little imagination to give it a sparkle. Now. Can we get out of this place?'

It was difficult to keep track of time in the caverns, but Eskra plainly thought that they had wasted enough of it. Bayrd replaced the pieces of Isileth's hilt and carefully, almost respectfully, hooked the *taiken*'s scabbard to the empty place on his weapon-belt. Then he looked about him, but there was nothing more to see – except for the fortress he saw in his mind's eye, rebuilt and restored to its ancient splendour.

His fortress.

It would have the ar'Talvlyn clan Colours fluttering bravely from its gates and walls and towers, but it would be his. Bayrd's duty had been less arduous than he had feared. There had been risks and hardships: no one could expect to travel through an unknown, hostile country in the brutal depths of winter and come out entirely unscathed at the end of it. Or say rather, entirely unchanged. In the past weeks, Bayrd's views had altered from what they were, so that he looked at his own folk and the people of the provinces through different eyes. But apart from that, he had been lucky, very lucky indeed. And – he glanced briefly at Eskra – there had been compensations he could never have imagined.

So far as he knew he was the first Alban to journey so far north into the province of Elthan and come back alive. Though that part of it still lay before him, he felt strangely unconcerned. He had completed the task he had been set and he had accomplished it with honour, so that it would not be unreasonable to presume that certain tokens of appreciation might be forthcoming as a conse-quence. It was seldom now that lords or Overlords asked faithful retainers to name their heart's desire as fair reward for duty done, but if Albanak or Gerin did so, Bayrd knew he would be torn between Eskra and the fortress of Dunarat.

With the fortress and its lands in his possession, he might stand a better chance of winning the woman he wanted as his wife. And if not, well . . . Well, he had married without wealth before.

And an optimistic man could always dream.

Horselord

BAYRD WAS STILL dreaming six months later when he eased his mare Yarak from a canter to a walk, then reined her gently to a standstill and dismounted. It had been more than half a year since they had last been here, standing side by side on the rise that overlooked the valley and the forest-bordered lake, with the vast dark bulk of the ruined fortress of Dunarat hunched and brooding on the ridge above. The sun was shining warmly and the snow would not return for another five months or so, but otherwise the scene was much the same. There was one difference: people were calling the place 'Dunrath' nowadays. As dealings with the ordinary people of the country grew more frequent and more friendly, it had become fashionable to speak Alban in the slurred fashion common to Elthan and Prytenon. And typically, the more the elder clan-lords fulminated against this corruption of the language, the more their younger warriors persisted. Mere age no longer had quite the same weight of authority as had once been the case.

Bayrd grinned at that, an expression without much humour in it. Much else had happened in so short a time, and first, most memorable – and finally most galling – had been his return in triumph as the hero who had found Albanak-*arluth*'s much-needed wizard. It was a triumph that had rapidly turned sour.

There had been some who had never expected him to return; who had hoped so, loudly and to the approval of others. They were stiff-necked old men for the most part, steeped in tradition, who regarded the Art Magic as a sin and defamation worse than murder. But others had been his own age, all too plainly jealous of his preferment, envying not just his success and survival, but even the sword he brought back. They were more than willing to use the completion of this dangerous and honourable duty as a proof that he was somehow unworthy of respect.

Bringing back a sorcerer to help against the Pryteneks was one thing, they claimed – people with that sort of mind never did learn to grasp the subtle difference between the terms – but bringing back a sorcerer who was a woman, and then making no secret of his plans to marry her when she finally agreed to his repeated proposals, was something else again. That she had refused him for more than six months now should have told him something. But he was ar'Talvlyn, of a clan notoriously stubborn and patient, and he would wear down her resistance at last. Though why he wanted to bother was more than they could understand . . .

People had said as much in his hearing, and in hers. Better by far, they claimed, if he had studied sorcery and the Art Magic himself, since at least he was ar'Talvlyn, of an *Alban* clan, and one of good repute despite all its faults. That had made him laugh grimly at what they would say if he ever put their suggestion to the test. She, however, was only a renegade foreign bitch who worked against her own people and did it for gold instead of honour.

That had stopped his laughter, and started the fighting. For direct insults, if for nothing else, clan ar' Talvlyn's patience had limits, and Bayrd's had already been reached. He had promised Eskra his name as a defence against the words of such idiots, and until she accepted that name and all else with it, the longsword Isileth had made a more than adequate substitute.

Bayrd fought five duels in as many days. They were duels in which, with sour memories of Serej ar'Diskan, he took care not to kill or even cripple his opponents and because of that restraint was almost killed himself. At the end of it all, he was simply given a wide berth. The fights might not have restored him to a position worthy of respect, but they at least had the advantage of putting a curb on unruly tongues. The talking hadn't stopped, he was sure of it, and there was little he could do to make it stop, short of killing everyone who even looked sideways in his direction. But it had gone behind his back again, and as a substitute for common courtesy that would have to do.

But those duels – and especially the reason for them – had other, unexpected repercussions. He could still remember how, at the time of the ar'Diskan affair, the other members of his clan had crowded around him and praised his boldness for standing up to the arrogant old clan-lord and accepting his challenge. It seemed that defending the clan name was all very well, but defending anything that clan disapproved of was not well at all. He had forgotten, or not cared to remember, how they had ostracised him for almost half a year after he had exchanged polite words with *Hospodar* Skarpeya. This was worse.

Ar'Talvlyn might well have been known as a clan of good repute, but that reputation had not extended to good manners, much less tolerance. Even though they had wrapped their opinions of Eskra in courtly phrases to blunt the crude edge – or disguise the crude meaning – of what they said, that meaning had been plain enough. Bayrd had taken two days of it; then he lost his temper, and one of his cousins lost an ear. As Companion and Bannerman to a high-clan lord, Bayrd had the right of challenge against anyone he pleased, even his own clan; but within an hour of the incident with Askel's ear, he was not a member of that clan any more. They had summoned him before a hastily convened council, and would have stripped him in the old phrases 'of name and fame, of house and hearth, of food and fire and family' – except that Bayrd invoked the privileges of his rank and did it first.

It had only occurred to him much later that he had acted much like Lord Ared, the tragic hero of the story Youenn Kloatr had told him on that winter afternoon in the village of Redmer. What Ared had merely threatened, as a means of gaining the acceptance of his wife, Bayrd had taken to its lawful conclusion. He had repudiated clan, and House, and family – and when in outrage they had forbidden him to call himself by their name again, he had assumed the Elthanek form instead, smiled maliciously, and defied anyone to take exception. The clan ar'Talvlyn might have proven themselves petty and small-minded enough to be an example to the rest of Alba, but they were not possessed of a death-wish. Neither then nor later did he hear a word about it. That throwing away of all his own past, and any heroisms that the clan's Book of Years had recorded, was an act which had shocked some.

It had surprised others not at all, and even gained the support of a few who followed his lead. For the most part they were the younger *kailinin* who deliberately spoke with the local accent, who felt leashed-in by the traditions of their elders, and who had been quietly insisting that old cusoms were for old times and old places. In a new time and a new Alba, it was time for new customs

– or at least different ones. Bayrd found himself playing the part of a hero all over again. This time, he hoped, it would last long enough for him to add a little credit to his newly chosen name of Talvalin.

He gazed at Dunarat up on the hill, Dunrath as he supposed he had better start calling it, and smiled a small smile to himself. They were this far north so fast, and without any of the strenuous fighting that it should have entailed, because Yakez the High Lord of Elthan was behaving as an ally. Well, not quite as an ally, but certainly as a man well-disposed to the Albans.

Or should that have been, ill-disposed to Lord Gelert of Prytenon.

Almost before Bayrd and Eskra got back to the safety of 'invader's country' there had been rumours of war between them, rumours that had swiftly become fact. Nothing had been confirmed as to the reason behind it, but the fact remained that in the early spring – so early as to be more like the dying days of winter – barely into what was acceptable campaigning season and with the Albans still firmly entrenched on his doorstep, Gelert had made sudden and undeclared war on his neighbour.

Bayrd suspected he knew why. After that fight at the gates of Dunrath-hold, Eskra had warned him to recover his arrows. Even though it had taken a dangerously long time to recover the distinctive Alban signalling arrows from where they had fallen far out in the ruins, he had cleared away everything that suggested anyone other than Gelert's and Yakez's man had been present. But he had done more than that. He had arranged matters so that the two groups of lord's-men appeared to have quarrelled and killed one another.

It was not a memory he was proud of, since it had required hacking at some of the corpses with their own weapons to conceal the marks of his arrows. None of them had been carrying bows, and those small, neat punctures would have provoked far too many questions. Close inspection by a skilled military surgeon might have uncovered the deception, but somehow Bayrd suspected that if there was a group of Lord Yakez's retainers riding bloody-spur back to the ruins, they would not have waited for medical assistance. Suspicion and the mutual antipathy of each lord for the other had done the rest.

So here they were in Elthan, and their march-camp was set up near Redmer village where Youenn the headman had expressed what looked like honest delight at seeing Bayrd again, along with poorly hidden surprise that he was still all in one piece. And despite the war between Prytenon and Elthan, despite the fact that they were by no means finished with Lord Gelert, two high-clan lords of Alba were once more ready and willing to kill each other over a piece of land.

The land in question was that surrounding Dunrath, to Bayrd's annoyance; and one of the lords was his own. Gerin ar'Diskan had laid claim to it on the strength of its having been discovered by his Companion and Bannerman, while Vanek ar'Kelayr, that notoriously quarrelsome man, was contesting his claim on the very same grounds.

Bayrd's daydreams about that land and its fortress had come to nothing after all. Despite Lord Albanak's praise on his return and the apparent success with which Eskra had turned aside all further sorcerous attacks – though she confessed to him privately that Gelert's wizards, if he had any left, had not made a single attempt – they had generated nothing more solid than an old-style granting of first choice in loot or plunder after battle. Gerin ar'Diskan had suggested that, and it only confirmed something that Bayrd had suspected since before he rode away. Gerin was cheap.

There was small chance of his getting rich on plunder in this war, the award itself cost nothing but a sheet of parchment and some ink – and whatever quantity of air had been required to read its rolling phrases aloud. Though not even the Overlord had the right to interfere in matters between a clan-lord and his Companion, Bayrd thought he had sensed an odd feeling of disapproval from Albanak at such a tightfisted display. Not that it would do him any good. This was a fact of life. Some lords were generous to their retainers, most were not. Generosity in the form of rank and status drained no silver from their coffers, and until this country was quelled and settled, being given any of it as a token of appreciation was unlikely. The land was for the lords and Heads of House, and anyone else had to wait patiently for what crumbs were left.

Well, ar'Talvlyns were good at being patient, and Bayrd saw no reason why a solitary Talvalin should be any different. He had been waiting for a long time for a lot of things, and one more wouldn't hurt. At least he still had his friends, Marc and Mevn. It was just as well. Without House ar'Dru he wouldn't have had a roof over his head this past half-year, not since clan ar'Talvlyn threw him out. Even though he had a bed to sleep in, it wasn't Mevn's. It amused her, in a sharp-edged way.

'Who are you trying to impress with this great strength of will?' she had said that first night, sitting at the foot of his bed but making no attempt to get into it. 'Me? The Elthanek? Or the gossiping tongues of the average Alban – which are going to wag no matter what happens between us?'

'I want to marry the woman,' said Bayrd, grateful for being able to say that to someone unshockable.

'So I've heard. And I've heard she's not interested. How many proposals now?' She grinned at him to take the sting from the words, though it didn't work as well as it might. 'Those tongues do wag, don't they? The lady's a difficult fish to land. You should change your bait. Duels and chastity aren't working . . .'

The first meeting between Eskra and Mevn ar'Dru had been something worth watching – from a safe distance. Marc had been given a solid elbow in the ribs when he leaned in and offered Bayrd odds of twenty to one that his sister wouldn't end the day the same shape or species as she had got out of bed.

For all her protestations that he was a free agent so far as his private life was concerned, the initial reaction from Mevn had been pure claws-out green-eyed jealousy. At the same time there had been fascination, interest, curiosity – and the definite feeling that no one who shared her lover could be all bad, wizard and foreigner or not.

Eskra didn't enlighten her on the depth or otherwise of their relationship. Indeed, she had very little to say at all; the only depth that concerned her was the one she was so far out of. Bayrd's attempts at an explanation of Alban life and culture had fallen far short of what was required, and other than setting up the necessary wards and spell-circles, she had shyly tended to stay near her quarters in the Overlord's household. It surprised and disturbed him to think that the brisk, tough, self-assured woman he had met outside Dunrath had been lost somewhere on the way home.

Bayrd sighed, and tried to push his private problems aside. There were other matters requiring his attention, and one of them was what had brought him to the hillside above the lake. Albanak had sent him, not to admire the view or even lust wistfully after the fortress which dominated it, but to examine the lie of the land. Or more correctly, the lie of the lake.

Vanek ar'Kelayr had been growing increasingly abusive over the matter of his property dispute with Lord Gerin, so much so that the Overlord had been forced to step in and act as a mediator. The last thing Albanak wanted was for an inter-clan feud to break out so deep into territory that had once been allied to Lord Gelert of Prytenon, especially a dispute over the division of land. Lord Yakez of Elthan was likely to take a dim view of anyone laying claim to what was after all still his land, and alliances could be renewed too quickly for comfort. The destruction of a sizable number of Alban *kailinin* by his erstwhile ally, and thus without loss to himself, would be of considerable advantage to Gelert.

Albanak's position was not an enviable one. For all his rank and status and the respect that went with it, he had very little real power, and only just enough men among his retainers and household troops to back up the power he did have. The Albans had dealt with kings too often to be ruled by one, or to grant any man among them kingly powers of decision without the approval of his high-clan lords. The Overlord could act as judge in this quarrel, but he could not save everyone time, expense and trouble by simply weighing up the merits of the case in his own mind and then deeding the land to one side or the other. That might easily lead to the losing party claiming bribery or favouritism, and declaring feud against *him*.

In place of the power he lacked, Albanak-*arluth* had developed cunning to something approaching an abstract art-form. When the land-claim first grew heated, Bayrd was summoned to the Overlord's pavilion, a large, starkly elegant officer's tent which was another acquisition from the barracks at Kalitzim. He had arrived, and was already rising from making his obeisance, when one of the senior *hanen-vlethanek* Archivists came bustling up with a somewhat older book than the one he wrote in nowadays. This one was open, Bayrd learned a few seconds later, at the page where, almost two full seasons past, the old man had noted

Bayrd's commentary on his first journey north into the province of Elthan. Indicating a few closely written lines with the butt of his pen, he handed the book to Albanak and then settled down to note what was about to happen now.

'There is some small mention made of racing, Bayrd-*eir*,' the Overlord said. 'In what connection – recreational, sporting, or competitive?'

'Sporting, Lord. There was gambling on the outcome of each race.'

'So.' Albanak glanced at the page again, tapping at occasional words as though he thought them poorly chosen. 'And was this a tradition? A custom of the country, perhaps?'

Bayrd gave him a weak grin and as much of a shrug as was proper. 'Lord,' he said, 'it was half a year ago, and this was just part of a child's story . . .'

'Remember, please.' There was no severity in the command, which made a pleasant change. Lord Albanak could be gravel-throated when he chose. 'This may be more important than you realise.'

'Then yes, Lord,' said Bayrd after a few moments of careful thought. It had been something to do with Lord Ared and the fortress. Something to do with the acquisition of land . . . and suddenly the slant of the questioning became quite clear, so clear that Bayrd silently cursed himself for being so slow. 'Yes indeed. One could make a case that it was traditional.'

He didn't elaborate any further until he was asked, for the very simple reason that having forgotten most of what he had been told, he needed time in which to make something up. But that was when Lord Albanak decided that the question of the land around Dunrath would be settled by a race. A boat-race. Greatly daring, Bayrd asked him why.

The Overlord's cool consideration settled on him again. 'Don't presume too much on your position with Lord ar'Diskan,' said Albanak in tones of mild reproof; but the man was plainly so relieved to find a way out of his present difficult position that he was speaking the lines of his accepted role rather than being truly irritated. 'And since he is not merely your liege lord, but one of the disputants, I ought not . . . But you deserve an answer, since you provided mine.'

With a quick wave of his hand, Albanak indicated that the Archivist should cease his scribbling for the time being. 'Firstly, I would as soon this matter was kept from the ears of High Lord Yakez.' Bayrd grinned crookedly and nodded understanding. 'Quite so. He might not take kindly to our dividing up his province . . . Anyway. The boat-race. Yes. The onus of winning or losing in a boat-race, you see, does not rely on any one man – except perhaps for the men who choose who will row each boat. And I intend, in this instance, that each clan-lord in this wretched altercation selects the rowers from among his own . . .'

'. . . Own household retainers.'

Albanak's address to the assembled crowd was almost word for word what he had told Bayrd in private two days before, except for his more disapproving references to the case. 'The race will begin at Lord Gyras ar'Dakkur's command, from the southern-most point of the lake, and will end here before me at the north. The first to strike shore will be adjudged the winner, and his claim to the lands and territories in question will be granted. My lords, I wish equal luck to both of you. Go now. Race with speed, race with strength, and above all else, race with honour.'

It was a holiday atmosphere in that armed camp, mostly generated by men, though there were some women warrior-archers as well. Bayrd was sorry that more of the women and children had not come with them to the north. But it had been considered unsafe, and only a few were here.

Mevn and Eskra were among them; Mevn having refused to be left behind under any circumstances, and Eskra as part of the Overlord's household in case Gelert of Prytenon should try any sorcerous tricks. They were somewhere in the crowd, and Bayrd had already seen a score or so of the villagers from Redmer, no doubt profiting mightily from selling the beer and foodstuffs they had been carrying. He grinned briefly at that; they were probably covering wagers as well. Old Youenn wasn't the man to let such an opportunity go by, and it had been the same, more or less, all the way up their route of march from Erdhaven and the coast. It was ironic, and only grew more so the more he saw of it: the peasants concealed their goods and fled in terror from their own lords and supposed defenders, but came out to meet the Alban warriors who had invaded their country. Invaders or not, their reputation for honourable fair dealing carried more weight than the fact that they were the enemy.

Bayrd led Yarak off to one side, and saw the little mare safely into a paddock well away from the milling people before sauntering down to the lakeshore. The two contesting lords and their chosen supporters had already galloped off, and the next time they would appear would be in the long, narrow boats he had seen brought to the lake earlier that morning. They were rakish things like infant warships, with high prows and sternposts and a row of oar-benches along each side of the slim hull. Bayrd didn't know where they had come from, or who had provided them, and he regarded someone's claim that they were just fishing-boats from the lake with some doubt. They might have been, but they looked too elegant for such workaday vessels. Had the Overlord not been set against Yakez of Elthan knowing what this was about, he could almost have believed that Albanak had borrowed a pair of pleasure craft.

And maybe he had. The man was devious enough.

Another gaggle of men and women on horseback cantered off towards the far end of the lake. They would be planning to ride alongside the speeding boats, shouting encouragement – it was scarcely courteous to shout anything else – or simply watching the race. Bayrd had no intention of doing anything so energetic. He would watch the boats when they came into view, and not before. Until then, he planned to find one of Youenn Kloatr's enterprising villagers and discover what beer they had this time. And if he met up with Eskra, or Mevn – or even both of them together – so much the better.

He met up with Marc instead.

'I would never have believed it,' said ar'Dru as they shared a pot of pale golden wheat beer, shot with green tints from an infusion of woodruff. 'My sister and your lady, walking arm in arm and chattering like old friends.'

'It sounds like a good thing.' Bayrd grabbed at the beer as it went by.

'Good?' Marc choked on a laugh that had encountered a swallow of beer halfway down. 'Speak for yourself. She's only my sister of course, but I still wouldn't want Mevn talking about me to any other woman.'

'At least they're talking. Eskra's been too quiet of late.'

'A woman can never be –' Marc started to say, then thought better of it. 'You're really very fond of her.'

'I love her,' said Bayrd simply. 'You know that. You both do.'

'Does she? Bayrd-*ain*, this one-sided affair has gone on for – what? – seven months?'

'Six. And it might go on for another six. She's not Vitya ar'Diskan, if that's what you're hinting at.' Frustration, annoyance, concern, disappointment . . . All of those emotions and more were so mixed up in Bayrd's words and the thoughts which had prompted them that he doubted he could have singled out one of them for particular notice.

'Few women are.' The thankful relief in his voice was so obvious that Bayrd's mood shattered and he laughed out loud. 'That's better.' Marc recovered the beer-pot and stared in dismay at its contents. 'There's a hole in this thing,' he said, 'and I don't mean the one at the top.'

'We need more, that's all.'

'That little fellow with the barrel is just over there.' Marc signalled frantically until he managed to get an answering wave from the beer-seller. 'We'll wait for him.' Then he studied Bayrd for a moment. 'It might be that she wasn't comfortable in Erdhaven. That she's just glad to be home.'

'This is just where she lived. I don't think it was ever her home. But it could be.'

'Meaning . . .?'

'Meaning that it's pretty countryside. When it's not under four feet of snow.'

'In other words, mind your own business. But did you ever tell her about you? About –' Marc made a fist with the index and little fingers extended, '– you know. *Bzzt!*'

'Somehow I was never able to steer the conversation around to it,' said Bayrd drily. '*Bzzt*, yourself.'

Marc ar'Dru grinned, and as the beer-seller came by he held out the pot to be filled. 'Don't you mean, go and –'

'Ssh! Listen! The race has started.'

The faint, distant sound of a long cavalry trumpet came floating over the water and through the muttering voices of five hundred-odd people. Some of them very odd indeed, thought Bayrd callously. There was a slow, general surge downward towards the water, but Bayrd and Marc made their way through the fringes of the crowd towards where Overlord Albanak and several of his high-clan lords were seated on camp chairs, shaded from the sun by an awning made up of all their banners. Keo ar'Lerutz glanced in their direction and inclined his head politely; both of the younger men sent a very proper salute in reply. It was hardly surprising that he was here; his reputation for ruthless impartiality was both proverbial, and slightly frightening because of it. When matters came to judgment, Lord ar'Lerutz would be as fair – and as cold and as unswayed by any emotion – as the edge of a razor.

And then they waited. And waited. And waited some more. The lake was not as long as some, but it was just long enough, that a proper level of tension and excitement built up before the first shout of 'There! There they are!'

It was a stage-perfect ending to any contest: the two distant specks burst suddenly from a bank of warm-weather haze hanging low to the water, each one rimmed with a white collar of foam from its plunging bow and frantically-beating oars. As they drew steadily closer, the sharper-eared could hear the drumming hoofbeats of each crew's supporters, their yells and cheers, and finally even the squeak and rattle of the oars against their thole-pins. After that nothing could be heard, for the entire crowd on the shore burst into a single roar of excitement, enough to drive the boats ashore by sheer force of noise alone.

They surged forward in a final effort, running together still, neither gaining on the other, and the two prows gouged into the coarse shingle beach so close together that the double crunch of their impact was a single sound. Men fell from their benches at the sudden jolt; oars broke; a rush of foam-streaked water rolled up the shoreline and soaked into the grass.

And the judges looked from face to face in bafflement at which one of them would dare to make a decision. When not even the contending lords were able to stake their honour on a claim that they had landed first, one by one the heads of all within earshot turned towards Lord ar'Lerutz. He would know, and his respect for justice was such that his verdict could not be regarded as other than fair. The old clan-lord sat still and silent for so long that the crowd began to shuffle its feet impatiently. At last he straightened up, looked at them with mild disapproval, glanced once at each of the lords still standing on the decks of their respective boats, and bowed his head to Albanak-*arluth*.

'Together,' he said. 'There is no question of it. They struck land together. The race is a draw.'

'My Lord,' said Vanek ar'Kelayr as politely as he could manage despite a face reddened by sun and excitement and anger, 'this race cannot be drawn. There must be a winner.'

'And a loser,' said Gerin ar'Diskan with a pointed glare at his rival.

Old Lord ar'Lerutz studied them as though they were some odd, unpleasant form of aquatic creature which had crawled up from the water and started to query his existence and function in life. He was not accustomed to having his judgments questioned by anyone. 'As there was neither winner nor loser,' he said severely, 'this race has *been* drawn.'

'But my lord . . . !' Lord Gerin ar'Diskan was ready to argue the point, though sensibly he shut up before that.

Ar'Lerutz shifted on his chair and fixed first one and then the other with a long, slow stare. 'If you want to see it, the answer is simple enough. Use horses to tow your boats back to the start line, then row another race. With,' and there was no contradicting that tone of voice, 'with the same crews. You may add one extra man. But no more than one. And I suggest you agree on evidence of victory that is somewhat less ambiguous. Let us say, the first man to set hand on the shore. Proceed.'

And a moment later, Bayrd heard his name being called.

'I want you to be my extra crewman,' said Lord Gerin, scrambling out of the boat so that a pair of horses could start dragging it back down to where Lord ar'Dakkur was waiting to hear word of a result.

'My lord? Me? In that? My lord, I've never rowed a boat in my life! This is hardly the time for me to risk learning. You would lose –'

'I don't want you to row, Bayrd-*eir*. But I might need you to . . .' He glanced from side to side, and saw Marc ar'Dru standing not quite far enough away, with an expression of imbecilic disinterest on his face that would not have fooled a blind man. 'Walk with me.' Gerin plucked at Bayrd's sleeve and led him away from the crowd, and the ears of the crowd.

'That old fool,' said Gerin ar'Diskan with a disdainful toss of his head towards Lord ar'Lerutz, 'wants no ambiguity this time. If I have to, I'll provide him with proof of my winning that even he can't deny. But I can't tell you yet. Not even now. I might not need it, and then the fewer know, the better.'

'How many know, my lord?'

'One. Myself. And that's enough for now. But I may give you an order during the race. You will obey that order without question.' That was an order in itself.

'Yes, my lord,' Bayrd said obediently.

'Your Word of Binding on it.'

A quick flash of resentment at this lack of trust shot through Bayrd. Normally a man's promise was good enough. But he nodded all the same. 'My Word on it.'

'Good. Then we had best get to the boats. And remember, I intend to win.'

Mystified, and more than a little unsettled, Bayrd Talvalin followed his lord down to the boat and the patient horses waiting in their harness.

Every time the oars dug at the water the rowing-boat bucked like an unbroken colt, and each time Bayrd staggered until he learned to flex with each jolting, irregular motion rather than try to brace himself against it. For men who had just completed this same course less than an hour before, Gerin's crew seemed to have lost none of their strength. If this was how they rowed when they were tired, then Light of Heaven! how much more had this cockleshell lurched to and fro when they were fresh?

Bayrd hated it. The movement wasn't regular enough to start him feeling queasy yet, but it affected him in other ways. His knees and ankles and the muscles of his belly hurt, from trying to wrench himself back to balance every time the deck rose or fell or pitched in some unforeseen direction. His wrists hurt, from the repeated shocks of grabbing things when keeping his balance became a lost cause. And his shins hurt, from being hacked again and again by the dozens of unnecessary wooden protuberances sticking out at odd angles from the hull.

If he felt like this after only ten minutes, then what state would he be in at the end of a race which last time had lasted almost half an hour?

Lord ar'Kelayr's boat was running as level as it had done the last time, less than two lengths to their left. As Bayrd glanced over to check its progress, staggering slightly when turning his head affected his whole balance, Vanek ar'Kelayr looked at him, worked his jaws and spat copiously across the gunwale in their direction. The insult was blatant, and yet if called on it, the excuse was just as obvious: in a race like this a man gets spray and water in his mouth, now doesn't he . . .?

Bayrd looked away and fought his anger back to calm. He had duelled a high-clan lord once in his life already, and doing so again would start to look like some sort of pattern for those with eyes to see such things. Eyes that saw them whether they were there or not, coupled to mouths to which the word 'ambitious' came as easily as breath. Ahead of him, Gerin ar'Diskan swayed with the motion of the boat, moving with deceptive ease that Bayrd almost envied. Almost, but not quite; even thinking of the amount of practice it must have taken came very close to making him feel sick at last.

He concentrated on the thin line of land just visible over Gerin's shoulder. That was their goal, and already it seemed closer than before. The thin mist played tricks with distance. As he set his teeth against the slow thick churn of discomfort building up inside him, he fancied he could see the lighter patterning of bodies and faces against the darker mass of the shore. Over the screech and thump of the oars, the hiss of the water past the hull and the boom as it struck against the planks, he could almost hear the cheering again. Imagination, nothing more.

Then Gerin swore and pointed out to the left. Bayrd looked, and saw something that was not imagination. Vanek ar'Kelayr's boat was moving ahead. It had not taken the lead by more than a quarter-length, but that was already enough to lose ar'Diskan the lands he coveted. His crew valiantly increased their efforts so that the spray flew from the bow, and cut their opponent's lead by maybe a foot.

And there they remained, unable to gain, able only to hold their position. If the lake had been half as long again, ar'Kelayr would have won honourably, by a clean margin. As it was, this was even more insulting than his white globule of spit. He would be slapping his hand against the grass at the Overlord's feet just as Lord Gerin sprang out of his boat. To be defeated by such a short distance was more than could be borne.

And it was a risk that Gerin had prepared for. 'Bayrd!' His voice cut through all the other noises of the racing boat. 'Companion, to me!'

Reeling, and trying with all his strength not to fall across the rowing-benches for that would surely give the race to ar'Kelayr, Bayrd struggled forward along the narrow deck. Lord Gerin half-turned and watched him approach, then when he was close enough held out one hand to steady him. Startled by the honour, Bayrd was even more unnerved at the colour of the clan-lord's face. He had seen that expression only once before, and in the shocked memories of afterwards he knew it had been once too many. It was white, not the clammy greenish hue of seasickness but the bloodless pallor of fear. And what made it worse was the look of determination locked onto the man's features. He looked like a theatrical mask.

'Your Word, remember?' Gerin's voice was pitched low for a degree of privacy from the rest of his crew, but it carried to Bayrd's ears well enough.

'I remember.'

'Then keep to it. Draw your sword.'

Bayrd Talvalin felt the sickness in his stomach give a sudden plunge, and it turned cold. For some reason, perhaps because this contest closely concerned his lord's honour, the *taiken* Isileth was riding at his hip. It was well covered against the spray, even though he was sure that after however many years in the crypt beneath Dunrath, water could not hurt any part of it.

'Companion, I said *draw*.'

The blade came from its scabbard with a metallic hiss that Bayrd could hear clearly over the noises of the water and the oars. It was a hungry, warning sound, the hiss of a viper leaving its burrow, and abruptly he felt afraid of what he would be asked to do. An awful suspicion was taking shape in his mind as it raced back to what Lord ar'Lerutz had said.

It was as if Gerin ar'Diskan had seen the thought form in his eyes. 'Yes,' he said, and forced his mouth into a sort of smile. 'The first hand to shore. Just the hand. How well –' the voice and the smile cracked together, and reshaped themselves into a horrid simulation of cheer, '– how well can you throw. . . ?'

'Far enough.' Bayrd swallowed, wondering how he had come to be trapped like this. It was not right. And yet it was: a Companion was permitted to do such things at the request of his lord. Worse things . . . Gerin glanced out over the bow, towards the land and the people, and Bayrd followed his gaze. He heard the clan-lord's teeth grinding together. Another five minutes, ten at the most, and then he would have to do as he was ordered. There was no honourable way to refuse. None at all.

The oars beat against the water, and still they could not gain on the other boat. It had not been able to draw any further ahead since that first dash, but it was ahead. Barely ahead, but enough. Vanek ar'Kelayr would win; the land would be his, and the old fortress, ready to be rebuilt. And once Yakez of Elthan had been persuaded by force to accept his loss, ar'Kelayr would have the villages as well. Bayrd's throat went tight. Redmer and all the other little places which had shown him friendship in the deeps of winter half a year ago, even when friendship would have cost them all they had if their own lord had heard of it. And ruled by ar'Kelayr, a man who would not keep the peace even with his own folk. He closed his eyes and saw flames, saw swords, saw blood. That would happen the first time Youenn Kloatr dared to raise his voice. It would happen within a week.

'Bayrd. . . ?'

The thoughts shattered like glass hit by a hammer: bright, painful, useless shards. 'My lord?'

'Soon now.' His voice was trembling with the anticipation of agony.

Gerin pulled a thong of braided leather from his belt and gripped it in his teeth while he fumbled with the fastening of his sleeve. Bayrd watched him; looked at the shore; looked at ar'Kelayr standing tall and arrogant in the bows of his speeding boat; and looked at last at Isileth. The longsword's edges glinted.

He knew how sharp they were; sharper than any other sword he had ever seen. Sharp enough that it would all be over before it even began to hurt. Bayrd made his choice.

Reaching out across a deck that suddenly seemed quite steady, he pulled the thong from between Gerin's teeth, and in the same movement reversed Isileth so that the long blade lay against his arm and the hilt was presented to his lord. Gerin stared for an instant, not believing. 'No,' he said. 'No. You can't mean this.' But suddenly his voice was steady again.

And then he took the sword.

Bayrd wrenched up the left sleeve of his tunic without troubling about the fastenings, and fabric tore as scraps of metal tinkled brightly on the deck. He wrapped the thong around his forearm twice, three times, four, and dragged it tight with right hand and teeth. Except for the thin pallid ring where the thong bit into flesh, his left hand began to darken with trapped blood. He looked at the shore, tried to see Eskra – *prayed* to see Eskra, and didn't – measured the distance to throw the . . . To throw, and measured the time to reach shore and a surgeon. Close enough. Soon enough. Make an end to the waiting.

He raised his left arm and extended it. His left hand was straight out to one side, hot and cold and tight, trembling as the blood tried to pump past the obstruction. He turned his head to stare fixedly in the other direction. Sweat trickled down his back, ran out of his hair. His heart had never been so loud. Something made him say, 'Forearm, not wrist,' and he was amazed at the calm in his voice.

Bayrd took six breaths very fast one after the other, and pushed the last from his lungs as hard as he could. 'Now,' he said on that final breath. 'Do it. *Now!*'

There was a sound like a bird's wing, and a sound like a gasp, and a sound like a ripe apple hitting the deck.

There was a sound like rain.

There was a sound like pain.

There was no sound at all . . .

He could hear the cheering swell to a crescendo; then it stopped on a high note and became scattered screams and silence.

Bayrd opened his eyes. He was lying on the deck of the boat, but it had stopped moving and someone was doing something to his

223

left arm. It felt cold and hot by turns, but the silver spike that had run up through his bones and into his brain had gone away. His head was too heavy to turn, so he looked up. There was a sky above him that was blue. It had been red before. Hot. Burning hot. The someone said, 'Good. It isn't bleeding any more.'

'So soon?' said someone else. They sounded relieved, but at the same time surprised.

'It couldn't be soon enough for me. He might have bled dry otherwise. Look at the mess . . .'

It went dark again, and when the light came back he was lying on grass instead of planks. It felt good, and smelt better than tarred timber. He breathed in the scent of the grass and the small flowers scattered through it, and felt better. Strong enough to sit up. So he did.

This time the surprise was louder, especially when he raised his left arm and looked at the bandage wrapped around it from the elbow down. It was shorter than it should have been. And then he remembered everything.

Almost everything. Though the arm-stump hurt atrociously, he had forgotten what the silver pain had been like. Bayrd was glad of it. Eskra was there; and Marc and Mevn; and off to one side, looking ashamed, was Gerin ar'Diskan.

Bayrd couldn't understand. He had given the clan-lord no more than what a Companion promised: service and honour and life and limb. He smiled at how appropriate that was, though it was a wincing sort of expression. But there was no reason for his shame. There was no sign of Vanek ar'Kelayr, and no sound of triumph, so it was difficult to tell what had happened – except for what he *knew* had happened.

'Did we win?' he asked. There was a ripple of nervous laughter that he suspected had more behind it than his innocent question. Gerin was still carrying Isileth. All of a sudden he handed it to Marc ar'Dru and hurried away. Bayrd didn't watch him go. Turning his head was too much effort.

'Albanak-*arluth* wants to see you outside his pavilion as soon as you're well enough,' said Eskra. There was an odd set to her face, and it was mirrored by Marc and Mevn. 'And we have your hand.'

'Ah.' Bayrd wasn't quite sure that he wanted to see it again. His last memory outside the silver pain had been of lying on the deck with his face all wet, looking at his own hand not connected to anything, and then Gerin bending down, lifting it, and flinging it out of sight. 'Show me,' he said at last.

It was the same hand he had known all his life; slightly scarred by the grazes and small cuts of growing up, one fingernail broken on an over-tight buckle, some traces of grass-smear over the knuckles. And a great deal of rusty-black dried blood that ran from the fingers right up to where its forearm stopped abruptly at a straight, clean cut. The flesh was horribly cold.

'Sharp sword,' said Bayrd, trying to make a joke and wondering what sort of funeral you gave bits of yourself.

Then his stump shot a needle of sensation up and down the length of the arm; not pain this time, not the silver pain, but a high, shrill tingling. It was like the difference between singing and screaming. He didn't know if he had screamed. He had done his best not to, but sometimes you just couldn't help doing things you didn't want to . . . And the tingling hit him again.

If feeling had colour, then this was hot, bright blue . . .

'Get this bandage off.' His voice was suddenly urgent. 'Get it off *now!*'

Eskra dropped to her knees beside him and began unravelling the knots – then paused, looked up at Marc ar'Dru and grinned at the knife which had suddenly appeared out of his boot. It wasn't an honourable blade like the three on his weaponbelt; it was just functional. The purpose of such a hidden knife is to cut things, and this one cut better than most. The bandages fell away in long loops until there was only a pad of cloth over the stump. Bayrd didn't want to see that part – strange that a warrior should be so squeamish, but then there was something rather less personal about other people's torn flesh and spilled blood – but the tingling was so acute and so constant that he pulled the pad away without waiting a second more.

It had covered another clean cut, a surface as flat as a polished mirror. He stared in wonder at the bones and muscles, the nerves and bloodvessels all severed and open to view, then looked at his hand. The next step was so obvious that it was foolish. It was also so obvious that there was nothing else he could do. He picked up the hand, pressed cut arm to cut wrist, and let go.

There was no flicker of blue flame, no brilliant flash of sorcerous power running a bracelet of fire around his wrist over the white line of the scar. Nothing at all.

But the hand stayed where it belonged.

The fingers moved properly; it began to grow warm again – and with the warmth came the sizzling of the worst pins-and-needles he had ever suffered in his life. When that was over, and the swearing it had provoked had died down to a muttering under his breath, Bayrd stood up.

Or rather, he tried to stand up and needed help from everyone near him.

'Carefully, carefully.' That was Mevn's voice, still amused at everything but also doing her best to mask her astonishment. It wasn't working. 'You've lost a lot of blood. You're going to be as weak as a kitten for a few weeks.'

'A kitten could take me two falls out of three.' They laughed, but he meant it. 'I'll have to stay on better terms with the kitchen cat.'

'Never mind the cat,' said Marc. 'Something's biting the Overlord, and from the look of ar'Diskan, Albanak's passing the biting along. Mind what you say. Oh, and while we're on that subject, Eskra put your hand back. Understand?'

'I think so.'

'Good. It's strange, though. You said something once, years ago. About sorcery and your hand. That the Talent was as much part of you as your hand, but you could always cut the hand off. It was the left hand, at that. Very strange . . .'

'It would appear we were worrying needlessly,' said Overlord Albanak, silkily. He stared hard at Bayrd, taking in details, drawing conclusions, making up his own mind as he always did. 'I doubt you could say the same.'

'Lord, I meant only – '

'We know what you meant. All of us.' Albanak leaned forward on his camp-seat with as much dignity as if it had been a throne. 'You are a remarkable young man.' Bayrd twitched inwardly at that choice of words, wondering how much more there was than the obvious meaning. 'Quite remarkable.'

'Of a sort I had thought had passed from the world,' put in Keo ar'Lerutz, which if all this was a compliment was high praise indeed. Bayrd just wished he knew for sure. All the comments were disturbingly oblique, at least to a guilty mind.

'Your display of honourable behaviour has been an example to every *kailin* in Alba,' said Gyras ar'Dakkur, back by now from his place at the start of the race, and Bayrd silently released a long sigh of relief. So it was a compliment after all, and not . . . Not the alternative. 'It reflects credit on your name.'

'My lord. . . ?'

'Talvalin, of course.' Lord Gyras smiled. 'I do not make that sort of mistake.' He glanced at Albanak. 'It is such credit, Lord, as deserves a reward.'

'We are all agreed on that, my lord ar'Dakkur. An honourable name deserves honour, so Talvalin shall be the name of your clan. Let it be so written. And you shall be its first clan-lord.'

Though he heard the sharp, delighted intakes of breath behind him, Bayrd didn't turn round. He didn't move at all – for if he did, he was certain he would fall down.

Albanak evidently thought the same, since he made the same gesture as normally acknowledged a full First Obeisance. 'I will take your courtesy as given, my lord,' he said. 'Now: a clan-lord needs land, and a fortress.'

Bayrd heard another gasp, but this time there was no pleasure in it. Gerin ar'Diskan's black brows lowered, and he gave his Bannerman and Companion a suspicious scowl. 'Lord. . . ?'

Whatever he had been about to say was cut short when the Overlord stared at him. 'They are not yours, my lord,' said Albanak quietly. 'You did not win them.' In the sudden silence it was possible to hear birds singing in the distance, and the murmur of voices discussing the day's remarkable events. Bayrd had eyes only for the expressions tumbling across Lord Gerin's face, and he was glad that Isileth was back on his belt.

'The first lord to lay hand to the shore,' ar'Diskan protested, and he was trying hard to keep his voice and his temper under control. 'I was that lord.'

'The hand was not yours.'

'I would have . . . My Bannerman made a gesture of great honour and service to his lord. *My* Bannerman. Who acts for *me*. Therefore the hand represents *me*. Therefore . . .' His face darkened and the dam broke. 'He knew this would happen! He tricked me! I am the first lord to set hand on the shore! *I* am! Not this cheat, this – '

'Be careful, my Lord ar'Diskan,' Keo ar'Lerutz said in a stern voice. 'I said "the first man". I did not say "the first lord". Had you done this yourself as you . . . claim . . . you intended – ' that hesitation was damning ' – then it would have been as much a cheat as now you accuse Talvalin of performing. But it would have been a splendid cheat, a valiant one worthy of securing victory. As it is . . .' ar'Lerutz indicated Bayrd's bloodied sleeve, 'you must see why we cannot award you the prize.'

'But, but, but . . .' Gerin ar'Diskan was absolutely stammering with fury. 'But it cost him nothing! Look – the hand is restored, as good as ever it was!'

'The rewards of virtue are many,' said Albanak. 'He is a generous young man, more generous than many I know with more wealth.' The Overlord put no special intonation into his words, but both Bayrd and Gerin stared hard at him. 'He is also most fortunate, because I doubt that he knew – '

'I did know, Lord.' Bayrd's voice was still weak and shaky from his ordeal, and the startling developments afterwards were making him feel no better. 'At least, I hoped the Lady Eskra might find it possible . . .'

'There! A confession! There, you hear him?' shouted ar'Diskan in triumph. 'Out of his own mouth! He confessed to the trick!'

'Not a trick, Gerin-*eir* ar'Diskan.' The anger in Albanak's voice was growing. 'Though he keeps his hand, yet he gave you the use of his losing it.'

'He knew what you would do when it wasn't my hand!'

'Ar'Diskan, be silent!' roared Albanak, surging to his feet in a passion. 'Do not presume to tell your Overlord and these worthy judges that any man is privy to their thoughts. The judgment remains. That is all.'

'If the hand was no use, Gerin-*eir*, remember that you had the use of his pain. You suffered nothing. Remember the pain.'

'I will remember,' said Clan-Lord Gerin ar'Diskan. He inclined his head in a bow as curt as he dared, then swung round on Bayrd. 'Rest assured, ar'Talvlyn or Talvalin or whatever you call yourself. I will remember it well.'

'I am truly sorry, my lord,' said Bayrd, and meant it. 'All this . . .

it wasn't what I intended. I had hoped only to serve my lord to the utmost of my ability. And . . .'

'And?'

'And you were afraid of the pain.'

It was the truth, and it was the wrong thing to say. Gerin's face went as white as it had been on the boat, but there were two patches just over his cheekbones that flushed as red as wounds. 'You were my Bannerman and my Companion,' he said softly, all roaring past and done. 'No longer. You are my enemy. And that I will remember most of all.'

'My lord . . .' Bayrd began to say to Gerin's back as the clan-lord stalked away from Albanak's pavilion to where his horse was tethered. Then he shrugged painfully and gave up the thankless task. Nothing he would say could change matters now, and he was disinclined to waste further breath in trying. There was just one thing left incomplete.

'My lord!' His voice was courteous enough, but it still brought Gerin to a stop with his horse's reins hanging loose between his hands. The man did not turn round to face him, but there was no need of it. 'My lord, I was your banner-bearer and your Companion and your conscience. You choose to dismiss me without just or reasoned cause. Therefore, my lord, I defy you, and renounce my faith and fealty, freely given and freely taken. I speak it for my name and for my clan . . . and for those who are my family, now and tomorrow.'

Gerin still did not turn, but he looked back over his shoulder, and he was smiling. 'A fine speech, my lord,' he said, swinging up into his saddle. 'Brave words from a man who makes so light of fear and pain. I advise you to enjoy the lands you gained, my lord. Enjoy them quickly. Enjoy them today. Because I swear that from this day onward, you will never be sure of tomorrow . . .'

Though Bayrd said nothing as ar'Diskan rode away, Marc ar'Dru stalked forward and spat on the ground in formal disgust. 'Just words,' he said disdainfully. 'Boasting. Threats. Nothing more than empty air.'

'Are they?' said Bayrd. 'I hope so.'

As Eskra made her way towards him through the crowd, he held out his hand – both his hands – towards her. As she took them gently he looked down at her, then gazed out across the lake to the

229

outline of Dunrath-hold along the crest of the distant hill. The sun would be setting behind it in a few hours, a glow of red against the jagged blackness of the tumbled ruin. Black fangs in a glowing red mouth, open to devour . . . what?

'I truly hope so,' he said again. 'Because he was right. We can never be sure. Not until the day beyond every tomorrow . . .'